"THIS BOOK WILL CHANGE THE WAY YOU RAISE YOUR DAUGH-TER. MACKOFF WRITES WITH TENDER WISDOM AND OFFERS INVENTIVE STRATEGIES THAT CAN HELP EVERY GIRL DEVELOP A WHOLEHEARTED BELIEF IN HERSELF."—Judsen Culbreth, editor in chief, *Working Mother* magazine

"PRACTICAL AND EMPOWERING, *GROWING A GIRL* IS CHOCK FULL OF GOOD ADVICE AND EFFECTIVE TECHNIQUES THAT CAN BE USED ON A DAILY BASIS BY BOTH PARENTS."—Nicky Marone, author of *How to Father a Successful Daughter*

"GROUNDBREAKING! IF YOU WANT A DAUGHTER WHO BE-LIEVES HER OPINIONS MATTER, HER FEELINGS ARE REAL, HER ACTIONS HAVE CONSEQUENCES *AND HER HORIZONS ARE TRULY UNLIMITED,* YOU *MUST* READ THIS BOOK!"—Jane Adams, author of *I'm Still Your Mother* and *Wake Up, Sleeping Beauty*

"DAUGHTERS NEED FATHERS: FATHERS WHO BELIEVE IN THEIR PERSONHOOD AND POTENTIAL. IN *GROWING A GIRL,* DR. BARBARA MACKOFF CHALLENGES OUR CULTURAL CONDI-TIONING BY OFFERING FRESH INSIGHTS AND ADVICE TO EV-ERYONE WHO HAS THE PRIVILEGE OF RAISING A DAUGH-TER."—Ken R. Canfield, Ph.D., president, National Center for Fathering, author of *The Heart of a Father*

HOW CAN I TEACH MY DAUGHTER
TO BELIEVE IN HERSELF?

As the parents of a young daughter, you have read about the dangers—the crisis of confidence, decreased self-esteem, and gender stereotyping—that your daughter may face as she approaches adolescence. Do you wonder:

- How do I keep this from happening to my daughter?
- How do I challenge the stereotypes that may limit her choices?
- Where will I find role models to inspire her?
- How can I encourage her to speak her heart and mind?
- How will I help her find comfort and joy in her body?
- How will I teach her to be safe—without scaring her?
- How can I guide her to discover her strengths in school?

Now, in this groundbreaking work, your questions are answered, as consulting psychologist Dr. Barbara Mackoff teaches you seven practical and effective strategies for avoiding stereotyped beliefs and behaviors . . . and raising a self-reliant, self-confident, and strong daughter.

D0595505

GROWING A GIRL

Seven Strategies for Raising a Strong, Spirited Daughter

Dr. Barbara Mackoff

A Dell Trade Paperback

A DELL TRADE PAPERBACK

Published by
Dell Publishing
a division of
Bantam Doubleday Dell Publishing Group, Inc.
1540 Broadway
New York, New York 10036

Library of Congress Cataloging in Publication Data
Mackoff, Barbara.
Growing a girl : Seven strategies for raising a strong, spirited daughter /
Barbara Mackoff.
p.   cm.
ISBN 0-440-50661-1
1. Daughters.   2. Parent and child.   3. Parenting.   I. Title.
HQ755.85.M235   1996
649'.1—dc20   96-21993
CIP

Printed in the United States of America

Published simultaneously in Canada

November 1996

10   9   8   7
BVG

For my daughter, Hannah
For my parents, Sam and Selma Mackoff
And always, for Jeremy and me

ACKNOWLEDGMENTS

"I am so glad you finished your book," says Hannah's note on the drawing taped to my office wall. And I am glad to gratefully recall those who joined me in writing this book.

I think lovingly of my father, Sam Mackoff, who showed me the garden and named my strengths; my mother, Selma Mackoff, for her generous spirit and for cheering me at every finish line; Mavis, who listens to my story; Cora, for sharing her special family and so many others with me; Valerie, who sees the best in me; and Jane, for her loving care.

My special thanks to all the families who told me about their wonderful daughters; to Diane Stein and Laura Kastner, for lighting my path as a parent; to my agent, Amy Berkower, for her warm and candid comments; to my editor, Mary Ellen O'Neill, whose delight in her daughter, Mary Kate, shines through her terrific ideas for these pages; and to Darlene Cox, for a decade of preparing my manuscripts with wonderful care and good humor.

I will always be grateful to you, Hannah, for letting me tell your stories and teaching me how to write this book. And to you, Jeremy: your no-holds-barred love for Hannah is a joyful lesson.

Contents

❦

STRATEGY 2.
BELIEVE HER STORY
*How to listen to the story of a daughter's life—and
teach her to honor what she knows and feels*

STRATEGY 3.
DECLARE HER INDEPENDENCE
*How to champion a daughter's self-reliance and
teach her to be safe—without scaring her*

STRATEGY 4.
BRING HOME HEROINES
*How to find and use role models to enrich
a daughter's sense of self*

STRATEGY 5.
WEAR GENDER GLASSES
*How to show and tell the story of
sexism—and counter our culture's
narrow views of women and men*

STRATEGY 6.
TELL THE TRUTH ABOUT BEAUTY
*How to teach your daughter to see beyond ideals
of perfect beauty—and celebrate her beautiful self*

STRATEGY 7.
LEARN WHAT SHE LEARNS
*How to discover your daughter's strengths as a learner
and build on her natural interest in math, science, and
computers*

Prologue:

The Girl in
the Elevator

"SUCH *enthusiasm*!" observed a woman, as the sound of my daughter's animated voice filled the elevator in The Pike Place Market. I nodded—remembering how many times two-and-a-half-year-old Hannah's joyful curiosity had engaged friends and smiling strangers. My reverie was interrupted when the woman stepped out of the elevator and turned to me with a smug prediction. "She will lose her enthusiasm, you know. They *all* do." "Not my daughter," I shot back as the door closed. "We won't let her." But why did I find her casual comment so troubling?

Perhaps because this encounter took place at a time when little girls were making big headlines—and very little of the news was good. The front page pictured daughters dancing to Mom's or Dad's office on "Take Our Daughters to Work Day." But if you turned the page, you found data about the free fall of a daughter's self-esteem during adolescence,[1] scenarios of teachers who short-change girls in the classroom,[2] polls detailing widespread sexual harassment of young girls,[3] or an interview with Harvard psychologist Carol Gilligan linking stereotyping with a disturbing loss of competence and confidence as girls approach adolescence.[4]

Those were not the good old days. Do you remember: Sleepy Sunday mornings—when you opened the newspaper to find yet another description of the doom and gloom that awaits your not-yet-adolescent daughter? As you read the latest article, you glanced across the room to your brave new daughter who was merrily climbing out of her playpen, or building a Duplo skyscraper, noodling on the computer, or teaching her cat to sing. Her confidence was higher than a kite and yet you wondered, "How can I keep all of this from happening to *my* daughter?"

FUTURE SHOCK

Everywhere I went, parents were comparing notes about these discouraging words. The mother of a two-year-old told me, "Sometimes, when I am holding my daughter in my arms, I get tears in my eyes when I think of the terrible things that will happen to her in high school." Her future shock reminded me of Merlin the Magician in King Arthur's court. Cursed by his ability to see the future, he lived the present preoccupied by the dangers ahead.

Writer Anita Diamant spoke for many parents when she announced her intention to go "on red alert" to protect her daughter Emilia's sparkle and snap. Her alarm sounded in response to the American Association of University Women's widely reported (and widely argued) finding that by high school, only 29% of the girls in the study agreed with the statement "I am happy the way I am."[5]

As she explained, "My high-spirited daughter, I have read, is in danger of turning into a washed-out version of herself, who obsesses about her weight, who answers, 'I don't know' when asked a simple question, and worries so much about being liked that she disappears."[6]

Like these parents, I caught myself watching Hannah for early warning signs of flagging self-esteem. And at times, agonizing about the role models my husband, Jeremy, and I had offered her.

I remember the evening when Hannah pointed to a picture of Batman in a magazine and proclaimed, "Only men can be Batman." I quickly countered, "Yes, but we can be Batwoman and climb to the top of tall buildings." But Hannah was unmoved. "Oh no," she said firmly. "Dad will be Batman; you and me will be princesses, and we will be scared."

"Where did that come from?" Jeremy and I wondered after Hannah had gone to bed. Was this predictable preschool fearfulness? Are there too many boys in her class? Has she overdosed on Disney (where all girls "grow up" to be princesses)? Was this the same girl who fell off her new tricycle last week and stood in the kitchen, crying and spitting blood, announcing, "And I want to get right back on my bike again"?

"Was it something we did?" we asked each other. Didn't we both work, chop garlic, fold towels, read her books about brave girls, pull worms from the garden, and chase alligators out from under her bed? At this point, Jeremy and I agreed: We refused to spoil Hannah's delicious childhood worried about whether she would be captured by the culture. We refused to obsess about our actions— even with the threat of Hannah's adolescent losses hanging over our heads.

Still, I chuckled sympathetically when I read writer Jane O'Reilly's account of her own future shock. "I tried to warn my goddaughter Zoe that eleven can be a dangerous age, and she said, 'I'm sick of this eleven stuff. I feel like a bug under a microscope. Cut it out!' "[7]

WILL IT BE DIFFERENT FOR MY DAUGHTER?

Then came the worst part: I began to experience a strange sense of déjà vu. I snapped at a relative when he suggested that Hannah "wouldn't be interested" in her cousin Nathan's trucks (and I was not-so-secretly pleased when she made a beeline for them). I complained that Baby Bop was even ditsier than Barney and that Daisy (one of the two female engines on the PBS series "Shining Time Station") wore too much makeup.

I stood in the aisles of Toys "R" Us, rolling my eyes at the girls' section, fuming about the boys pictured on athletic equipment. Not wanting to overemphasize Hannah's appearance, I began to respond to the frequent "Isn't she pretty," with a peevish, "and *smart*, too!"

My laundry list of familiar complaints disturbed me—and reminded me of the angry shocks of recognition in my first glimpses of sexism twenty years ago. Yet I couldn't stomach the prospect of spending my daughter's youngest years rounding up the usual suspects and complaining about postmodern sexism. Nor could I face a daily microanalysis of Jeremy's and my actions as role models.

I didn't want to hide behind the fashionable "I'm not a feminist, but" disclaimer, yet I recognized that over the years I had become more selective in my battles. Two decades ago, I taught an anthropology course offering a fiery feminist critique of sexual and cultural stereotypes. But in the years that followed, I altered my habit of bursting into a chorus of "I Am Woman" every time a man called me a "girl."

I now reserved my stereotype sightings for situations where genuine learning and change were possible. In my work as a consulting psychologist, I have traveled even further—urging women to use humor as a professional tool to tackle sexism on the job. I felt safe in assuming that the world would be a different place for our daughters. But I was wrong.

THE GLASS MEZZANINE

I was a member of the generation who had expected our daughters to shatter the "glass ceiling" that had blocked women's rise to top-floor careers. Instead, we were stunned to read the studies such as those of psychologist Carol Gilligan, who called our attention to a lower floor—I thought of it as a glass mezzanine—where girls between the ages of eleven and thirteen got stuck and lost their strength and spirit.[8]

I alternated between shivering and fuming as I read Gilligan's descriptions of the silencing of daughters as they approached adolescence: the playing dumb, the diets, the depression, and the crisis in confidence. This slump in self-esteem was linked to the all-too-familiar fallout of living in a sexist society. Our culture tells girls to keep quiet and be beautiful and loving, says Gilligan—to notice the absence of women and say nothing.

But why, I wondered, would a spirited two- or eight- or ten-year-old—so sharp and clear in what she feels and knows—grow into a tentative, silenced thirteen-year-old? It seems that a daughter's fall in self-esteem is linked to a rise in impossible expectations for young women.

"Eleven-year-olds are not for sale," notes Gilligan. But then, as a girl's body begins to change, parents and teachers suddenly begin to treat her *as a woman*—and present her with stifling standards of perfect beauty and boundless love.

As a young girl comes to understand these narrow norms of feminine goodness, she can become increasingly self-critical and silenced. She may wonder, How can I trust my own thoughts and feelings and stay connected to the people I love?

In addition to her depressing dance with the ideal woman, by the time a daughter is twelve or thirteen, she will have noticed the lesser presence and power of women in society. She may wonder, Can I really grow up and be anything I want to be? As a daughter encounters what Gilligan calls the "wall of Western culture," she is at risk for losing her confidence and exuberance.

When I read Gilligan's studies, I heard an eerie echo of the woman Hannah and I had encountered in the elevator ("She will lose her enthusiasm; *they all do*"). Still, I had little desire to reexperience the long-abandoned anger and pain of scanning for sexism. Like so many of you, watching my daughter grow had filled me with the purest sense of wonder. I didn't welcome any information that would undermine my joy of being Hannah's mother.

Everywhere I turned, I saw the images and experiences that could erode Hannah's budding sense of self. Did I have to become what I used to call "a street fighter"—ever alert to gender typecasting—to make the world a safer place for Hannah to grow? And then, along came Barbie.

THE PERILS OF POLITICALLY CORRECT PARENTING

Everybody has a Barbie story. Funny, isn't it, how Barbie has become a kind of voodoo doll in the ceremonies of raising "free" children? But there was nothing funny about my Barbie outburst on the day that Hannah and Jeremy brought the dreaded doll home.

When he saw my double take, Jeremy quickly telegraphed a "Let's discuss this after dinner" look; but I could not be stopped. "How could you get her a *Barbie doll*?" I demanded, and listed all of the clichéd complaints: She's passive, an invitation to anorexia, a clotheshorse—a symbol of perfection no girl can match.

Jeremy agreed, but reminded me that we had promised her a Belle doll (from *Beauty and the Beast*) and that Belle was a wonderful role model: brave and bookish, streetwise and loving; it just happened that Mattel used the same mold for Barbs.

Hannah began to cry; she sensed the possible loss of the doll. I folded them both in my arms and offered a rather lame explanation, "Let me tell you why I don't like this doll. She doesn't look like a real girl; she's too skinny, her hair can't get messy, she's in a party dress, and she can't really go out and play." Hannah listened solemnly, nodded her head, and then said, "But *I* like her."

I had never felt more wooden and foolish—and less loving and enlightened as a parent. At last, my discomfort with being a "streetfighter/mother" came into sharp focus. Perhaps Barbie was simply an insult to my feminist vanity (I had spent years skewering stereotypes and here was *my* daughter toting the ultimate passive plaything). I could picture Hannah's preschool and then preteen years as an endless, joyless horizon of Barbie Redux: similar lectures, sexism sightings, censoring of books, power struggles about videos.

True, each of these activities might loosen her sexual straitjacket. Yet these were acts so humorless and judgmental—so far removed from the unconditional regard we believed would nurture Hannah's special spirit and strength. As one loving aunt explained, "When I complain about stereotypes in her books, she thinks I'm mad at *her*."

But what was the alternative? How could we counter the culture that might cripple Hannah's confidence—without constant snarling about sexism? How could we plant the seeds of sturdy self-regard (the ones that will strengthen her to weather the winds of adolescence)? Like you, my bottom line was this: What kinds of experiences will teach our daughter to develop a wholehearted belief in herself?

THE SEARCH FOR STRATEGIES

So pressing were these questions that I began the search for the stories and strategies that I can now share with you. On my search, I read hundreds of conflicting studies about sex differences. I even discovered data that cast doubt on the alarming studies about adolescent girls' crisis in confidence.[9] I read dozens of intriguing and soulful books; yet many books were too political, clinical, or metaphorical to be practical.

More to the point: Every book emphasized girls facing the challenges of adolescence—none focused on parenting and preparing the littlest girls. As a result, I found myself writing the book I wanted to read.

For the last three years, I have explored my questions in interviews with parents, daughters, psychologists, and educators. I've reviewed carloads of books, magazines, and curriculum resources. Parent discussions blossomed into my designing and teaching a workshop called "Growing a Girl."

With each step, I had more questions: How do parents provide love, recognition, and a sense of belonging, and at the same time create more equal opportunity? How do we counter the socialization that limits our daughters, yet nurture their own special kind of femininity?

How can we confront our future shock, responding *before* the age of twelve or thirteen? How do we strengthen a daughter—from day one—to stand on the "glass mezzanine" and not lose her amazing grace? (I even dared myself to try to answer all these questions without once using the word "empowerment.")

At each stage, this search for strategies to strengthen Hannah's emerging sense of self was a humbling experience. Whether I tackled a literature review, interpreted a stack of questionnaires, began an interview, or faced a classroom full of parents, I was aware of my arrogance in approaching the unfinished business of generations: sex differences, self-esteem and stereotyping, beauty myths, role models, adolescent slump! Only Hannah could inspire my audacity.

Yes, I was trained as an anthropologist and psychologist—I had the clinical tools. But Hannah was my child, not my longitudinal study. I wondered if I could respect Hannah's privacy in my writing. I felt queasy writing a parenting book—I could just imagine a teacher or acquaintance observing Hannah in the midst of a "meltdown" and murmuring, "And *her* mother wrote that book about daughters." I felt less like an authority and more like a mother eagle, trying to teach her eaglet to fly away from predators.

And so you see, the strategies I have discovered were disciplined by my training but colored by the pride and prejudices of a parent— driven by the need to be practical.

The writing of this book has been the most demanding work of my life. Every chapter forced me to confront my history, my fears, and my limitations. Yet my resolve was strengthened by watching Hannah grow: by her shouts of laughter, her bravery, her quirky works of art and tender wisdom. For me, the book has been a labor of love.

I can't wait to tell you what I have learned.

GROWING
A GIRL

Introduction

Equalist Parents: Seven Strategies for Raising a Strong, Spirited Daughter

Hannah has always loved trains. Thomas the Tank Engine (from "Shining Time Station") was one of her first and favorite toys. Several birthdays and holidays later, she had accumulated quite a number of the show's engine "characters." Yes, only a few of these characters were female, but this was balanced by the juicy personalities of each train and the "every train" moral lessons of the episodes. Best of all was the train talk—answering Hannah's questions such as "Where is Thomas's boiler?" and "What does 'ready for shunting' mean?"

One afternoon, Hannah gathered all her trains with great excitement and placed them in a large circle on the living room floor. Then, with a series of deft moves, she set a small teacup and saucer in front of each. "I'm inviting my trains to tea," she explained and asked me if I wanted a piece of "green pistachio cake."

I admit I felt a stab of disappointment in my first glance at this train tableaux (they might as well be dolls, I thought). But this whiff of boy-worship became a sense of wonder as I watched her. Hannah's eyes and cheeks burned brightly as she offered each train refreshments asking, "And how was *your* day?" and then she launched into a long shaggy-train story of her own.

At that moment, she seemed so-very-Hannah: focused, funny, affectionate, imaginative. It occurred to me that these were the very qualities that we cherished and hoped to protect from the erosion of stereotypes. How pointless to wish that she play on another track.

THE PITFALL OF POWER PUMP PARENTS

As I reflected on my reaction to the Train Who Came to Tea, I realized that nonstop scanning for stereotypes was not the only pitfall for parents of daughters. I can track my response ("boys' play is better") directly to the fact that I cut my career teeth in the era of those loopy outman-the-men business books for women.

In machisma classics such as Betty Harraghan's *Games Your Mother Never Taught You*, strong women were told they could not afford the nurturing behaviors typical of traditional female caretaking. I realized that when parents believe that only boys are bound to succeed, they find themselves acting as if it's never too early to polish a daughter's power pumps.

Just listen to this chilling advice offered to us in a parenting book of that era:

> If you cannot resist [buying a doll and carriage], then do it, but recognize that you are contributing to the stereotypical image of each girl becoming a "mommy," rather than an independent professional woman who may *also* be a mother. Little boys grow up to become *fathers*, but it is not made the focal point of their existence.[1]

When we read this advice, we realize how much we have been encouraged to undervalue the nurturing actions of our daughters. For example, the couple who bought their daughter a basketball were disappointed when, after she shot a few baskets, she sat on the ball and announced that she was "hatching an egg."

Another thoughtful mom described her seesaw of values. "I was watching my daughter cuddle with her doll and I thought, how wonderful that we have helped her learn to be so loving. And then I panicked, wondering, 'But what about all of that BOY stuff?' "

Two things troubled me about this kind of boy-worship for parents and daughters. First is the error of making male behavior the standard of success in play, work, and love. Even worse: the doubting and devaluing of what have been called traditional "feminine" qualities—those linked with the nurturing and expressive actions in our private lives.

Still, I find it equally troubling to see the pendulum swing in the opposite direction. I've noticed a growing number of books that detail a distinctly "feminine" and—these books imply—a superior feminine work style that is more cooperative and caring.[2] Parents searching for strategies for raising a competent and caring daughter must be wary of all such stereotypes.

It is one thing to raise a daughter to play and win on her own terms—"You don't have to act like a boy to do your best." It is quite another matter to encourage her to succeed with another set of limiting stereotypes: "Women make better managers; they are more cooperative than men." Or, "Men are sharks; women are dolphins." A daughter deserves our support if sharks are more her speed. Or if she wants to invite her trains to tea.

EQUALIST PARENTS

Thinking about Hannah's tea party allowed me to understand an essential metaphor of parenting a daughter. If play is the work of early childhood—the earliest expression of her unique vision and voice—then it is our job to provide equal access to the trains (and dolls, puzzles, blocks, and computers) and encourage her in her job of finding her own special way to play with them. Our biggest challenge is to strengthen her resolve to play it as she sees it.

One mom explained the importance of letting her daughter make her own choices in play (and books and clothes). "We try not to put limits on her choices; we want to teach her to look within herself. We hope that as she grows, she will be more focused on how *she* views the world than how it views *her*."

Here I found a name for the kind of parent I wanted to be—an *equalist parent*—one who creates more equal opportunities for her daughter through loving exposure. An equalist parent honors her daughter's unique experience in the world, and encourages her to define femininity in her own terms.

Still, I was convinced that equal exposure and loving regard would not be enough to navigate the minefield of stereotypes that awaited our daughters. We still needed to be able to offer a "second opinion"—to share our "gender glasses" with our daughters and show them the cultural slights of stereotyping.

As one mother explained, "Whenever we read or watch television, I point out who is missing. Already she's coming to me saying, 'Mom, look, there are no girls in the story.' "[3]

A SECOND OPINION

When Hannah selected *Sleeping Beauty* at a bookstore, I had my first chance to offer a second opinion. Although Sleeping Beauty, like Barbie, evoked my "red flag in front of a bull" response, I tried a less doctrinaire approach. I read the book to its treacly finale, and offered another interpretation.

"You know what bothers me about this story, Han?" Hannah shook her head, only slightly interested. "It's that when Sleeping Beauty goes to sleep, *she doesn't even try to wake herself up*; she waits for the prince to come and do it. You know how when Dad and I come into your room in the morning and say 'Cock a doodle doo,' you open up your eyes all by yourself?

"And you know how you feel so proud when you do your circus puzzle all by yourself? Well, maybe Sleeping Beauty should try to do things on her own. Maybe next time we read, we should say, 'Hey, Sleeping Beauty, open up your eyes.' "

Following this interpretation, I admit that I put the book in the bottom of the book basket. Yet several times, when she found the book, Hannah would say, "Mom, we have to tell Sleeping Beauty: 'Open up your eyes, all by yourself!' "

The mom of a six-year-old offered a wry description of this strategy of second opinions. "Sure, I let her read the old-fashioned sexist fairy tales—and even see the movies of them. But I don't let her watch or read them on her own. I'm always sitting right by her side, passing the popcorn, asking questions, countering stereotypes."

PREVIEW: THE PRINCIPLES OF EQUALIST PARENTING

When I began to design a seminar for parents of young daughters, I wanted to share my view of equalist parenting. I wanted to teach parents how to expand a daughter's horizons—by nurturing her uniqueness and independence. In the book that follows, you will find many stories and strategies that were inspired, argued, embraced, and road-tested in my "Growing a Girl" Workshop. You will find practical techniques to challenge the power of the early experiences that can diminish a daughter—or direct her to the "Glass Mezzanine."

Most of the parent strategies are designed for girls from birth to age twelve; yet many of the approaches will be useful for the rest of her life. You will also notice that the choice of techniques was shaped by several principles I discovered during my own search for solutions.

INHERIT THE WORLD FROM YOUR DAUGHTER

My father, who raised four daughters with a wise kindness, once shared his view of parent-child history with me: "When you are young, you must inherit the world from your parents; but as you grow, *we* must learn to inherit the world from you." For the equalist parent, this marvelous advice urges us to balance our interpretation of the world by understanding the fresh view of our daughter's.

My father's advice also reminds us of the perils of raising a daughter in your own image and reminds us that her story is not our story. Self-esteem is not "passed down" from parent to child; it is found in the support we offer our daughter to build her own.[4] As equalist parents, we cannot insist that she carry our political torch or finish our business with our parents. In the chapters that follow, you will find methods to believe a daughter's story, to view the world as she does, and to identify and cherish her unique strengths.

PARENTS HAVE INFLUENCE, BUT NOT CONTROL

Let's take a spin around an overused proverb. The idea that it "takes a whole village to raise a child" succinctly states the horizons (and limits) of equalist parenting. The truth is this: No matter how loving and balanced the opportunities or interpretations you offer— no matter how often you celebrate your daughter's strengths—there is a world outside that will seem to unravel your good work. Your daughter will always live in a cultural village that bombards her with images and experiences that threaten to uproot her growing sense of self-respect.

As equalist parents, we are forced to acknowledge the difference between influence and control. Throughout this book, I will identify ways to expand your sphere of influence in the years she lives under your roof (for example, in the behavior you model, and in your interpretations of the village to her).

Yet we must also accept the fact that some of the seeds of esteem we plant will not flower. Her cultural encounters may fail to nourish them, her temperament may uproot them. In later chapters—as we learn to honor individual differences in daughters—we are humbled by the limits of our loving influence.

LITTLE THINGS MEAN A LOT

Recognizing the power of the village does not prevent an equalist parent from propriating the power of my mother's marvelous axiom: "Little things mean a lot." My mother, who is a great observer and celebrant of people, often called our attention to the generous or callous acts that bespoke volumes about a person. As equalist parents, we also understand that "little things" add up.

We can refrain from hissing at every schoolbook without a heroine—yet we know the damaging impact of what educators Myra and David Sadker call "thousands of repetitive inequities."[5] Consider this book as a big list of the little things in your village and family life that can nurture or diminish a daughter's sense of self. We will find a balance between being in a state of constant agitation ("He said *what*?") or smug retreat ("I'm not prickly about feminist issues").

In the pages that follow, I also want to tamper with your beliefs about what constitutes a "little thing." I'd like to suggest some criteria for selecting your battles and viewing the models you offer. Barbie and Sleeping Beauty offer convenient cultural artifacts to attack, but I will also ask you to look at the "little things" you model in your behavior.

Barbie will never be an honored dinner guest, but do you talk (within earshot of your daughter) about your "diet," how "fat" you are, your "cottage cheese thighs"? Do you snub Sleeping Beauty, but quickly jump up to rescue your daughter in her play? Equalist parents must be show *and* tell parents.

MEN ARE NOT THE ENEMY OR THE IDEAL

For twenty-five years, my dear friend Ray has reminded me how tough it is to grow up to be a strong and nurturing man. I can clearly recall a typical scenario for us—home from a first semester of college—talking until dawn in the driveway of my parents' house in Phoenix. We were having our usual conversation about spirituality, drugs, and sexual politics. Ray always listened to my scenarios of how sexual stereotypes stifled women and then asked, "Do you think it's any better for men?"

I argued then (as I would now) that it is hard to feel sorrow for those men in power and that patriarchy has its privileges. The next time we talk, I will pepper my argument by adding that it is little girls, not little boys, who suffer a breathtaking loss of self-esteem in adolescence.

Yet as you continue reading, you will see little space devoted to bashing boys or men. You will also see no "special" sections written for fathers or sons. To reduce a father to a footnote is to deny your daughter her first experience that all men are *not* alike.

Instead, the chapters ahead assume: Boys/men have their own

"narrowing" and tough games to play; girls do not thrive by mimicking male standards of strength; women are not the experts in raising a daughter; *and the biggest difference between boys and girls is how we treat them.* I will be suggesting techniques to help a daughter find joy in being a girl and detail the many ways that boys and men can be the allies of even the littlest girls.

ALL GIRLS ARE NOT THE SAME; WOMEN ARE NOT THE SUPERIOR SEX

Being an equalist parent means discovering how your daughter is different from both the boy *and* girl next door. We must nurture her uniqueness. Listen to the wisdom of this workshop parent. "Even if the 'average' boy has different talents or learning styles than the 'average' girl, each child deserves to be treated as an *individual*—not as the average boy or girl."

Parents must also avoid the idea my friend Jane calls "women are protein, men are carbohydrates." It is a belief that reflects two of our era's most hyped and divisive stereotypes: the idea that adult women and men inhabit different worlds[6] and the conceit that a woman's "world" and "women's ways" are not only different from men's, but superior to them.[7]

What's wrong with the idea that sisters are superior? Let me count the ways. First, a view of women as wonders assumes that girls and women are all alike—that they speak in the same (instinctive, nurturing, cooperative) voice.[8] This belief keeps us from cherishing a daughter as a unique, precious person.

Next, this view of women conveys contempt for men as a group. One dad admitted how easy it is to reinforce this women-are-beatific and men-are-beasts view. "I have to make a concerted effort with my daughters to stop myself from sighing with sarcasm and saying, 'Well, that's just men. . . .'"

A view of women that celebrates—and refuses to devalue—the historic caretaking roles of women is appealing. Yet parents who think in terms of the superior sex—whether men or women claim the fame—will look to children to confirm their beliefs about grown-ups' sex differences. Then, they can shortchange a son or a daughter's growing sense of self. In this book, I invite you to let your daughter's individuality light her way of becoming a wonderful woman.

IS THIS BOOK FOR YOU?

The strategies of equalist parents can be used by single parents, nuclear families, aunts, uncles, teachers, neighbors, or loving friends of a girl under twelve. Readers looking for a book about how to shrink sexism without surgery or tame a teenager will be most disappointed.

Instead, you will find these pages suggest that nurturing a young girl's unique strengths and spirit—while focusing her ability to see (and rise above) cultural limits—are the most powerful weapons in the struggle for self-esteem as she grows toward her adolescence.

HOW TO READ THIS BOOK

The book is divided into seven strategy sections; each strategy details a course of action in raising a strong and spirited daughter.

The division into seven strategy sections is not meant to imply a seven-step guarantee that your daughter (or mine) will avoid the trap of the glass mezzanine. Instead, each chapter is designed as a path to action—to embolden parents *to act now,* rather than fearing or waiting for a potential crisis in her adolescence.

Within each section are dozens of parents' stories, perspectives, and specific action plans for raising a strong and spirited daughter. You will also be hearing from Hannah—who flew from age two-and-a-half to five-and-a-half as I wrote these pages.

Some of the strategies were developed in my "Growing a Girl" workshops and are adapted from techniques used in cognitive and behavioral psychology; some are drawn from the resourceful work of organizations such as Operation Smart, the Women's Action Alliance, and The Ms. Foundation. Other strategies are the ideas of loving and gifted parents like you.

Strategy 1. Discover Your Own Stereotypes

Why the biggest difference between girls and boys is how we treat them—and how to help your daughter find joy in being a girl.

Strategy 2. Believe Her Story

How to listen to the story of a daughter's life—and teach her to honor what she knows and feels.

Strategy 3. Declare Her Independence

How to champion a daughter's self-reliance and teach her to be safe—without scaring her.

Strategy 4. Bring Home Heroines

How to find and use role models to enrich a daughter's sense of self.

Strategy 5. Wear Gender Glasses

How to show and tell the story of sexism—and counter our culture's narrow views of women and men.

Strategy 6. Tell the Truth About Beauty

How to teach your daughter to see beyond ideals of perfect beauty—and celebrate her beautiful self.

Strategy 7. Learn What She Learns

How to discover your daughter's strengths as a learner and build on her natural interest in math, science, and computers.

HERE'S LOOKING AT YOUR DAUGHTER

Like so many of you, when Jeremy and I spend time away from our daughter, we're talking about her. In most cases, we marvel at

Hannah's special "take" on the world. This includes endless variations of incidents only a parent would appreciate ("Don't you love
the way she taught her bugs the alphabet?"). One night, I caught
myself midsentence, and asked Jeremy, "Do you think that *all* parents believe that everything their child does is so special and
unique?" He smiled and said, "I hope so."

To Jeremy's hope, I will add my own. Although this book began
as a search for my own parenting strategies, my wish is that what I
have learned will enable you and I to take our daughter's strengths
seriously, while nourishing her spirit and capacity to care. Most of
all, I hope that the ideas on these pages will bring a sense of wonder
and joy to your adventure of raising a daughter.

Strategy 1

DISCOVER YOUR OWN STEREOTYPES

*Why the Biggest Difference
Between Girls and Boys
Is How We Treat Them—
and How to Help Your Daughter
Find Joy in Being a Girl*

1

❦

Approach the Gender Puzzle

SARAH (age eight) and her mother, Amy, were shopping for Halloween costumes. As they combed the hangers of princess, bride, and bunny costumes, Sarah grew increasingly irritable and sullen. "Why is she being so bratty?" Amy wondered, but asked, "What's wrong?" And Sarah explained, "Remember I told you how some of the girls at school are 'girly girly'—they like to wear frilly clothes and draw flowers on everything? Well, all of these costumes are for girly girls and none of them look like me!" The solution? A search for Sarah's fantasy: a brilliant red devil's costume, a shiny pointed trident.

Sarah reminds us of a central lesson of equalist parenting. *All girls are not alike.* Our first priority as parents must be to help her find ways to express her ideas, fantasies, and feelings in a voice that is uniquely her own. We must let our girls be girls—on their own terms. Yet treating your daughter as an *individual* in a culture obsessed with differences between *groups* of boys and girls can make parents feel like a salmon swimming upstream in a tsunami.

For this reason, the first strategy helps us explore how our ideals about sex differences can shape a daughter's development. When we watch our daughters, like Sarah, approach the puzzle of gender, we hear an urgent call to examine our own theories about the differences between boys and girls.

SEX DIFFERENCES: EVERYONE HAS A THEORY

Have you ever noticed how quickly a discussion of how to raise a strong daughter turns into a discussion of how girls are different from boys? Listen to a teacher the day before my "Growing a Girl" workshop: "I'm so glad you are doing this. Before I worked here, I believed that boys and girls were really alike. But you go into those classrooms and the boys are yelling, grabbing for trucks, and the girls are quietly feeding their dolls."

Everyone, it seems, has a theory of sex differences. In my classes, parent and teacher theories often confuse two questions about sex differences: *What* is different (beyond physical/sex characteristics) and *why* does this difference exist? This confusion between effect and cause is clear in four popular parent theories.

Each of these theories predicts how parents will label and shape their daughter's behavior. As you will see, three of them lead to narrowed choices for a daughter.

SEX DIFFERENCES: FOUR POPULAR PARENT THEORIES

1. The Toy Theory

"I don't buy the idea that sex roles are learned. No matter how many trains and blocks and trucks I buy her, she's just not skilled or interested in using them. She's only two years old—too young to have been sullied by the system."

Sex difference effect observed: She doesn't like visual-spatial, active "boy" toys.

Implied cause: This is an innate biological difference in cognitive abilities and play preference between boys and girls.

2. *The Testosterone Theory*

"It's got to be testosterone! I would have never believed it till I had a son. He's just so much more aggressive and wild than my daughter."

Sex difference effect observed: He's aggressive; she's not.
Implied cause: This is an innate, biological difference caused by the "male" hormone, testosterone.

3. *The Kinder, Gentler Theory*

"I'm so glad I have a daughter. When I watch her cuddling, nurturing, talking, and listening to her dolls—and hear the praise she gets for being so caring—I know we will never have to deal with a 'bang-bang, you're dead' thing like we would with a son."

Sex difference effect observed: She is loving and caring with her dolls.
Implied cause: Girls are born to be nurturing and peace-loving; they are rewarded by the culture as well.

4. *The Power of the Culture*

"She stayed at home until nursery school. She always played with trucks and balls *and* dolls; she loved to climb and wear pants. After six months in school, she will only wear skirts and refuses to play ball; I can't believe how quickly she got socialized."

Sex difference effect observed: A change in sex-typed choices in clothes and activities after attending school.
Implied cause: Socialization creates sex differences.

CAUSE OR EFFECT?

It is easy to understand the confusion and passion surrounding our theories and questions about sex differences—especially the "nature versus nurture" issue. We confuse cause and effect because of the consequences for our sons and daughters.

Just think: If there are no personality or cognitive differences between boys and girls, can there be a valid reason to kick girls out of the treehouse or trigonometry class? Yet if differences in ability are wired into physiology, is your daughter destined (no matter how many microscopes you buy, or science museums you visit) to kiss frogs, but not dissect them in biology?

If compassion and cooperation are in a girl's hormonal hope chest, can only women make the world safe for democracy or stop to ask for directions? But then again, if all sex differences are learned, can we reeducate the village—move both sexes toward achievement and tenderness?

HOW THEORY BECOMES PRACTICE

Each of these questions is a detour on the road to equalist parenting. Instead, we must map a course that asks: *How do our own theories of sex differences shape our expectations and actions with our daughters?* How do our theories translate into parent practices that narrow or expand her opportunities to grow?

I must tip my hand to tell you this book will argue for the "power of culture" theory. Because after trekking through hundreds of sex differences studies, I found the only point where most scientists agreed was about the strength of socialization in offering gender lessons.

So I'm convinced that the question of *whether* boys and girls are different cannot be separated from the question of how our culture's emphasis on sex differences creates a self-fulfilling prophecy. We *expect* boys and girls to be different and so we *treat* them differently—and then, they have different experiences and do, in fact, behave differently.

SELF-FULFILLING EXPECTATIONS IN ACTION

In their research on sex-linked (and self-fulfilling expectations), educators Myra and David Sadker interviewed a mother of eight-year-old twins who discovered her own stereotypes.[1] Her son and daughter were riding bikes, collided with each other, and fell. When she ran over to check if either was hurt, she responded in two dramatically different ways. She told her son to get back on his bike ("Up and at 'em, Tiger.") and told her daughter to sit with her on the steps ("Honey, are you all right? Come sit with me a minute").

As she and her daughter sat, watching her son race his bike, Mom was appalled at the different messages about risk and recovery she had conveyed. She tried again, telling her daughter how important it was to get back on the bike again after a fall. As she watched the twins both riding again, she wondered: *What about all the times when I expect different things and don't even know I am doing it?*

Responses like these create what psychologists Sandra and John Condry call a "reality defining quality." In other words: Without this mom's "Aha!," her son and daughter would be likely to grow up fulfilling her gender type-cast expectations.[2]

YOUR THEORY OF SHE AND HE

Homework: Take a moment to explore your current theory (and expectations) of sex differences. How do you think girls and boys are different (beyond physical parts)? Do you think boys and girls have different abilities? Personality traits? How do you explain the reasons for these differences? How do you think your daughter's life would be different if she were a boy? How do you think your observations of men's and women's behavior influence what you see in the behavior of boys and girls?

Reflect for a time on your answers. How could your theory (e.g., thinking girls as a group are "more sensitive" than boys) translate into a self-fulfilling gap of experiences? How might they influence the books and toys you buy, the family outings and after-school experiences you choose, how you praise, criticize, and comfort her, deal with her anger, help her with homework, talk about her future?

In her groundbreaking book, *Unlearning the Lie*, Barbara Grizutti Harrison invites parents to observe their theories of sex differences in practice—to see how they might shape a daughter's (or son's) development.

> A fire engine rushes past your house. Whom do you call to see it? Your daughter, or your son?
>
> You drive past a wedding party. Whose attention do you call to it? Your son's, or your daughter's?
>
> You are given flowers. Whom do you ask to arrange them prettily in a vase? Your son, or your daughter?
>
> Out walking with your children, you pass a woman with a small baby. With whom do you share your pleasure in the infant? Your son, or your daughter?
>
> A building is under construction. To whom do you point out the crane, the workers, the details of construction? Your daughter or your son?
>
> Relatives come to visit. Do they hug and kiss your daughter and tell her how pretty she looks? Do they shake hands with your son, toss him up in the air, and jocularly mess up his hair? Why?[3]

As parents, we must explore our theory of and search for our own stereotypes. We must keep our eyes on the prize: What can we learn from the sound and fury about theories of *group* sex differences to nourish our daughter as an *individual*? How can we help her to create her own ideas about being female?

HER THEORY: A FEMININE PUZZLE

You may be wondering, do we have to prove that boys and girls are exactly the same to get equal treatment for our girls? Or do we have to exaggerate the differences between men and women (and find women to be superior) for our daughter to find strength and joy in being a girl? Or even, does this mean I can't take my daughter to *The Nutcracker* wearing a velvet dress? The answers, my friends, can be explored while looking at two pieces of the puzzle of your daughter's femininity.

Each piece pictures a prime time when girls use their newly developed cognitive skills to crystallize their own theories of sex differences—what it means to be a boy or girl.[4] In the first, we see girls in early childhood who seem to reflect adult's stereotyped ideas of differences. Here, the littlest girls are struggling to organize their impressions of what it means to be a "good girl." In the second, we see girls in early adolescence, diminished as they struggle to understand why impression management is what it means to be a "perfect woman."

THE PRESCHOOL PUZZLE: "GIRLS CAN'T . . ."

If you placed your daughter in a room full of infants dressed in red, it would be nearly impossible to identify girls and boys based on behavior[5] (although you'd notice strong individual differences in temperament). Three or four years later, when you walk into your daughter's preschool classroom, you will encounter boys and girls thoroughly typecast by sex in behavior and play.[6]

The four-year-old daughter who loved to shoot hoops will tell you emphatically, "Girls can't play basketball." Once, she spent hours building skyscrapers out of blocks. Now, she wants to pretend to cook and iron; she greets you in pink satin pumps, and refuses to wear pants. This is the time when parents ask, *"Where did that come from?"*

One encouraging way to answer the question of the preschool puzzle is in terms of Swiss psychologist Piaget's view of cognitive development. In this view, preschoolers' rigid theories of boys and girls reflect a leap in their cognitive ability to categorize themselves and others. Piaget calls this ability "concrete operations." Stay tuned for a translation.[7]

You probably noticed that by age two, your daughter separated the boys from girls by noticing physical characteristics—clothes, hair, jewelry. Her sense of gender was reversible. She thought she could change sex by changing her hairstyle. By three and a half, she was aware of genital differences. If someone asked whether her dinosaur was a boy, she might answer, "No, she doesn't have a penis."

By age four, she was suddenly a walking encyclopedia of sex-typed restrictions in behavior, play, and personality: "Girls can't be pirates, boys don't cook, girls don't yell." As Eleanor Maccoby points out, kids at this age seem to be *exaggerating sex roles "to get them cognitively clear."*[8]

The bad news is that many of her new, rigid sex roles accurately reflect our culture's preoccupation with sex differences. The better news is that she may grow out of them—kids' thinking gets more flexible with age. Because a preschooler's rigid view of the sexes is just one example of the limits of "concrete operations."[9]

You've already seen concrete operations in action—your pre-school daughter's lack of flexibility and difficulty understanding exceptions. Remember when you tried to explain why you talked to a stranger in the grocery line and she said, "But you told me *never to talk to a stranger*!"

Like her view of the stranger in the supermarket, a child under seven views the sexes' differences through concrete operations: simplistic, rule-bound, and exaggerated. Don't despair. As your daughter approaches eight or nine, this thinking will give way to more abstract thinking (what Piaget calls "formal operations"), including the ability to understand exceptions and role reversals.

Here's an example of how her thinking can change. In one study, a group of fifth graders held fewer stereotypes about whether men or women can do various jobs than first graders. The study suggests that older children are more flexible in their thinking and don't rely on the either/or thinking reflected in their preschool theories of the sexes.[10]

Do remember: Preschool is the age where many parents give up. "My daughter is only three and she is obsessed with wearing dresses, refuses to wear pants, and refuses to touch a baseball! I can't fight it." When parents understand that our little one's stereotypes are a cognitive stage, we are released from several unhappy choices. We don't have to blame ourselves; we can stop saying, "She didn't get that from *us*!" Even better, we need not see defeat in her stereotyped behavior—or view it as an expression of biologic destiny (and stop trying to level the playing field).

Parents who want to put Piaget's theory into practice can stay busy while awaiting a daughter's more flexible view of sex roles. We can "listen to her words"—as preschool teachers love to say—acknowledging, for example, how important it is for her to wear what she calls "girls' clothes."

Yet we can still show her how to hammer a nail or climb a tree wearing tights. We can offer a gentle second opinion ("But your dad is a boy and he loves to cook"). Soon enough, she will have the cognitive keys to reject stereotypes and find femininity on her own terms.

THE EARLY ADOLESCENT PUZZLE:
"THEY ALL HAVE BOYS' NAMES."

Your ten-year-old has moved beyond the gender typecasting of early childhood to become a lively, sure-footed, play-to-win girl—full of what Annie Rogers calls "ordinary courage" in speaking her heart and mind.[11] Three years later, she may become confused, self-critical, less confident; she won't confront her friends; she keeps her opinions to herself.

The mirror is her enemy and she may tell you, "My breasts are too small/too big, my hair is too straight, my nose is odd, my thighs are giant." This is the age where parents ask, "What happened at school today?" and hear a story like Myra's.

Everyone in Myra's sixth-grade class was given a peanut to "adopt." The assignment was to name and nurture and have complete responsibility for this adoptee for twenty-four hours. Myra overheard one of the teachers whispering to another, "Can you believe, all of the kids named their peanut with a *boy's* name?" Myra named her Peanut "Susan," and explains, "After that, I got really depressed. *I could see that girls didn't matter as much as boys.*"

In addition to the development of her body, an adolescent girl has a blossoming of her cognitive skills—in particular, her ability to see herself from the outside. This increased intellectual ability brings her closer to the glass mezzanine in two ways (and makes her need your support—despite her denials—more than ever).

First, as Elizabeth Debold, Marie Wilson, and Idelisse Malave explain in their book *Mother Daughter Revolution,* "With this new capacity [to see themselves from another's point of view] they begin to monitor themselves incessantly, looking at their looks, witnessing their every movement from the perspective of the boys, who have increasing power in their lives. This potential allows them to become self-conscious, to create a self they can compare to the ideals they see."[12]

Then, like Myra, a daughter's understanding of adult ideas and expectations about the sexes can reach a critical mass. Her newly sharpened cognition offers her a view of what Carol Gilligan calls "the wall of western culture." She sees women being less valued ("all the peanuts have boys' names"); she sees others reacting to her womanly body and understands that she is now expected to meet the standards of being a beautiful and impossibly good woman.

Her blossoming cognition offers your daughter two possible and opposite outcomes: If she has your support to talk back to cultural pressures, she can use her abilities to understand (and resist) the experiences that will unsettle her belief in herself. But if she walks the wall alone, or if you increase the pressure to be pretty, polite, and perfect, she has enough cognitive firepower to master the terrible art of "impression management. She will learn to present a false image of herself to gain acceptance."[13]

Then, she begins the act of living two lives: At adolescence, she notices the lesser power and presence of women and does not complain; she silences her voice to stay connected to loved ones. Later—as a grown woman—she finds she can't remember the words or the music of her joyous, zestful girlhood.

Yet we can't despair about our preschool or preteen girl's view of gender. Both show a sharpening of cognitive skills. Your preschooler may live in dresses because she discovers she's female. Your preteen may seem to live in the mirror because she's discovered our culture's ideas of perfect women. With your support, both daughters can develop the skill to reject stereotypes and find joy in being a girl.

While our daughters make sense of the gender puzzle, we must consider two issues that are messier than her room: Is there scientific "proof" for sex differences? And how can our ideas about sex differences honor our daughters?

2

Study Sex Differences

I must confess: I almost ruined my friend Liz's birthday dinner trying to refute one of her guest's "theories" of the differences between boys and girls. In Round 1, Steve held forth about "how different girls and boys are," and I offered a tight-lipped recitation about how even scientists can't agree about sex difference in the research literature. In Round 2, he opined, "The *researchers* may not agree about sex differences; but my *experience* is that boys and girls are very different. My son and his friends are completely different from my daughter and hers."

His wife, Linda—trying to be more festive—added, "But men and women *are* so different. I jog on the waterfront every day and hear conversations breezing by. The men are always talking about *work* and the women are always talking about their *feelings*."

By now, I had argued this angle so many times, I could see where we were headed. Steve and Linda would listen politely to my case for seeing children (or adults) in terms of individuality—rather than sex differences. And then, with a look of condescension reserved for folks who have never traveled beyond their hometown, one of them would tell me, "You'd feel differently if *you* had a son!"

I reminded myself that this was a party, yet that didn't stop me from making a preemptive strike, asking, "How will you be able to see your daughter as an individual if you think that all girls are so much alike?"

I know that Steve and Linda would have loved to change their place cards—to share dessert with someone who hadn't spent the winter slogging through hundreds of conflicting studies about sex differences or interviewing parents about their strategies for raising strong daughters. Because in my review of the scientific research and in my conversations with parents like Steve and Linda, I had discovered three things:

- All parental ideas about sex differences can be both proved *and* debunked by the data.
- No matter what science says, parents base their ideas on their own child's sex role behavior—or their opinions about adult sex differences.[1]
- Parent theories of sex differences lead to self-fulfilling—and limiting—expectations for daughters.

In this chapter, I want to state my own theory of sex differences: *The biggest difference between boys and girls is the way we treat them.* As we explore the truth and consequences of parent theories of sex differences, I will show you what I mean.

PLAYING WITH THE TOY THEORY

You remember the Toy Theory:

"I don't buy the idea that sex roles are learned. No matter how many trains and blocks and trucks I buy her, she's just not skilled or interested in using them. She's only two years old— too young to have been sullied by the system."

The Toy Theory combines what/why questions of sex differences with great economy. This parent theory assumes two things that are at the heart of the differences debate: (1) that girls and boys have different cognitive abilities and interests, and (2) that cognitive abilities and interest are biologic facts—they are innate. Sharpen your pencils, because whether or not you believe in the Toy Theory, you can find a scientific study to encourage you.

If you tout the Toy Theory, you will be interested in studies that found girls to have greater verbal gifts—and boys to be more skillful in math and spatial thinking.[2] You will be fascinated by the numerous sex-divides-the-brain studies. For example, data suggesting that your daughter's left brain hemisphere (the site that processes verbal and sequential thinking) develops before her right. And that a son's right hemisphere (home of visual and spatial relationships) develops first—thus increasing his odds at besting his sister in building Lego skyscrapers, laying train tracks, and finding Waldo.[3]

On the other hand, if you refuse to believe that your daughter was born to hate blocks or suffer from math anxiety—you'll be interested in the growing number of studies that suggest that verbal and math ability differences between the boys and girls—the ones that are supposed to prove differences in the brain—are shrinking or disappearing.[4]

Two more powerful reasons not to buy the Toy Theory: First, the studies that explain how *practice can erase sex differences* in the ability to perform spatial tasks such as puzzles.[5] Next, the data that describe how early experiences (say, whether she plays with trains and trucks) can directly alter the direction of brain development.[6] There's enough to send you to the Tonka truck aisle.

Is the Toy Theory true? That depends on which scientist you ask. The more important question: How do parents behave when they believe the toy story?

THE TOY THEORY IN PRACTICE

A dad admits his disappointment that he and his wife are expecting a girl. "I was hoping to have someone to give my old electric train set to."

Five-year-old Isabelle has spent the morning building a three-foot Duplo dinosaur. "Great work," says her mom. "That must have been hard for you."

In both examples, we see how the Toy Theory (girls are born with different interests and abilities than boys) influenced parent actions—and can create limiting expectations for daughters.

The dad mourning about the model trains can be derailed in two ways. First, he has resigned himself to segregated parenting—even before his daughter is born. If his "a boy for you, a girl for me" thinking continues, he will miss many wonderful, playful moments with his growing daughter. His daughter may miss even more.

If he believes that she is born to be bored by electric trains, does he also decide not to buy her boats or trucks or tool sets? Does he assume that she will not be interested in building bridges or understanding electricity, engineering, or physics?

Still, the daughter who built the Duplo dinosaur is at even greater risk. Since the most alarming consequence of the Toy Theory—its belief that boys and girls have innate abilities—is *underestimating a daughter's intelligence*. The danger for daughters is created when parents and teachers convey their belief that boys are born with math and science ability (and that girls can achieve, but they have to try harder). Girls, especially the brightest girls, learn to underestimate their abilities.[7]

Consider, too, how the Toy Theory sets the stage for sex segregation. When you assume that girls and boys have innate abilities and interests, you buy them different toys. When you buy different toys, you offer sex-linked expectations and preparation for school. You also teach boys and girls to see each other as different—even opposite. They play with different toys, develop different play styles, and eventually prefer their own sex.

In time, "she wouldn't be interested in trains" can become "let's not invite the boys to the party." As years go by, this sex segregation shapes playground politics. Have you seen this child's play: "Cootie Tag," "The He-Man Woman Hater's Club," pollution rituals ("Yech, she touched me!"), devaluing femaleness ("Tommy is a girl!"), girls against boys, bra snapping, girls chasing boys, "Kiss or Kill," and "Let's spy on the girls"?[8]

As you will see in later chapters, sex segregation on the playground is reflected in the classroom and can dramatically limit the horizons of your daughter's education. So before you put the Toy Theory into practice, you might ask:

- What toys and games have I assumed are mother-daughter, father-son pastimes?
- Do I expect my daughter to have to try harder to piece together a puzzle or add up her Scrabble score?
- Have I been avoiding certain toys or computer software—assuming she "wouldn't be interested"?
- Have I bought her nontraditional toys (a chemistry set or a carpenter's bench) without showing her ways she might play with them?

By now, I hope you are wondering if your daughter is a potential math whiz and maybe you've decided to shop for a tool kit on your lunch hour. Still, you may be thinking, *Just don't try to convince me that boys are not more aggressive than girls.* Welcome back to the "Testosterone Theory."

THE TYRANNY OF THE TESTOSTERONE THEORY

"It's got to be testosterone! I would have never believed it till I had a son. He's just so much more aggressive and wild than my daughter (or niece)."

Parents convinced of the Testosterone Theory may propose the time-honored "testosterone equals aggression" argument. Like the Toy Theory, this is another example of the biology-is-destiny approach to sex differences. It is used to explain everything from why "all little boys like war games" to why no one ever talks about a "football widower."

Science homework for testosterone believers is a now classic study: Female monkeys who took a tad of testosterone acted out male monkey business.[9] In the human version of the data, mothers who took an androgen-based (male hormone) drug during pregnancy had daughters who were more aggressive and independent than the daughters of mothers who were not exposed.[10]

But if you refuse to believe this theory of hostile sons/docile daughters, you'll be delighted with other kinds of data: For example, studies that report that the *significant production of both tes-*

tosterone and estrogen doesn't begin until puberty—that during childhood both androgen (male hormone) and estrogen (female hormone) are relatively low.[11]

You may want to read data from the rat pack—studies where male rats injected with testosterone began to show "maternal" grooming and nest-building with their baby rats.[12] But it is the human version of the data that may send the tired Testosterone Theory packing. Take a peek at studies that suggest that *low levels* of testosterone, rather than an overload, seem *related to the aggression* linked with the so-called male hormone.[13]

Is the Testosterone Theory true? That depends on which scientist you ask. A more urgent question asks, How does expecting boys to be more aggressive—thanks to testosterone—contribute to encouraging the growth of such aggression? Pull up a chair and consider a short sample of how this belief can cause us to shape girls' and boys' behavior.

TESTOSTERONE THEORY: EXPECTING AGGRESSION

Jean, an attorney, brought her two-year-old daughter Kate, dressed in blue sweats, to a last-minute meeting with opposing counsel at the courthouse. After the meeting, they stopped in a coffee shop, filled with mostly male attorneys and judges. As Jean paused to greet a colleague, Kate expressed her frustration by angrily throwing her milk cup across the room.

The men were admiring, "With that arm, he could play for the Seahawks!" Jean then addressed her daughter, "Kate, we don't throw cups." Next, Jean reported, "There was a stunned silence. The men gave us a disapproving look, turned back to their food, and we became invisible."

Many parents, like the gang at the coffee shop, believe and expect boys to be more aggressive than girls. If you are among them, I invite you to study the ways you might be shaping this sex-linked aggression. Do you:

- Play more roughly/actively with your newborn son—more gently with a newborn daughter?

- Buy more action toys and encourage more outdoor time, more physical risk-taking, and more independent exploring for boys than for girls to "work out a boy's aggression"?
- Express bemused tolerance (and even encouragement) for a boy's aggressive play fantasies, or requests for violent video games: ("Boys will be boys . . .")?
- Admonish and discourage aggressive risk-taking and exploring play or fantasies in girls: ("That's not very *nice*!"; "Girls don't . . ."; or even "That's not ladylike.")?
- Endorse male aggression as the norm by peppering your everyday commentary with questions like: "Isn't that just like a man?"

In fact, one study suggests this very scenario of adult tolerance of aggressive "boys will be boys behavior." When researchers camouflaged the sex of three- and four-year-olds (by dressing them in snowsuits) and asked adult viewers of videotapes to rate the aggression levels of a child who was hitting and throwing snowballs at another child, the results were a stunning example of gender expectations.

When the child was thought to be a boy hitting a girl or a girl hitting anyone, the scene received a negative rating. But when the same child (now labeled as a boy) was thought to be hitting another boy, adults did not disapprove of the fight.[14]

In sum, the consequence of both the Toy and the Testosterone Theory are gender prejudice. Because in both theories, parents limit their daughter's or son's development by acting on the belief that simply *being* a girl or boy determines a child's behavior or ability. Gender prejudice is also hard at work in the "Kinder, Gentler Theory" of sex differences.

KINDER, GENTLER GIRLS

"I'm so glad I have a daughter. When I watch her cuddling, talking to, and listening to her dolls—and see the praise she gets for being so caring—I know we will never have to deal with the 'bang, bang, you're dead' thing we would with a son."

On first glance, the Kinder, Gentler Theory of sex differences seems like the Testosterone Theory in a dress. Look again. This theory oozes a parent's beliefs about innate female superiority—a theory where boys and men "don't get it," and girls are born to. Step into my parlor, and you will see how difficult it is to use scientific studies to separate nature from nurture.

If you believe your daughter was born with a gentle nature or a superior disposition, you will want to underline studies that report girls to be less aggressive than boys.[15] And you won't be surprised to read research findings that report by age two, girls are using more words about feelings than boys.[16] You'll want to read the study showing three-year-old girls (in a task matching story characters' feelings with a photo of feelings) performed as well as five-year-old boys.[17]

But if you don't believe that kindness is a daughter's exclusive birthright, you will want to sample the studies that suggest girls to be as aggressive as boys—but they show it differently.[18] You will be intrigued with studies that demonstrate how girls, from birth, get a better emotional education than boys.

You'll see, for example, studies where mothers of daughters prepared them to read emotions by displaying a wider range of emotions to them than to sons.[19] You'll also discover data reporting that parents offer daughters a bigger emotional vocabulary than sons, by using more feeling words while reading to them.[20]

Is the Kinder, Gentler Theory of sex differences true? That depends on which scientist you ask. But before you send me a mash letter, let me be clear about questioning how culture gives girls the emotional edge. I am not advocating equal opportunity aggression for kids—or suggesting that empathy is of less value than a noisier activity. The essential question is this: How does seeing a daughter as kind and gentle limit our ability to see her as a woman of action (and a son as a gentle soul?).

A GENTLE THEORY IN ACTION

The exquisite dollhouse that Grandpa Dan lovingly crafted for Hannah is in need of a remodel. The stairs are rickety, the bathtub is legless, the chandelier is hanging by a thread. The main reason for the disrepair is the high volume of visiting friends. The other reason may be a game Hannah invented called, "Where's Baby?" In it, the resident Babydoll refuses to hang out in her high chair. She hides and seeks in and outside the house. Hannah adores her dollhouse, and this rowdy little game of hers. She tries to engage kids and adults to play with her.

The adults are fun to watch. Some respond by finding even wilder hiding places ("Aargh, she's in the chimney!"). Others recoil, telling her to "be gentle," to "play nicely." Jeremy and I—who never expected her dollhouse to be a wild thing—have agreed to respect (within reason) the way she wants to play. She has to be gentle with the furniture and no, "Baby" can't peel off the wallpaper.

We see Hannah as both a raucous and a gentle child, whose hearty laugh punctuates our dinner hour. She's also a person who ministers to her stuffed animals with the concentration and kindness of a "veterinarian" (her current career choice). She is fiercely competitive—whether drawing "the best cheetah" in her class or learning to add.

When I watch Hannah in action, I am reminded of how the Kinder, Gentler Theory of sex differences can keep parents and teachers from understanding how complicated a daughter's thoughts, words, and deeds can be. It is also a theory that keeps us from being attuned to her feelings or her unique ways of playing or learning. Do you remember:

- a day your daughter stormed home from school, announcing, "I hate Julie; she called me a copycat. I'm never inviting her over again!" And you responded, "That wouldn't be very nice," or "I thought Julie was your friend!"
- the teacher who spoke at a parenting conference and said, "We all know that girls learn differently than boys" (meaning, they are more cooperative; you know: kinder, gentler).

These moments direct us to see the dangers of believing girls to be gentler: We shush daughters, squirm at their rowdy ("unladylike") play. We deny them strong, messy feelings and we discourage them from sticking up for themselves. We can ignore their unique learning style.

As you can see, the Kinder, Gentler Theory of sex differences, like the Toy and Testosterone theories, lacks scientific certainty. But you can be sure all three theories are self-fulfilling stereotypes—they treat girls as members of a group, not as individuals.

Consider psychologists Sandra and Daryl Bern's nervy analogy. They ask us to imagine how outraged we would be if every African American boy was socialized to become a jazz musician, based on the assumption that he had natural talent. But suppose, they wonder, that it could be demonstrated that African Americans *on the average* did possess an inborn better sense of rhythm? *"Would that justify ignoring the unique characteristics of a particular youngster from the very beginning and socializing him to be a musician?"*

The Berns' conclusion is a wake-up call for parents who want to describe their daughters or sons by sex. Similarly, when a woman's socialization treats her as a member of a group on the basis of some *assumed average characteristic,* she will not be prepared to realize her potential.[21]

But is there a theory that sidesteps stereotypes?

A THEORY YOU CAN PRACTICE

Last Saturday, Hannah and I took our bright yellow ball to the grade school playground down the hill. As we kicked and caught the ball, Hannah began to stare at the painted mural on the wall facing us. "How come all of the girls in the painting are petting animals and all the boys are playing ball?" she wondered.

My first response was silent anger, "Here I take my daughter to play ball and she ends up staring at a two-hundred-foot pictorial of the Kinder, Gentler theory of sex differences." Then I applauded her observation and told her, "You are right. That's really not the way boys and girls are. *You* love to play ball *and* pet animals." We listed girls who played ball and boys (including Dad) who loved pets. We agreed that the picture on the wall wasn't true.

I was stunned by this reminder—that Hannah is growing up surrounded by our culture's narrow ideas of how girls and boys should be. Yet, I felt ready to counter the culture—armed with the two ideas that find agreement among virtually all sex differences researchers. These two ideas must light our theory and practice as parents of young daughters.

Differences between individuals are far greater than differences between male and female.[22]

Nobel Prize–winning researcher Roger Sperry has suggested that individual brains may be even more unique in their structure than fingerprints.[23] Can you imagine a more marvelous motivation to let your daughter's strength and spirit as an individual define her femininity?

Biology cannot be considered apart from culture.[24]

Even the researchers who argue that biology can be destiny will add that biology cannot be considered apart from culture. Nurture, it seems, can transform the force of nature. So won't you join me for a front-row seat to challenge the socialization that can surround and limit our daughters?

By now, you must know that my own parenting theory combines the power of culture with the glory of the individual. I call my theory "Let Girls Be Girls." For a closer look, just step up to the nearest stroller.

3

Let Girls Be Girls

HANNAH was born a blue-eyed, nearly bald eagle—easily mistaken for a boy. Yet we were determined not to surrender to pink, scratchy lace or bow headbands. Our earliest shopping trips brought home a rainbow of soft cotton blues: periwinkle, turquoise, Robin's egg, cobalt. As my pride in having a daughter grew, I became bored with the hail-fellow question, "How old is your son?"

So I bought a few dusty pinks, and two things happened: I found out that pink is a wonderful color for Hannah (especially on cloudy Seattle days), and I joined the legion of parents whose daughters are greeted with stereotyped salutations like, "Will you look at those eyelashes!"

My friends Rob and Beth's newborn daughter wore her wonderfully spiky hair unadorned and her clothes unisex. "Does it bother you if Katy is mistaken for a boy?" I asked, looking at Katy's blue overalls festooned with footballs. "Not at all," said her mom. "We'd like to protect her from the Barbie doll syndrome, and if she's treated like a boy from time to time, this may help her keep a full range of options in defining herself."

Two families, two responses, one reality: From the moment of your daughter's birth, her sex is the most important determinant of the way the world responds to her. In this chapter, we see the power of culture in determining how we treat boys and girls differently from day one.

YOU MUST HAVE BEEN A BEAUTIFUL BABY

Although studies indicate no clear-cut differences in the way newborns behave,[1] try telling that to your cousin Ben, who proclaims your infant daughter a "heartbreaker" and your newborn nephew a "linebacker." Psychologists Edward Tronick and Lauren Adamson explain this frustrating phenomenon in their book *Babies as People:* "We adults do not treat the sex of the baby as a trivial clue. To us it is a central organizer, a potent description of who the new baby is."[2]

Upon learning the sex of the baby (or thinking they have learned), an adult takes nature's first projective test—investing the "boy" or "girl" with their theories about the typical behaviors and goals for each sex.

Family therapist Olga Silverstein has noted that with the advent of amniocentesis, socialization can begin five months *before* birth.[3] We see families who are expecting girls talk to the unborn children more, and stroke the mother's belly more often. " 'Hey, how ya doing in there, big guy?' is about all the typical in utero boy can expect," says Silverstein.

MEET BABY X

Once the baby is born, the power of culture begins to build. A number of "Baby X" studies—where the *same* infant was labeled either a boy or a girl—suggest that from the moment of their arrival, adult caretakers provide dramatically different social and emotional experiences for infant sons and daughters.[4]

Consider one study, where adults looking at the same baby ("Beth" dressed in pink, and "Adam" dressed in blue) judged the

baby's sex by behavior. Beth was described as "sweet" and "feminine" and Adam as "sturdy" and "vigorous."

How about another study, where adults watched the same baby
(variously labeled "girl" or "boy") play. The "girl's" response to
the pop of the Jack-in-the-box was labeled "fear" and the boy's was
labeled "anger."

Still not convinced of how early socialization begins? Read the
results of an experiment where male and female parents played with
a fourteen-month-old baby. When the baby was labeled a girl,
"she" received more cuddling and chatting, while "he" received
more encouragement to be more active and play with typical boy
toys.

Or review the research where mothers of newborns were video-
taped playing with a baby identified as either a girl or a boy while
the infant's true gender was concealed by clothing. Baby boys were
encouraged to move more than girls. And the mothers, too, became
movers and shakers when playing with boys.

In each study, only when the baby was believed to be a boy did
adults point him in the direction of activity and capability. Such
studies define what Carrie Carmichael calls "gender prejudice"[5]
with stunning clarity: Actions based on the idea that simply *being* a
girl or boy determines how a child thinks, feels, and acts.

Parents who read the "Baby X" studies quickly discover three
things, First, how early sex stereotyping begins (making it impossible to argue sex differences purely on the basis of biology). Next,
how gender prejudice is the direct result of our own theories about
how boys and girls are different. And then, If we had a nickel for
every time *we* used a child's sex as a cue for our actions or expectations, we wouldn't need a college fund for our daughters.

Some parents read the studies and become self-conscious for
months—appalled at their sex-typed small talk with babies and toddlers. Others see themselves responding to how girls look and how
boys act, or softening their tone with girls, toughening their timbre
with boys.

THE POWER OF CULTURE:
HOW BELIEFS BECOME ACTIONS

Still, there are parents who ask, "What is all this fuss about the diaper and pins set? Aren't they too young to understand?" Yet how much adults read into even the littlest girl's gender is a critical issue since her first buds of stereotyped behavior don't open to full blossom until preschool. By that time, she has taken a good look around her social world—a world chock full of our theories about how boys and girls are different. Just look at how we put our theory into practice, the moment we become parents.

In her book *The Courage to Raise Good Men*, Olga Silverstein talks about her beliefs in action.

> When the nurse brought my newborn son in for a feeding, she said, "Oh, boy, is this guy strong willed! He knows what he wants and he wants it now . . . he's got a temper . . ." Believing absolutely in that will and that temper, I did feed him right away.
>
> When my next baby, a girl, started screaming from hunger, the nurses would bring her in to me with the explanation that she was upset and needed soothing. So I would croon to her, "Oh, sweetie pie, you're unhappy. What's the matter? Tell mommy all about it," and I would continue to talk quiet nonsense to her and stroke her and sing to her until she quieted down. Only then, did she get the nipple.

With wonderful candor, Silverstein concludes, "So from day one, I was active in establishing and adhering to the male/female instrumental/expressive divide—which is a product of the belief that boys and men are primarily oriented toward activity, achievement and power and women toward nurturance and relationship."[6]

For a crash course in how parental ideas socialize their children, consider a survey that studied the rooms of children *under age two*. Researchers found boys' rooms full of sports equipment, play vehicles, building kits and tools and girls' rooms full of kids' furniture, dolls, and play kitchen utensils. Boys slept on sheets of blue and girls slept on multihued sheets of pink and yellow.[7]

It's clear that parents bring up boys and girls in radically different environments—selecting different toys for female and male children even before the child can express a preference. For a fresh view of your own beliefs about girls, go to your room or office (wherever you keep the flotilla of family photos). Which photo ops feature your daughter: Is she all dressed up? or in action?

These stories and studies provide provocative evidence of the power of culture. They demonstrate that parents who act on their theories of sex differences treat boys and girls differently. This contrast in treatment creates a culture gap between boys and girls—one that will be described in scenarios throughout this book.

As you will see through the book, the cultural gap between boys' and girls' experiences grows wider as your daughter moves from cradle to circle time, and wider still as she approaches the glass mezzanine. As the gap widens, the options for girls seem to narrow. But what's a parent to do?

LET HER CHOOSE HERSELF

Equalist parents know what they wish for their daughters. As writer Anna Quindlen explained, "I would like to help make my daughter a person who could look around the panoply of personality traits in the characters of both men and women and choose—herself. Her true self, not some lipsticked version of it."[8]

Parents who want to join a daughter in challenging the stereotypes of our culture must look closely at how they define femininity. Consider first, the folly of these four approaches. Each one focuses on comparing girls with boys—rather than helping a daughter "choose herself."[9]

LET GIRLS BE LIKE BOYS

My 12-year-old twin girls are dedicated to doll play . . . but I felt the dolls were limiting and too girlish. What we really wanted was for them to do traditional "boy" things. We bought them blocks and trucks and balls, but they kept asking for dolls. I sometimes felt like this was a sign of failure in our quest to raise non-traditional girls.

I didn't realize for many years that by devaluing and trying to discourage their relationship play, I was teaching them a cultural rule: What you like to do (relationship learning) is not as interesting as boy's play.[10]

In her story, Nancy Gruver, co-founder with Joe Kelly of the ground-breaking girls' magazine *New Moon,* points out how parents who seek to minimize the differences between boys and girls approach the sticky wicket of boy worship. In the "Let girls be like boys" approach, Father knows best, boys are the standard of best behavior, and mothers know only how to be mothers.

Here, the expression "Wait till your father gets home" takes on a new meaning as growing girls are encouraged to assume men are the superior sex and overvalue the activities associated with the public sphere where men have traditionally dominated: achievement, abstraction, agency, action sports, aggression.

Daughters are discouraged from developing the nurturing, expressive activities associated with the tradition of women in private life. This approach echoes the "power pumps" parents' attitude: "It looks like men succeed in business, so let's help our girls grow up to be men."

Parents who teach a daughter that she can only look *outside* her sex for strength offer a lesson in self-contempt. As Nancy Gruver explains, "Ironically, in trying to help our daughters overcome the disadvantages of being female, we perpetuated the cultural devaluation of typical female activity."

If you reject all feminine associations with home and hearth as "powerless," you will limit the joyous expression of your daughter as an individual. You may raise a young girl who feels she must someday choose between work and love.

LET GIRLS AND BOYS BE THE SAME

I feel determined to encourage my 5-year-old daughter to enjoy typical girl stuff—while at the same time give her lots of nontraditional alternatives. But sometimes I feel like I have to balance ballet with basketball or have her *build* the dollhouse she wants to play in. It's just too much pressure for me—and for her!

Many parents hedge their bets against unequal treatment by minimizing differences between girls and boys. Yet, as this parent laments, the biggest problem with gender-free "androgynous" parenting (besides trying to pronounce it) is that instead of acquiring one set of sex-typed behaviors, your daughter would be expected to master two. It's the Supergirl Syndrome.

Parents must make every effort to level the playing field. But being equal doesn't mean being the same. Still, the question of how your daughter can be the same as the boy next door is another example of girls measured by a male yardstick. We must ask instead, "What special qualities does my daughter bring to the neighborhood?"

Another possibility: If we insist that boys and girls are the same, we will send our daughters into the world without what psychologist Dana Crowley Jack calls "Gender Glasses"[11]—without tools to see and resist the ways in which boys and girls are treated differently.

LET GIRLS BE GIRLISH

At a holiday party, I asked a father about buying presents for his young daughter, "Are you able to find interesting toys and strong role models in books?" He smiled, "Oh, we are not concerned about that, we *want* her to be feminine."

Many parents maximize the differences between boys and girls in a (sometimes) defiant choice of a fixed idea of femininity. Barbie knows best and the secrets to the universe are in the kitchen and the mall. In this view, fathers are only useful as flirting foils—they're practice prom dates. Here is a route that is perilous to both the girls who beg to wear party dresses to school and to the girls who live in the trees. It fails to nurture a daughter's individuality and her view of women and men as juicy, complicated people.

Still another pitfall: Parents who encourage their girls to be "girlish" often fail to distinguish enjoyable and powerful aspects of traditional femininity from defeating ones. It is one thing to admire your daughter's storybook hairstyle—and another for her to tie her self-image to the ribbon in her hair.

We must see the difference between the experiences of a daughter who "cares about people" and those of the daughter who feels pressure to be a "good girl" and silence her true thoughts and feelings.

The very idea of being "girlish" implies the crazy-making command to "be a lady"; to muffle yelps of joy, to label her moxie as "sassy," or to submit to a dress code. A worst case scenario: In your battle to get her out of the horse's stable (locker room, library) and into a dress, you misread her unhappiness and anger at not being seen. You assume she would be happier if she were more girlish.

LET GIRLS BE BETTER THAN BOYS

Twelve-year old girl on a talk show: "In my class, the girls love math. Our scores are higher than the boys'."

Adult response: "Well, that proves, once again, that women are superior to mcn."

Girl: "That's not what I meant!"

Many parents maximize sex differences in the hope that a separate-and-superior (girls are kinder, gentler) view will strengthen a daughter's sense of self. On the surface, this women-are-the-superior-sex strategy seems supportive. Look closer: You are asking your daughter to exchange one set of stereotypes for another. The assumption that *all* girls learn, love, and relate in the same way is as narrowing as the notion that boys are best in math, science, and soccer.

In this approach, parents project their views of how adult women and men act. In "Mother knows best" and Father "doesn't get it," we hear the tired echoes of blaming all men for all wrongs. If you want your daughter to be treated as an individual, you can't afford to group and dismiss half of the population as purveyors of patriarchy.

We don't have to teach a daughter that she is superior to men to celebrate the seasons of her body—to nourish the tenderness associated with women's traditional caregiving role, to seek her specialness. I must ask: Do you really want to position your daughter for a future where she lands on a counseling couch, complaining that she is from Saturn and he is from Pluto? What a lonely, angry destination.

All four of these approaches (in contrasting how she is different from boys) won't help her "choose herself." Consider, instead, an approach that will help her emerge from her adolescence with her true colors shining.

LET GIRLS BE GIRLS

Helping a daughter find joy in being a girl doesn't mean: boy worship, blinders about being a girl, exaggerating feminine stereotypes, or elevating traditional feminine strengths to Sainthood. Are you wondering what's left? Just take a look at Emily's dress.

> Eleven-year-old Emily happily lived in her jeans—a fact loudly criticized by a teacher who urged her to wear dresses and look "more feminine." After several rounds, Emily repeated her teacher's discouraging words to her mother. Suzanne's brilliant response: to make light of this teacher's typecasting by making Emily a Cinderella-style gown from a crinkly shower curtain. The day she wore it to school, her teacher trilled, "You look beautiful! Where did you find that fabric?" "It's an old shower curtain," said Emily with a sly grin. Her teacher got the point and never mentioned her wardrobe again. And Emily returned to her comfortable clothes.

Here's what Emily's mother understood: to let girls be girls means to celebrate a daughter's uniqueness. For her, *individuality defines femininity*. But we are surrounded by roadblocks to this goal; we live in a culture preoccupied with fixed theories of sex differences—reflected in our behavior, in books, and by the messages of the "4M's": music, movies, magazines, and Madison Avenue.

Yet we must begin with the assumption that you can have a strong influence (though not control) in how your daughter finds meaning and magic in being a girl. The focus of the chapters that follow is to help parents create a "counterculture," a sanctuary where you can let your girl be a girl and where she can:

- Learn to recognize and be guided by her own authority and experiences.
- Declare her independence; test, explore, risk, find answers on her own terms.
- See herself as the author of her accomplishments.
- Gain an understanding of the culture of the "village"—how its theories of sex differences and emphasis on female beauty and body can limit her opportunities.
- Blossom as a learner, and discover her unique style and strengths of mind.
- Find comfort and joy in a rich, expansive definition of femininity. Try out many interests and roles.
- Stay connected to loved ones—especially when she dances away.

Letting girls be girls requires a passionate belief that your daughter knows herself best. This means making room at the table for a whole range of behaviors and experiences: the authority linked with the tradition of men in public life; and the tenderness tied to the tradition of women in private life. We can champion her behavior as an *individual*—without devaluing any of her qualities, believing she was born to have them, or elevating them to sexual superiority.

Yet we must also question the experiences that exaggerate traditional femininity. We must ask, when does sensitivity to others mean giving up on her own needs? How can the desire to be loving and connected lead to a silencing of her self—of looking outside for approval?

We must also use our influence to narrow the gap in experiences and expectations between boys and girls. And all along the way, we must somehow deal with the "Fluff Factor."

BUT WHAT ABOUT THE VELVET DRESS AT THE BALLET?

What about the loaded question of "looking feminine"? You didn't know whether to cheer or fear your daughter's discovery of barrettes, patent leather, and dress-up clothes. She sashayed away from the mirror and toward you, asking, "Aren't I beautiful?" You answered, "Oh, yes, darling," but the pleasure of the moment was diminished by the future you envisioned: the agony of her adolescence, where she stands in front of the same mirror and feels neither pretty, witty, nor bright.

The very idea of "looking feminine" seems an easy stereotype to skewer. You fear that someday she will suffer from the fallout of feeling judged by her appearance. So one escape route is to hide her in plain sight with a no-nonsense haircut, no-frills clothes. This may temporarily divert attention from her appearance; until the day she announces that she "only wears skirts," and that she won't leave home without one. Or that she wants to grow her hair long like her friend Julia.

Do remember that the dress she wore to the ballet—the one she insisted on wearing to school or even sleeping in—is not the uniform of the glass mezzanine. You must ask, first of all, how old is she? (Remember how preschoolers exaggerate ideas of femininity and masculinity to understand them?) More important, do her clothes limit her activities or friendships?

Are you (or she) selecting clothes that wear *her*—they are so fussy, stylish, and pretty they become a frequent source of conversation? Are her presents largely geared to her appearance? Is her view of herself increasingly focused on "looking beautiful"? What is your investment in her beauty?

We'll explore questions about beauty more in later chapters. In the meantime, you don't know whether to be relieved or worried that your seven- or ten-year-old absolutely refuses to wear a dress and shows no interest in ruby slippers. You don't want her to trade on her appearance, but she looks like, well, one of the guys. Instead of the clothes wars, let's reconsider the wisdom of Emily's mother, who created the Cinderella shower curtain dress to tweak her daughter's teacher.

We admire Suzanne's decision to nurture her daughter Emily's confidence and pleasure in making choices about her appearance. In creating a shower curtain Cinderella costume for Emily, she offered both her support and a good-humored model for resisting—and talking back—to her teacher's stereotyped ideas about femininity. She understood Emily's style as self-expression—it was not just about wearing jeans, but enabling Emily to be what the French call "comfortable in her own skin."

Suzanne also understood that style is an expression of her daughter's vision of herself. And if you don't encourage your daughter to develop her own sense of style, she will become more vulnerable to society's narrow, numbing standards. She will be less able to, as one mom put it, "make her life a work of art."

Writer Carrie Carmicheal evokes this art of letting girls be girls—of guiding kids to define themselves by personality instead of sex. As she explains, "Raising a child free of gender prejudice has as its goal celebrating the myriad differences between *girls and girls* and *boys and boys*—not blunting the differences between girls and boys. . . . It is freeing the personalities and helping children sustain their own differentness in the face of adversity."[12]

I keep coming back to what one dad told me, "Sex is a disguise—a distracting one. The mystery of the self isn't sex based—it's larger than your body. My daughter's life direction isn't rooted in her sex, but in her spirit."

Now, enough talk about our theories as parents. Let's find out more about your daughter—and why there is no one quite like her in all the world.

KEY IDEAS

Strategy 1
Discover Your Own Stereotypes

Why the biggest difference between boys and girls is how we treat them—and how your daughter can find joy in being a girl

- Even scientists can't agree about sex differences—you can find studies that prove (or debunk) any theory.
- See your theory in practice. Question how your beliefs about girls and boys might nurture (or limit) your daughter's development.
- Close the gender gap. Ask yourself: "How would I be praising, criticizing, or expecting my daughter to be different if she were a boy?"
- Remember that all girls are not alike. Celebrate your daughter's uniqueness.
- Don't despair about your daughter's rigid view of gender. Both preschoolers and preteens are sharpening their cognitive skills.
- Let girls be girls. Join your daughter to create joyous, expansive choices in becoming a woman.

Strategy 2

BELIEVE HER STORY

*How to Listen to the Story of a
Daughter's Life—and Teach Her to
Honor What She Knows and Feels*

4

❦

Make Her the Authority

AFRICAN-AMERICAN poet and educator Beverly Jean Smith has written lovingly about her mother, who believed her story and "backed my voice." She remembers when Mom lost half a day's pay to come and tell her kindergarten teacher that if Beverly wasn't sleepy, she couldn't be forced to take a nap. She came to school again in sixth grade, when Beverly's teacher had been calling her a liar—questioning her about a fight in the school yard.

Beverly writes, "I reported the teacher's questioning to my mother. She always told us to tell the truth and anything can be dealt with. She came to school and assured the teacher that *my version of the story was the truth as I knew it.*"[1]

In our second strategy, we approach the art of Beverly's mother. We will learn to discover and believe the story of a daughter's life. When we listen to the tales our daughters tell, we understand the individual differences (rather than sex differences) that shape each daughter's unique presence in the world. In the chapters that follow, you will find techniques for mirroring the truth of her thoughts and feelings, and for understanding her temperament and her energy.

All of our actions are aimed in one direction: *to make her the authority about her experiences*[2]—to teach her to honor what she thinks and feels. We begin by witnessing the risks to the daughter who dares to tell the truth as she knows it.

THE DARE OF TRUTH: DAUGHTERS WHO DISAGREE

Hannah wants my advice. "Today Alice asked me, 'Don't you just *love* the Power Rangers?', and I thought, well, I like the way they rescue people, but they get into too many fights—they are pretty violent. I didn't know what to say, because she really likes them. Should I tell her that I don't like them?"

My immediate response was a split decision. At first, I wanted to hug Hannah and say, *"Just tell her why you don't like them.* You and Alice will be friends long after her Power Ranger lunch box is morphed into the garbage bin!" Instead, I decided to second her emotion: "You are wondering what will happen if you tell her that you don't like something she likes?" We peered into the mirror of her confusion for a few minutes, and then role-played telling her friend both feelings.

As we talked, I felt unsettled by a moment of future shock— preschool Hannah was clearly describing the dilemma documented in the literature about preadolescent girls. To wit: Girls—as contrasted with boys—sense that the telling of their true thoughts and feelings—"I don't like the Power Rangers"—will put their relationships in danger.

PERFECT GIRLS

In their book, *Meeting at the Crossroads*, Lyn Mikel Brown and Carol Gilligan write eloquently about how young girls are urged by adults to measure themselves against a phantom "perfect girl." Has anyone actually seen this girl? She is always calm, controlled, quiet, never noisy, bossy, braggy, or aggressive. She has no bad thoughts or feelings—she's not anxious and doesn't cause trouble. Everybody wants to be with her, praise her, love her.

The dangers of trying to dance with the perfect girl are clear: Girls begin to silence themselves to avoid conflict. As Brown and Gilligan explain, "A girl [near adolescence] begins to show her reluctance to know what she knows *and the fear that her experience, if spoken, will endanger relationships and her survival.*"[3]

Take Jesse, for example. She's an eleven-year-old who had little trouble speaking her mind at eight—but who now sees "niceness" and covering up strong feelings as a way to gain love and stay in relationships. "Saying something wrong—or saying something in the wrong way—is terrifying," says Jesse. The phantom of the perfect girl haunts Jesse and she advises, "If a girl doesn't like another girl, she should pretend she likes her."[4]

HAPPY GIRLS

Psychologist Harriet Lerner, in her book *The Dance of Deception*, offers a chilling portrayal of how parents can instruct daughters to replace their genuine feelings with inauthentic, more "ideal" expressions.

> Whenever Bea got down in the dumps, her mother Ruth would approach her with false brightness and say, "Who is this unhappy girl? This is not my Bea! My Bea has a pretty smile on her face! Let's make this sad little girl go away so that my *real* Bea can come back!"
>
> Whenever Bea shared a problem, Ruth would reflexively rush in to fix it, or she would offer unsolicited advice or glib admonitions to "look on the bright side" and "keep a positive attitude." In response to her mother's allergic reaction to depression, Bea had long ago stopped sharing real feelings with her.[5]

As we study these scenarios, we yearn for strategies to prevent our daughters from learning to silence themselves—or fashioning a false "ideal" self to comply with family or cultural demands. How can we help our daughters show what Annie Rogers calls "ordinary courage": the ability to speak one's mind by telling all one's heart?[6]

MIRROR, MIRROR

I'm convinced that a parent's most potent tool in countering our culture's demands for "perfect" and "happy" daughters lies in a special kind of listening. Psychologist Hans Kohut calls it the act of "mirroring," offering a daughter an emotional mirror that reflects her experiences "without distortion or fear."[7]

Haim Ginott, a pioneer in parent education, defines our mission in mirroring. "A child learns about his/her physical likeness by looking in the mirror. *She learns about her emotional likeness by hearing her feelings reflected by us.*"[8]

Listen to Jeffrey explain how mirroring emboldened his daughter to trust her own feelings and dare to disagree: His daughter Ellie was a "math hotshot," who changed schools and had to retake a class. When her new teacher tried to get her to solve problems in a different way than she had been taught, she asked her dad's advice.

Jeffrey told me, "I sensed that *she knew in her heart that her new teacher was wrong*, but she wondered, Should I take a stand? Is it okay to argue and draw a line in the sand? I said to her, '*You* know you are right.' And she asked, 'So, it's okay to be aggressive?' I said, 'Why not? You are right, aren't you?' "

In Jeffrey's encounter with Ellen, we see that mirroring is equal parts empathy and education. When we reflect and interpret a daughter's feelings to her, she feels understood—we have heard the feeling *behind* what she says.[9] In this process, she also learns to recognize, name, and trust her own experiences. Over time, as she listens to her own voice, she becomes the authority about her experiences; her reflection of self will come from within.

In our mirroring, when we urge her to voice what she feels, we offer her an alternative to the "perfect girl." We also provide a model of a relationship where she can stay connected (and still be loved by us) even when she expresses strong, angry, messy feelings—especially feelings that are different from ours.

Miles explains, "I have always encouraged Rhianna to be comfortable arguing or being mad at me. I figure if she has lots of practice getting mad at a six-foot-two male, she'll be able to say what she thinks to anyone."

THE ESSENCE OF EMPATHY

In her brilliant book *The Drama of the Gifted Child*, Alice Miller explains the emotional riches of a child who receives adequate mirroring. The child whose parents can empathize feels:

- My parents respect me and regard me as the person I am at any given time—and as the central actor in my own activity.
- My parents understand me when I try to express my feelings and they do not laugh at me.
- My parents are rich in their own talent and courage and not dependent on my achievements; they do not need me to be like them, they do not need my comfort or my smile—or to see themselves mirrored in my admiration and love—to feel strong.
- I can be happy or sad when anything makes me happy or sad. I don't have to look cheerful for someone else and I don't have to suppress my anxiety or distress to fit other people's needs. ⌐
- I can be angry and no one will die or get a headache because of it; *I can rage without losing my parents.*[10]

As I read Miller's words, I recalled many shining stories of empathy that parents have told me. Two examples illuminate the essence of empathy. In the first story, Jane joins nine-year-old Amy to mirror an unsettling feeling that has no name. We see how seriously Jane regards Amy's feelings—she doesn't demand that Amy deny her distress.

Earlier this year, Amy started telling me about what she called "my feeling." I noticed that when she was stressed, she might say, "I have my feeling, my stomach hurts." I didn't know whether she was feeling anxiety or guilt, but I just kept acknowledging how uncomfortable she felt. I refrained from telling her not to worry about it—I took it seriously. Then, one day—after a particularly long conversation, she wrote me a note saying, "Thank you for helping me with my feeling. I love you." She hasn't mentioned "her feeling" since then.

In a second story, eleven-year-old Maya shares an angry secret with her mother, Cathy, and finds an embrace of acceptance. She is able to rage without losing her mother.

> When Maya's father and I divorced, she found herself caught in the middle—not just going between two houses—but feeling as though she had to choose between her father's (African-American) and my (white) ethnic identity. One day, she told me she had been carrying a secret; she blurted out that she wished she could have a black mother.
>
> Once the secret was released, she cried, laughed and cried. I sat, holding her, appreciating her. I thanked her for telling me; I told her I was proud of her sharing, and congratulated her for letting it go. I was hurt, but not angry. I understood that she was an ethnic person and she needed to identify with that.

Cathy's experience conveys the challenge of reflecting—and not overreacting or rejecting—a daughter's deeply felt secrets. Yet we see that mirroring is not an act of martyrdom. Cathy could regard and value Maya's wish, but still authorize her own pain. Parents can say, "What you tell me hurts [or angers or worries] me, but I'm glad you decided to tell me."

MIRRORING IS HARD WORK

We see that mirroring can move mountains. Yet as you already know, it is easier to rhapsodize about empathy than practice using it. Raise your hand every time you recognize one of your own responses.

Instead of affirming feelings, we often respond by denying, advising, shushing, and shaming.

Psychologist Betsy Cohen suggests that we might have more sympathy for sleepy Snow White if we understood that she was "without anger or direction" because her stepmother—busy studying her own reflection in the mirror—did not adequately mirror Snow White's feelings.[11] Without mirroring, says Cohen, our heroine

Child	Parent
"There's a witch under my bed!"	"Don't be scared; witches aren't real."
"I'm hot."	"How can you be hot? It's thirty-two degrees; I'm freezing!"
"I'm not hungry."	"Just eat a few bites."
"I hate Susan! I'm not inviting her to my birthday party."	"Well, you've *already* invited her and I thought you two were such good friends."
"My teacher is always picking on me."	"What do you think you are doing that is bothering him so much?"
"I'll never finish this paper on time."	"You should have started it last week. Why don't you cancel your sleepover with Kathy so you have more time?"
"I'm not in the mood to go to the party."	"That doesn't sound like my happy little girl."
"The next time he makes fun of me, I'm going to punch him in the face."	"Calm down; we don't hit people."
"Why did it have to rain for the picnic?"	"Stop whining. There will be other sunny days."
"Robin is the meanest sister in the world; all she does is boss me around."	"That's not nice, I know you love your sister."

lacked self-reliance and looked outside of herself (the guy on the white horse) to point her in the direction of the sunset.

But let's not blame Mother—or wonder why Snow's father was not listening more artfully. Instead, let's ask, Why is it a struggle for parents to mirror a daughter's emotional likeness? First of all, remember that many parents find that mirroring does not reflect their own temperament or personal style.

As Jean explains, "I'm an attorney, a problem solver. I'm here for the solution. Kate had to teach me how to be reflective, empathic. When she was younger, she would tell me a feeling and I would try to argue with her, or resolve it. Then we started a journal together, and every night, when I put her to bed, we record the feelings and stories she tells me."

The Ghosts in the Nursery

Another scenario: Parents hold up the mirror to show their daughter her likeness and instead see themselves acting like their own parents. Child analyst Selma Fraiberg calls this experience "seeing the ghosts in the nursery." "These ghosts reflect the repetition of parents' past in the present," says Fraiberg.[12]

Many parents struggle not to repeat their parents' patterns of discounting their feelings. Yet parents can rewrite their own ghost story, explains Fraiberg, when they acknowledge the childhood pain they felt. Then, they will be able to improve upon their past rather than recreate it.

Jane (who skillfully mirrored Amy's unnamed "feeling") understands this dynamic. "My expressiveness was not encouraged by my family: whenever I would cry—out of sadness or anger—my father would make fun of me, calling me 'Sarah Bernhardt.' I *know* how painful and puzzling it is to have strong feelings discouraged and I have integrated this into my personality and my parenting with Amy."

For many parents, the ghost story finds a happier ending when they express empathy for their own parents. This happens when they realize that Dad and Mom were unable to reflect feelings because *they* lacked a model for mirroring—they did not have parents who honored their feelings.

Lea explains, "My mother still has a certain look when she disagrees with me; it's a look that always made me feel unloved. It still unsettles my stomach. But one day, I saw her mother give her the same look, and I began to understand that no parent listened to my mom without strings attached either. How can she give me what she didn't get? Understanding this doesn't take the pain away, but it soothes the anger."

INVITING EMPATHY

What's right with these responses? (See chart on page 50.)

In every example, the parent response mirrored the truth of a child's "inner" experience. In each response, a parent accepted a daughter's invitation to enter her world.

THE MECHANICS OF MIRRORING

Jeffrey Lustman, a psychiatrist at Veterans Hospital in West Haven, Connecticut, talks about the mirroring relationship—and how the invitations to enter a daughter's world change as she grows. As he explains, "Parenting is a lot about whether you are capable of responding to the invitations your children tender with each new chapter in their development. When my daughter was younger, she wanted me to take her point of view—to speak her feelings out loud and give them a language. Now [at sixteen] she often seeks me out to share her world—rather than validate it. With each stage, I discover a new person in her that allows me to be very different with her; it's like going from caterpillar to butterfly to caterpillar to butterfly."[13]

How do we accept these invitations to listen? The parents I meet want to understand the mechanics of mirroring. They want to know: What actions will help me to mirror my daughter's experience—and allow her to see her emotional likeness? How can my empathy push her envelope of expression past the "perfect happy girl"? Here's a short list of ideas for polishing your listening skills.

Child	Parent
"There's a witch under my bed!"	"Seeing things in the dark can be scary. How can we keep the witches away?"
"I'm hot."	"It's cold, but shooting baskets keeps you warm."
"I'm not hungry."	"That big lunch really filled you up."
"I hate Susan! I'm not inviting her to my birthday party."	"You seem really mad at Susan. You two must have had a tough time today."
"My teacher is always picking on me."	"You feel like he is not being fair to you—and you can't figure out why."
"I'll never finish this paper on time."	"The paper turned out to be more work than you thought."
"I'm not in the mood to go to the party."	"Tonight doesn't feel like party night to you."
"The next time Andy makes fun of me, I'm going to punch him in the face."	"You've had enough of Andy's teasing."
"Why did it have to rain for the picnic?"	"How disappointing; you were really looking forward to eating outside."
"Robin is the meanest sister in the world; all she does is boss me around."	"Sometimes it's hard to be Robin's sister."

Make Her the Authority

Terry recalls when Jessica (age seven) told him her dream about her newborn sister. Instead of being specific, his broad statement allowed her to accept her feelings.

> *Jessica:* I'm so scared, I dreamed a bear was going to eat Caitlin and I had to save her!
>
> *Dad:* You must have a lot of strong feelings about your new baby sister.

When we RSVP with empathy, we make her the authority about her feelings. Invite her to explore her feelings with general statements: "Today didn't go the way you planned. Susan acted differently than you expected." Or: "I'll bet you have some strong feelings about getting a new teacher."

With older girls, mirroring can discourage the expression of false feelings. For example, when you say, "It seems like what you are thinking and feeling is different from your friends." With younger daughters, our listening can be a lesson in labeling.

Name the Feeling

Deborah described Lauren as a "high-spirited intense child. At age three, her tantrums were really wild."

> I wanted to acknowledge her anger; but also teach her to channel it, take charge of it. So one day, when she was furious, I asked, *"Does it feel like a volcano is going to explode?"* Then, for a long time, we used the volcano as code for being really angry. She might say, "That volcano is in my tummy." As she has grown older, she can simply say, "I'm really mad, what can I do about it?"

Deborah is wise to use her mirroring to offer her young daughter a emotional metaphor—a specific name for her anger.[14] When we join a daughter in naming her experience, we see empathy as education; we are teaching her to express, recognize, and rely on her feelings.

Listen to the Feeling, Not the Event

Six-year-old Gloria came home from school and told her mother about how some kids had pushed her friend Dori into a muddy gutter. Psychologist Ginott describes what happened next, "Instead of asking for more details about the event, her mother responded to her daughter's feelings. She said:

> 'That must have upset you.'
> 'You were angry at the boys who did it.'
> 'You are still mad at them.'
> To all of these statements Gloria responded with an emphatic 'Yes!' When Mother said, 'You are afraid they may do it to you too?', Gloria answered with determination, 'Let them try, I'll drag them with me. That would make a splash.' And she started to laugh."[15]

Daughters come home to us complaining, grieving, raging, or elated about friends, tests, teachers—close encounters of every kind. When we acknowledge the feelings—rather than asking questions about the event—we create a safe harbor for her to express her exuberance, anger, confusion, envy, fear. When we confirm her feelings, she often finds the confidence to handle the situation on her own.

Affirm Mixed Feelings

Terry recalls:

> When my father was dying, I was spending a lot of time with him, and Caitlin was upset about my time away from her. When he died, she felt guilty about her anger and I told her, "Of course you loved Grandpa, but I'm sure that you also felt angry and jealous that I was getting on the train—that I wasn't there for you."

Terry describes his conversation with Caitlin as "affirming a range of feelings." He elaborates, "I try to give my daughters permission to have complex feelings—without specifying there is one right feeling."

Parents who want to mirror a daughter's mixed feelings can say, "You seem to have two feelings about your little sister: you enjoy playing with her *and* you are jealous I spend so much time with her." Or: "Your feelings about Randy go back and forth. You like to have him come over, but sometimes he gets on your nerves."[16]

When parents can acknowledge mixed, messy, not so "nice," feelings, daughters will learn to express and trust their own inner experiences. They will also trust you to share them.

REFLECT FEELINGS IN FANTASY

Educators Adele Farber and Elaine Mazlish, in their book *How to Talk So Kids Will Listen*, offer a marvelous strategy for mirroring: granting children in fantasy what we can't give them in reality. As the authors explain, "Having someone understand how much you really want something makes reality easier to bear."[17]

Young Child: I really want to go to the beach. Why did it have to rain? This whole weekend is wrecked! Why does this have to happen?

Parent: I can see how disappointed you are. I wish I had a magic wand and could make the sun come out.

Child, laughing: Can your wand make rainbows, too?

Older Child: The binoculars I got for my birthday are lousy! I can barely see that nest.

Parent: We can't really afford another pair. I wish we could win the lottery—then I could buy you a pair that are so strong you will be able to see a hummingbird wink!

Child: They'd be so strong I could see a hummingbird's eyelashes!

Even the youngest daughters understand that reflecting feelings and spinning fantasies are not the same as *agreeing* with them. Still, as Faber and Mazlish write, "When we grant a child's wishes in fantasy, we let them know we take their longing seriously."[18]

Mirror Her Behavior

Mirroring also means looking for the emotional logic behind a daughter's behavior. When I interviewed Kara, she didn't know how to respond to her twelve-year-old daughter Molly's recent confession: "Some of my friends are starting to smoke." I encouraged Kara to wonder, "Why is Molly telling me this? Is she wondering how her friends will treat her if she doesn't smoke; or is she already smoking with them—and trying to test how I will respond?"

In his book *Playground Politics*, psychiatrist Stanley Greenspan urges parents to understand how a child's actions fit into her experience of the world. He suggests that we view troubling behavior as a "coping strategy to minimize pain."[19] Greenspan's questions for empathic parents include: What's in this behavior for her? Why does she see the world this way? What goals does this serve? What does she assume?

Then—when she appears in a fashion victim's ensemble—we can ask, "Tell me why you want to wear that outfit to the party." Or after meeting the friend that any parent would love to hate: "Tell me what you like best about Jennifer." In the face of pained and troubled acts, we can begin a dialogue, saying, "You must have had a very good reason for what you did."

HOW EMPATHY INSPIRES INDEPENDENCE

Parent educator Nancy Samalin offers a fine example of how reflecting feelings emboldens a daughter to act.[20] She explores the experience of eight-year-old Susan, whose classmates' teasing wasn't helping her accept her new glasses.

One day, Susan came home sobbing, "They called me four eyes!" Her mother, Julia, hoping to ease the hurt, said: "You look just fine; don't let them upset you." Julia continued her supportive statements for several days until her daughter ran from the room shouting, *"You don't understand!"*

At that moment, Julia realized that she wasn't listening to her daughter's hurt feelings—she was trying to make them go away. Later, she sat on Susan's bed.

> *Julia:* Boy, I guess it is a horrible feeling to be called "four eyes."
>
> *Susan:* I hate those kids! If I cry, it gets even worse.
>
> *Julia:* Yeah, when I was about your age, my big brothers teased me, and crying made them even meaner. I wonder what you could say the next time that would be different.

Over the course of the next half hour, they came up with a strategy. Later, Julia thought about the role of empathy in helping her daughter master a hurtful situation. "I really wanted to build a protective bubble around her so no one could hurt her. But the only thing that really helped was acknowledging Susan's hurt and helping her stand up for herself."

Julia shows us the difference between sympathy and empathy. Sometimes daughters don't want (or need) a cheerleader. They want us to listen to angry or hurt feelings without minimizing, judging, or advising. The paradox is that recognizing feelings often leads to a solution. Once a daughter's feelings are recognized, she can find the solution on her own.

HER OWN TRUTH

As we have seen, mirroring is the art of telling a daughter that we believe her story. I was deeply moved by how Jane described this kind of listening. "I operate on the assumption that Alice is telling me the truth—that her emotions and observations of her world and the people in it *create her own kind of truth* (although it is not 100% literal truth). There is a circle here; I'm not sure which came first. But when I confirm what she tells me, it seems to reinforce her willingness to tell me the truth."

5

Discover Her Temperament

CAROL and her daughters, Kelly (six) and Christa (nine), arrived at a sunny summer picnic in the park at twelve-thirty. At two-thirty, Kelly tugged on her mother's sleeve, saying, "I really have to go home now." As Carol explains, "I really wasn't surprised—Kelly is so much less social than Christa. But the extroverted parent in me was judging her and wanting to scream, 'This is fun; what's wrong with you?' Instead, I asked her what she wanted to do and she said, 'I want to go home and alphabetize my Berenstain Bear books.' I looked at her solemn face and realized that she had socialized as much as she could. It was hard for me to leave; but she was maxed out and I had to honor that."

In Carol's response, we see the wisdom of understanding the individual differences, rather than sex differences, that define our daughters. In this chapter, you will find tools to discover a daughter's uniqueness in the rich details of temperament. We will explore how to mirror—and help her manage—the voice of her experience in the world. Let's start with a closer look at how Carol believed her daughter's story.

First, Carol understood Kelly's "temperament"—her typical style of responding.[1] She knew that her daughter was slow to adapt to new situations and people. Next, she reminded herself that Kelly drew her energy from within and preferred to recharge her batteries by being alone.[2] Alphabetizing bear books was the perfect antidote to the people-intensive picnic.

Most important, Carol honored the difference between mother and daughter by matching her expectations with her daughter's experience.[3] She could have danced all night, but Kelly was about to turn into a pumpkin.

WHY TEMPERAMENT IS A WINDOW TO HER WORLD

Do terms such as "temperament," "extrovert," or "energy from within" make you feel as if you were filling out a personality quiz in an airplane magazine—or reading a dizzy New Age pamphlet? Turn the phone over to voice mail, and let me explain why dimensions of personality—such as temperament—are a window to your daughter's inner world. Consider the following:[4]

- Understanding her temperament and energy preference help us see not just what she does but also her *experience* of what she does.
- Kids notice their temperament; they worry about their quirks, and get teased about them. Your discoveries can help both of you avoid limiting labels.
- If you can recognize and confirm her own experience of her temperament, you can coach her to be self-reliant in managing her temperament.
- Discovering a daughter's temperament and energy increases an awareness of your own. Here lies the opportunity to celebrate, or at the very least build a bridge between, your differences by creating expectations that allow her to grow.

HER TEMPERAMENT'S PICNIC

From the moment she was born, your daughter has been different from every girl and boy at the picnic in a variety of ways. One of the most intriguing ways is her temperament, her first and preferred way of responding to her experience of the world. Seattle psychiatrist Diane Stein once told me, "If you want to understand temperament, just watch when a nurse drops something on the floor of a newborn nursery." Some babies will be startled, awakened, wide-eyed, disturbed by the noise, others will look around briefly, and some babies will be blissfully undisturbed.

The idea of temperament was defined in a now classic study in the 1950s by psychologists Stella Chess and Thomas Alexander and detailed in their readable book *Know Your Child*. To Chess and Alexander, temperament revealed what they called the "how of behavior." They saw it as a style of behavior—present from birth—that revealed the way children respond to the world around them.

The nine temperament traits they described are "rhythm of body functions, intensity, persistence, sensory threshold, distractibility, adaptability, initial response, energy, and quality of mood." For parents of newborns and toddlers, the very jargon of temperament leads to a resounding *"Aha!* Yes, sir, that's my baby" response. Here's a short sample:

> *Rhythm of body functions:* "She immediately slid into a breast-feeding schedule" and "She always needed a diaper change during dinner." *Or:* "She was hungry at the oddest times; I never knew when we would need a changing table."
>
> *Intensity:* "She had a howl you could hear at the South Pole." *Or:* "She cried so softly, she sounded like a mewing cat."
>
> *Initial response:* "She never minded new baby-sitters; she ate anything we offered." *Or:* "She's going bananas with a new baby-sitter; remember when she would only eat Gerber's turkey and chunky vegetables?"
>
> *Quality of mood:* "She was a happy, smiley baby." *Or:* "She was often cranky; it was hard to get her to smile."

When you see how early your daughter displayed her traits of temperament, you can forget the Dr. Frankenstein feeling—you did not create your daughter's temperament; her behavioral style was built into her hard-wiring. Your response can only minimize or exaggerate the more challenging temperamental traits. Remember, too, that temperament is not destiny. A number of studies suggest that the emotional lessons we offer children can reshape their temperament.[5]

Long-term studies with slow-to-warm, slow-to-adapt children are a cheering case in point. One study reports that one out of three infants who displayed these traits outgrew them by kindergarten. When the parents of these changed kiddos were observed at home, it was clear their parents had put gentle, gradual pressure on them to behave more boldly.[6]

HER TEMPERAMENT AT PLAY

To discover more about your daughter's preferred style of responding—how her temperament shapes her unique experience of the world—let's imagine both of you at the picnic and playground with Kelly and Carol. Now consider eight of the dimensions of temperament. What might you see as her preferred style of responding?[7] (If she is too young to sit at the table, picture a future picnic.)

1. *Intensity.* What is the level of energy in her response to situations?
   High Intensity: She laughs joyously on the slide; wails if she scrapes her knee on the picnic table; bristles with frustration if she has to wait for swings or for dessert.
   Low Intensity: She smiles quietly on the slide; whimpers as she scrapes her knee; waits patiently for the swings or strawberry ice cream.
2. *Sensory Threshold:* What is the level of stimulation it takes to evoke her response to sounds, smells, textures, other people's stress?
   Low Threshold: She reacts immediately to stimuli in her environment. She whips her head around to see who is cry-

ing; complains about the smell of barbecue; won't eat the "goopy" potato salad; complains about the scratchy label in her shorts; wonders if the girl on the swings is mad at her. *High Threshold:* She is unruffled by stimulation around her. She doesn't notice the crying child, the smell of the barbecue, or the runny potato salad. Her shorts feel fine; she ignores the scowling girl on the swings.

3. *Persistence and Attention Span:* Does she continue an activity—even in the face of obstacles? What is the length of time she engages in an activity?

Low Persistence: She shoots a few baskets, misses, and stops playing. When you tell her she can't have any more cookies, she accepts the news with mild protest.

High Persistence: She shoots a basket, misses, but doesn't stop until she can slam-dunk the ball. When you mention the cookie cutoff, she locks in, debates, and may cry until sunset.

Short Attention Span: She spends two minutes on the slide, three minutes on the jungle gym, and five minutes making sand castles.

Long Attention Span: She sits for an hour making sand castles, then spends thirty minutes on the jungle gym.

4. *Distractibility:* How easily does an outside stimulus interfere with (or direct) her activity?

High Distractibility: On her way from the jungle gym to the picnic table, she stops to watch a robin, pick up a candy wrapper, and listen for five minutes to music from a radio across the street.

Low Distractibility: She is so involved in climbing the jungle gym, she doesn't want to come to lunch. Or she is hungry and you can't distract her by playing catch until lunchtime.

5. *Adaptability:* What are her responses to new situations? How does she adapt to transitions and change?

High Adaptability: She moves easily from playing pirates to having lunch; welcomes new kids into the game. She eats chicken without complaint—even though you had promised burgers. She leaves the picnic in a no-tears departure.

Low Adaptability: She protests when new kids join the pirate play, complains loudly when she is asked to stop for lunch. She refuses to eat the chicken, laments the lack of burgers, and cries when it's time to go home.

6. *Initial Response:* What is her first response to new situations—approach or withdrawal?

   Withdrawal: She is slow to warm up: refusing to talk (at first) to kids and adults she doesn't know; watching kids play pirates on the sidelines before joining in. She takes one look at peach pie and says, "I don't like it."

   Approach: She warms up easily: talking to kids and adults like old friends, joining in play immediately, eager to try the peach pie.

7. *Energy:* What is the balance between her active and inactive times?

   High Activity Level: She squirms in the car, makes a beeline for the swings, and plays full-throttle until lunchtime—where she wiggles, eats a few bites, and jumps up on the table, spilling her milk.

   Low Activity Level: She gazes out the window on the way to the picnic, slowly makes her way to the slide, and sits a long time before going down. She makes careful sand piles until lunch—where she sits at the table until she's finished eating.

8. *Quality of Mood:* Is her typical mood positive—expressing pleasure, joy, and friendliness—or is it negative—more serious, analytical, less joyful and friendly?

   Positive Mood: After two hours at the picnic, she raves, "They have a great climber"; "I made five baskets"; "the kids here are cool"; "did you taste those cookies?"

   Negative Mood: She offers a list of grievances—delivered in a whiny or joyless tone: "The slide was too hot"; "the kids wouldn't let me play"; "they ran out of cookies"; "next year they should . . ."

RESPONDING TO THE VOICES OF TEMPERAMENT

As you leave the imaginary picnic, think about your daughter's unique and rich (or exasperating) combination of these traits. Reflect about how they contribute to her individual style of responding to the experiences in her life—and how they may contribute to your experience of aging in dog years as her parent. Still, the discovery of her traits of temperament is a scenic route to understanding and validating her voice and worldview. She is trying to tell you how it feels to be her, how the world looks to her.

Mary Kurchinka, author of *Raising Your Spirited Child*, explains how understanding temperament is critical in honoring what a child feels and knows. "Identifying your child's temperamental traits is like an X ray. It helps you understand what's going on inside of your child so you can understand how she is reacting to the world around her and why. Once you understand the reasons behind his/her responses, you can learn to work with them, ease the hassles, teach new behaviors when they are needed. Most important, you can help your child understand and like herself/himself."[8]

We can strengthen a daughter's self-reliance by acknowledging the voice of her temperament. Yet parents who discover her temperament must be of two minds. We must balance confirming and accepting temperament—avoiding negative labels—while coaching and challenging her to have insight and mastery of her style of responding. Let's consider some dangers and opportunities of responding to the voices of temperament as your daughter moves from the toddler to the preteen years.[9]

Intensity: Difficult or Dramatic?

The biggest danger for *high-intensity* daughters is that they will be seen as "loud" and "unladylike" instead of "zestful," "out-of-control" instead of "enthusiastic." They are the little girls who get shushed and the older girls who learn to silence themselves. Parents of daughters with an intense temperament must find opportunities to nurture the depth, humor, and magical delight of feelings that set your daughter apart.

Help her find comfort in her intensity by using labels that speak of your comfort. Teach her positive words to describe and confirm her intense voice: "You love to laugh," "you feel things so strongly," "you have a great imagination" or "sense of drama." Coach her to recognize and channel her intensity in a positive direction. "You're really charged up about this, let's go outside where we can jump and shout."

Persistence: Never Say Never

Our biggest concern for daughters with *low persistence* is that they are quick to give up or say, "I can't," and adult caretakers or teachers will be quick to rescue them (or expect less of them). They may be labeled as "dependent"—even "lazy"; their temperament can lead to reinforcement of passivity. Let your daughter know you see her frustration—"I know how hard it is to hang in there"—yet coach her by teaching her to break tasks into smaller, more doable pieces.

On the other hand, daughters who are *high in persistence,* who dig in their heels, require our Olympian restraint to keep from labeling them as "sassy" and "stubborn" rather than confirming them as "assertive" and "independent." The closer your daughter moves to adolescence, the more important it will be to pause, midargument, and say, "I don't agree, but you are a great debater!"

Sensitivity: The Princess and the Pea

Our tenderhearted daughters struggle with sock bumps, scratchy labels, loud noises, yecchy smells, the pat that feels like a slap. Their *low threshold* for stimulation reminds us of the princess who is bruised by the pea under a stack of mattresses.

She is at risk in two ways. First, her strong reactivity to sights and sounds and smells can cause her to be seen as "prissy," "hysterical," or "impossible." Next, as she approaches her adolescent struggle to preserve relationships, her exquisite sensitivity to what friends and family do and say will complicate her struggle to stay connected to loved ones—without losing her sense of self.

We must coach her to recognize and manage the signs of sensory overload, yet confirm the unique spirit and strength of her sensitivity. We can say: "You hear and see so much"; "you have a beautiful heart"; "you have an eagle eye"; "you feel things so deeply"; "you really notice how other people are feeling."

Distractibility: The Daughter of Detours

Keep your eye on the daughter whose *high distractibility* creates dozens of detours on her way to getting dressed or setting the table or doing her homework. Count to twenty before labeling her as "lazy," "uncooperative, "not a good listener," or even "not bright." We must educate ourselves, teachers—and especially our daughters—about the creative potential of her wiry alertness.

We have two tasks. First, we must confirm the strength of her experience of being observant. We can say, "You really use your eyes and ears." Or: "I would have never noticed that if you hadn't shown me." Next, we can coach her: helping her reach her goals by allowing more time, creating less stimulating environments for school study, and helping her focus on one essential event at a time.

Adaptability: "She Wears Tights in Summer."

The daughter of *low adaptability*—who wears winter clothes into July, who experiences meltdown with an unexpected change of en-trée for dinner, who finds it equally hard to go to the party and hard to leave—may be labeled as "rigid," "difficult," uncooperative," "a terrible-two at twelve." These are the daughters who seem especially vulnerable to the truckload of transitions during preadolescence.

As she grows, we can coach her on two fronts. First, we can make transitions less troubling through extra time, advance warnings, and rehearsing. Next, we should help her confirm and give voice to the authentic feelings that drive her standing-in-place behavior. We can say, for example, "It's hard for you to give up what you had planned"; "you like to know what's coming next"; or "you felt like that just snuck up on you."

Initial Response: Shy or Slow to Warm Up?

Do you have a daughter who never fails to reject and *withdraw* from the new and unfamiliar: a new kid in school, a new recipe, a birthday party, or (most embarrassing) an old friend of yours whose eyes she won't meet? She is in danger of being limited to labels of "shy," "not adventurous," "fearful," or even "rude" or "anxious." The reality is that she is "slow to warm up" and her initial response of withdrawal is not her destination.

The balance between confirming and coaching lies in your ability to initially take "no" for an answer and then gradually expose her to new situations. Make her the authority about her experiences; but convey a confidence in her ability to warm up. You might say, "You like to think things through"; "you like to get started slowly"; "you enjoy watching first"; "you take a while to warm up, but then you are red hot."

Energy: She Can't Sit Down

The daughter whose *high-energy* temperament helps set her in perpetual motion can be limited by the labels of "aggressive," "uncooperative," and even that old standby "tomboy." The task here is twofold: First, coach family, daughter, and teachers to incorporate her need for motion (jujitsu after school, having her pass out papers, bring dessert from kitchen). Then confirm the positive experience of this trait: "You can accomplish so much with your energy"; "if I had your energy, I could . . ."; "you've got energy to spare."

Quality of Mood: The Oh-So-Serious Daughter

If your daughter of *negative mood* is seldom a happy camper (she's full of analysis, grievances, and suggestions), she is likely to be labeled as "whiny," "picky," "cranky," or even, "thinking too much." Parents of an oh-so-serious daughter need to go in three directions at once.

First, confirm her heartfelt critiques of people and places—but don't reinforce her negativity. (Say, for example, "The play was not what you expected.") Next, help her confirm her analytical strengths: "You like things to be just so"; "you have high standards"; "you think a long time about things that happen to you." Then coach her to anticipate problems: "What can we do to make the picnic fun for you?"

THE BALLET OF TEMPERAMENT: BEING AUTHENTIC/BEING ADAPTIVE

In each of the eight examples above, the discovery of temperament is a ballet of balance. As you begin to understand your daughter's behavioral style, you move in two ways. First, as parents who wish to nurture a daughter's unique strength and spirit, we must confirm (and encourage her to recognize) the *authentic* story of her experience that speaks through her temperament. At the same time, we must challenge her to become *adaptive*—to take charge of her temperament. As we coach her, we nurture her self-reliance, and her ability to trust her own experience and judgment.

But where will you both get the energy to tackle her temperament?

6

Explore Her Energy

LIKE most parents, my discovery of Hannah's temperament traits and energy preference led to the recognition of my own. I remember a snugly 2 A.M. feeding when Hannah was several weeks old. The heat thermostat switched on with a crisp loud click and Hannah and I both jumped out of our skins. This was the first of many clues that Hannah and I both had a low sensory threshold: we smell popcorn a block away; our attention is diverted by a crying child; we both try on and buy shoes and (too late) decide they are uncomfortable. We both want to pull out the scratchy tags in clothes; we both ask Jeremy, "Why did you shrug?"

I also discovered my energy preference (for introversion) by noticing how both Hannah and I get pooped by the party—and how we each recharge with our own version of alphabetizing bear books. On the other hand, I am a highly persistent, it's-not-over-till-it's-over kind of person. Sometimes, Hannah's "I can'ts" worry me: What can I do to encourage her stick-to-it self-reliance?

Still, I am filled with questions; I am suspicious of my glib comparisons. Just because Hannah does or doesn't act like me, does that mean I understand the story of her experience? How do I recognize

her temperament traits—the ones that are different from mine—and
still coach her to develop coping strategies?

In this chapter, we will examine how a daughter finds and refuels
her energy to manage her experiences in the world. We will also
consider occasions when her temperament and energy collide with
ours. We begin at Rachel's birthday party.

THE ENERGY TO CELEBRATE:
INTROVERTED AND EXTROVERTED DAUGHTERS

Jane's parents had arrived for a belated birthday celebration for
her eight-year-old daughter, Rachel. Jane answered the door, calling, "It's Grandma and Grandpa!" Then she heard the distinct click
of Rachel's bedroom door closing. After a few minutes of Jane's
frantic coaxing, Rachel emerged from her room, smiled, circled,
and then kissed her guests. When Grandma asked, "How was your
day?" Rachel offered a monotonic "Okay." To Grandpa's question,
"What are your summer plans?" she shrugged, "I don't know." As
Rachel opened her presents, Grandma moved her chair closer—and
Rachel moved her chair away.

Seated at dinner, Rachel surprised everyone: volunteering a long
story about a kid in her class and describing a summer computer
camp her teacher had mentioned. Then, halfway through the chocolate birthday cake, she grew quiet, excused herself, and retreated to
her room. But Jane was hot on her trail, hissing, "Aren't you glad to
see Grandma?" and "Don't you want to kiss Grandpa goodnight?"
And then, "You are embarrassing me," and "You're hurting their
feelings." But Jane returned (daughterless) and offered her parents
an apology by way of a lie: "Rachel's probably coming down with a
cold."

In fact, Rachel was very well, thank you; she probably enjoyed
the party, and was quite happy to see her grandparents. She was
simply displaying what Swiss psychologist Carl Jung called a *personality preference* for finding and maintaining her energy. Rachel
was showing a preference for what Jung called *introversion*.[1] She is
someone who relies on her inner world for energy, can quickly tire

of socializing, and recharges her batteries by being quiet or spending time alone.

HER PREFERRED BEHAVIOR

Like the temperament studies of Chess and Thomas, Jung's work on psychological preferences, or "types," describes early and persistent aspects of personality. Similarly, the idea of preference offers parents a way of observing not just a daughter's behavior but also her experience of her behavior. For parents, the focus is finding a balance between listening to the voice of preference and coaching her to find self-reliance by pushing the envelope.

Jung's original theory described four preference pairs. They have been popularized (and at times, misunderstood) through the wide use of the "Meyers-Briggs"-type indicator[2]:

1. *Extroversion vs. Introversion:* How we get energy and prefer to relate socially.
2. *Judgment vs. Perception:* Our preference for organizing and giving structure to our lives.
3. *Sensing vs. Intuition:* How we prefer to gather information about the world.
4. *Thinking vs. Feeling:* How we prefer to make decisions about information.[3]

Jung believed that the contrast between introversion and extroversion—the source, focus, and direction of a person's energy—was the most important of the preference distinctions between people. The difference between the two is most frequently explained in this way: *Extroverts* are energized by being with people, *introverts* can be drained by being with people and get their energy being alone or with a small circle of friends.

In other words, "time out" for an extrovert is Siberia; for an introvert, it is Nirvana. Parents with several children are experts in the different ways energy preference plays out. Here are some examples.[4]

Extrovert	Introvert
Leaps before looking	Watches before joining in
Thinks by talking	Reflects for a time before talking
Territory/boundaries are fluid (low need for privacy)	Protective of territory, high need for privacy
Tells all immediately	Finds it difficult to explain feelings; waits for hours or days to talk

Do you recognize your daughter in these descriptions? Does she have a tendency to be retiring, to need privacy, to drop her head when meeting someone, to be frightened and silent when swooped down upon by an adult? Do you also recognize your own attempts to correct and change her?[5]

THE PERILS OF THE INTROVERTED DAUGHTER

So now we understand that when Rachel goes to her room when her grandparents visit, she is probably not going to be lip-synching to Barbra Streisand singing "People." More likely, she is introverted, replenishing her energy bank by being alone. True, your extroverted daughter is in some danger of being labeled as "loud," but she meshes more easily and is more easily understood. She also outnumbers her introverted brothers and sisters by a ratio of 3:1.

For this reason alone, it is our introverted daughters who are most often misunderstood and who feel the most pressure from teachers and parents to change. They are most vulnerable to what Jung called "the falsification of self"—an experience of disharmony, lack of self-awareness, or lying to oneself to please others.[6]

From this view, it is easy to see that urging a disappearing daughter to "be nice" or to "kiss Grandpa" goodnight encourages her to develop a false sense of self. To move beyond a position of pressure,

take a moment to reconsider not just Rachel's *behavior* during her
grandparents' visit, but her *experience* of her behavior.

ENERGY AND TEMPERAMENT: FIVE PARENT TRAPS

It is tempting to view these four tableaux as a choice between
personality preference and politeness. You may be thinking Rachel
is downright rude. But let me frame the question in another way:
How do you honor your introverted child—once you understand
her preference for managing energy—and still challenge her to be
self-reliant? How do you teach her to tackle her temperament and
meet the social challenges in her life? You might start by looking at
your own reflection.

Take a moment and revisit the traits of temperament and energy
preference. This time, reflect on your own responses. *What happens
when her temperament and energy meet yours?* Listen to parents'
voices and imagine five tender traps.

Intrusion: "*I know how she feels.*"

> I see Eve at parties—standing on the sidelines, holding back and
> watching—and I feel for her. I've spent many an evening with a
> knot in my stomach when I had to meet new people.

A preference match between parent and daughter is a mixed
blessing. On one hand, the opportunity for empathy and confirma-
tion are strong. Yet the assumption of sameness leads to the trap of
intrusion ("I know how you feel") and projection ("When *I* was in
that situation, *I* felt . . .").[7] Both behaviors ignore the voice of her
temperament and energy; both narrow her opportunity to learn to
manage her preferences in her own unique way.

Reinforcement: "*We're both like that.*"

> Candace and I are both so intense, we're born to yell—going at
> it, full throat, all day long.

A parent-daughter preference match can be incendiary. A daughter's intensity can bring out your own, her fears can kindle your anxiety; her persistence can rankle your rigidity. When parent and daughter simply reinforce each other's preferred responses, a daughter misses the opportunity to look to her parent as a model for coping strategies in managing her own responses.

Disappointment: "Why can't she be more like me?"

I had really looked forward to having a daughter to chat with. I love to tell Sarah about my day; but she never really seems to want to talk about hers.

The lack of match between a parent and a daughter can evoke a sense of loss. The understanding of a daughter's distinct temperament and energy can unleash a litany of lost hope: "She'll never want to share her feelings, enjoy parties, try to travel to exotic places." Your sadness and disappointment—the wish that you two were more alike—can convey a disconfirming and damaging message to your daughter.

Embarrassment: "Why can't she even say hello?"

We were in the park and a man bent down to ask Laura about the dinosaur on her sweatshirt. She lowered her head and didn't answer. The man looked at me and said, "She's not very happy, is she?" I sighed. "She's just tired."

Many parents whose daughters' preferred responses don't match their own suffer from adult stranger anxiety. "What must they be thinking?" we wonder as we apologize or offer a running commentary on a daughter's behavior. Instead of this tyranny of politeness, we should be asking, Why do I care so much about what a complete stranger thinks of my daughter? Parents who disconfirm a daughter's experience—talking about her as if she weren't there—must examine the message they deliver to daughters: "Being true to your experience is an embarrassment to me."

Revisiting Grandma

---

1. "How was your day?"

Behavior: Didn't want to talk about her day; volunteered a story later in the evening.

Introverted preference trait: Finds it difficult to describe feelings and experience; needs time to reflect before talking.

Her most probable experience: "I haven't had time to think. I'll talk when I'm ready."

2. "What are your summer plans?"

Behavior: Didn't respond to question about summer plans.

Introverted preference trait: Needs time to think about decisions; mentally rehearses decisions.

Her most probable experience: "I'm working this through; I need time to make a good decision."

3. Musical chairs.

Behavior: Moved away when Grandma moved closer.

Introverted preference trait: Strong sense of territory.

Her probable experience: "I feel crowded, invaded."

4. Retreat.

Behavior: Grew quiet after a brief time at the table, then returned to her room.

Introverted personality trait: Drained by being with people.

Her probable experience: "I'm exhausted by responding to people. I need to recharge my batteries by being alone."

Overprotection: "She can't handle it."

> Every time Ellie goes on a field trip, she cries the whole time. We know that new places are hard for her; maybe she should just stay at school.

Overprotection, based on a daughter's temperamental traits, is an equal opportunity trap. When parents who differ from their daughters come to understand her experience of her temperament or energy (for example, how much transitions stress her), they may try to shield her from the pressure. By contrast, parents who share a temperamental trait can be paralyzed by empathy. In both cases, overprotection denies a daughter the opportunity to gain the confidence to manage her own temperament and energy.[8]

THE REAL MATCH: TEMPERAMENT, ENERGY, AND EXPECTATIONS

Psychiatrists Chess and Thomas view the potential traps of temperament from the vantage point of what they call "Goodness of Fit." For them, the issue is not whether parent and child are similar, but what kind of demands are placed on the child and what reactions the child's behavior creates in the parent.[9] So the issue is not so much the match between parent and daughter on a given trait but the match between your daughter's preferred responses and your expectations.

Here's a wonderful example from a parenting class:

> I could never understand why Leah would disappear into her room whenever people spent the day with us, until I learned about introverts and extroverts. Yesterday, I put that information to work for us. I was taking care of a little girl. . . . Leah had just gotten up and was not ready to talk or play. Normally I would have told her, "We have a guest. It isn't good manners not to talk with her and play with her." But this time I respected Leah. I told the friend that Leah had just gotten up and would be ready to play in a bit. . . . After thirty minutes, I

went to her room and told her it was time to play. By then, she was ready and they played beautifully.[10]

A GREAT MATCH

Like Leah's mother, we can find a balance of expectations that help our daughters be both authentic and adaptive. We can honor the unique voice of her temperament and energy *and* help her build her self-reliance. We do this by teaching her skills to cope in a world that is not necessarily like her. Here are some great expectations.[11]

• *Share Information.* Help her shape a better fit between environment and temperament by letting her, and maybe her teachers, know what strategy you've discovered: "I've noticed things seem to go better when you know what to expect . . . when we take a break for you to move around . . . when we don't pack too many activities into the same day."

• *Cut your losses.* Letting go of the fantasy of a perfect parent-daughter match can allow you to create what is possible. Your sadness that your slow-to-adapt daughter may never share your vacation delight in hitting five museums in a day. But couldn't she visit one, refuel at the motel, and venture out again?

• *Model your own comfort and mastery of her responses.* Let her see that you are not unglued by her temperamental traits[12]; offer a model of coping strategies. When your intense daughter sobs over a death in a story or movie, don't overrespond. Hug her, acknowledge the depth of her feelings, and move on. (First say, "That was so sad to see," pause, and then: "Did you like the scene where the kids played in the snow?" Later, if she stays stuck on sadness, you might say, "Maybe we can go on a bike ride and chase the blues away.") Parents of intense daughters must balance between confirming feelings and inflaming them.

• *Prepare rather than protect.* Don't shield your daughter from the stress of managing her temperament; prepare her to succeed. On the eve of a grandparent visit, do some strategic planning with an introverted daughter. You might say, "You know how Grandpa always has a million questions for you; is there anything you want to tell him about?"

Or with a younger child, "Let's find one of your paintings to show Grandma." And take it further: "I know sometimes you need privacy when we have visitors. How can we explain that to Grandpa so he knows you are glad to see him but just need to be alone for a while?"

• *Don't mind her manners.* Avoid the tyranny of niceness by demanding only what one parent called "minimal politeness." To the slow-to-warm or introverted child, you can say, "When Darlene says hello, it's good manners to say hello back; but you don't have to talk if you're not in the mood." Avert your own stranger anxiety by labeling and modeling a positive view of her behavior: "She's thoughtful"; "she likes to look before she leaps"; "she takes a while to get going, but then she dances all night."

BEDTIME STORY

Carol reminds us of how mirroring a daughter's temperament and energy enables us to believe a daughter's story—and honor what she feels. This bedtime story took place about a year after her daughter Kelly wanted to leave the picnic to alphabetize her Berenstain Bear books. As Carol tells it: Kelly (now seven) was having a slumber party for about six of her friends. Around midnight, Kelly came to Carol's room and said, "Mom, I'm sick of my friends, can you please take them home?"

Carol explains it, "I couldn't imagine feeling the way she did. I'm such an extroverted person; I get my energy and satisfaction from verbal sparring and chatting. But I could see that Kelly needed to be on her own. I wasn't going to take the girls home so I set her up alone—in the corner of her room—with some books. She sat in her corner and read, I chatted with the girls for a while and went to bed."

KEY IDEAS

Strategy 2
Believe Her Story

How to listen to the story of a daughter's life—and teach her to honor what she knows and feels

- Encourage her to tell the truth about her feelings and ideas.
- Make her the authority about her experiences and her opinions.
- Be her mirror: help her name her feelings, and accept her strong and mixed emotions.
- Acknowledge her temperament—her typical style of responding—but also coach her to take charge of her behavior.
- Recognize how she recharges her energy. Respect her boundaries, but teach her to manage the social situations in her life.
- Adjust your expectations. Understand how your own temperament matches or differs from your daughter's.

Strategy 3

DECLARE HER
INDEPENDENCE

How to Champion a Daughter's
Self-Reliance and Teach Her to Be
Safe—Without Scaring Her

7

Consider Her Conditioning

Ellen Wahl, director of Operation Smart, tells a wonderful story about a group of ten-year-old girls who were out in the backyard of the Schenectady Girls Club, fixing their bicycles in a bike repair class. Wahl recalled, "Three eleven-year-old boys walked by. 'Hey, what are you doing?' challenged one of the boys. 'That's not girls' work!' Wrench in hand, Deborah looked up and scowled: 'It is so girls' work. Or are you going to be around every time I need to fix my bike? No way!' "[1]

Deborah has offered us a dazzling declaration of independence—made up of equal parts competence and self-reliance. Her defiance echoes psychologist Judith Bardwick's definition of independence: "It results from learning that you can accomplish things by yourself, can rely on your own ability, and can trust your own judgment."[2] Deborah also reminds us of the struggle of daughters and parents who want to talk back to cultural expectations that girls "need help." How can we challenge assumptions about the dependence of our daughters?

In this third strategy section, we will explore dozens of ways to join a daughter in declaring her independence by nurturing her competence and self-reliance. But first, join me in the nursery to look at the lessons of dependence that begin on the day she is born. Let's look at how these lessons condition both parent and daughter to view girls as fragile, helpless, and dependent.

DEPENDENCE TRAINING: THE CINDERELLA CURRICULUM

Thanks to Colette Dowling's classic book, *The Cinderella Complex,* many parents refrain from using the expression "Cinderella story" when they mean a romantic, happy ending. Dowling has insisted that we relearn the prince-saves-girl story as a fable of many women's failure to become independent. She defines "The Cinderella Complex" as a "girl's belief that there will always be someone to take care of her."[3] I can't think of a more succinct definition of unhealthy dependence in a daughter.

Parents searching for the origins of overdependence will find the research to be a cautionary tale about our brave new daughters. When we examine the data on dependence, we see—once again—a story shaped by different assumptions and expectations for boys and girls.

CONDITIONING IN THE CRADLE: BABY, PLEASE STOP CRYING

As our story begins, we see parents whose actions are influenced by the false assumption that girls are more fragile, when, in fact, the greater sturdiness of the female infant has been amply demonstrated.[4] Yet studies report that male infants are handled more frequently and more vigorously than females.[5] Still other studies suggest that if girls are receiving less stimulation, they may also not be receiving the same kind of encouragement to explore that their boy pals are. But girls do, however, get attention for crying.[6]

In her review of research about how we train children for independence, psychologist Lois Hoffman highlighted data that described how girls, but not boys, received more handling and attention when they cried. Here, Hoffman saw the beginning of a pattern of emotional independence in girls: The girl babies learn that help arrives quickly if you cry out for it. Also, mothers of daughters discover that crying will stop if you hurry to help.[7]

For Colette Dowling, this pattern is the female foundation for looking outside of oneself for emotional rescue and problem solving. She points out that since male infants are thought to be tougher, moms don't seem to rush to comfort them. As a result, boys don't receive reinforcement for the idea that "help arrives when I cry." Dowling writes, "There are times when a boy has to solace himself. This *works* for him; he is able to comfort himself on a regular basis. Bit by bit, he (unlike his sister) learns to become his own emotional caretaker."[8]

SEE HOW SHE DOESN'T GROW

As a daughter grows, the direction of the Cinderella Curriculum continues to be shaped by different expectations for each sex. Consider, for example, a study of families at the zoo, reporting that girl toddlers were more likely to be carried or stroller-borne than boys. Boy toddlers, especially those with dads, were more likely to walk.[9]

More disturbing data is found in the study that asked parents of four-year-olds about what age they would permit various independent behaviors (for example, using a sharp scissors without adult supervision or playing away from home for long without first telling an adult). Mothers of girls responded with older ages than those with boys.[10]

The direction of the data—though flawed by an emphasis on mothers—is clear. Girls are not learning the same lessons as boys. Among the differences: Girls receive less encouragement for exploration and more attention (and reinforcement) for being damsels in distress than boys; parents expect and grant the age of independent acts as later for girls than for boys.

As a result, sisters are not expected (as the song goes) to "do it for themselves." We see this dependency training follows her to school. Here, a daughter's independence is critical to her education; yet in the classroom she gets more help than she needs with her home-work.

THE TOO-HELPFUL TEACHER

Equity educators Myra and David Sadker offer a sample of how girls can learn to learn in the classroom:

> A fourth grade girl doesn't know how to put a disk into the computer. She raises her hand for help. The teacher stops at her desk and puts the disk in for her.
>
> In a eighth grade science lab, a girl can't adjust her micro-scope. The teacher asks a boy to show her how to do it. He goes over and adjusts it.[11]

This kind of Cinderella curriculum was first described twenty years ago, when psychologists Lisa Serbin and Daniel O'Leary found that preschool and kindergarten teachers offered boys de-tailed explanations about how to finish tasks at hand. Girls—in-stead of being offered directions—watched the teacher *do* the task for them.

One scenario has become a classic. Serbin and O'Leary observed a group of kids going up to the teacher's desk to staple party bas-kets. The boys were shown *how to use the stapler,* but when the girls didn't staple on their own, the teacher *stapled the handle to the basket for them.*[12]

In a more recent study, Marta Cruz Janzen made several visits over the course of a year to a kindergarten class of Hispanic chil-dren. She compared kids' assistance in using the classroom VCR and found than when girls wanted to watch a tape, the male aide set it up for them. When the boys wanted to watch, he gave them detailed instructions about loading, starting, and rewinding. The obvious outcome: At year's end, the girls still went to the aide to start the tape and boys could command the VCR by themselves.[13]

Whether teachers are stapling or VCR surfing, overhelping girls in the classroom can interfere with their developing the learning habits (such as persistence) that are the keys to success in math and science.[14]

PARENTS AS TEACHERS: LEARNING TO DEPEND

When we turn from insights about the research data to understanding our day-to-day experiences with our daughters, we must be willing to see the part we play in teaching the lessons of dependence. Even though the practices we preach seldom seem as obvious as those I've described in the classroom, I expect you to wince along with me in recognizing these three parent-teachers.

Careful Captains

You see them everywhere; sometimes you hear them before you see them. "Be careful!" they caution as a daughter practices her wobbly walk. "Be careful!" they warn as a daughter walks through a puddle or approaches the jungle gym. "Be careful!" they call out as she stands on the edge of the diving board. Oh, just once, I want a daughter to shout back, "Be careful of *what*?"

Careful captains convey a mix of anxiety and lowered expectations of independence. Even worse, they can project their own anxiety onto their daughters. "You weren't even scared," they say. Thus a daughter thinks: "If Dad or Mom thinks this is so scary, maybe I should too." She learns to be motivated by fear; not trusting herself to evaluate her own safety.

Careful captains are teaching a powerful dynamic of dependence because a daughter doesn't learn how to be safe by trusting her judgment, or how to profit from her trials and errors. She grows up wary of mistakes and risk-taking—the very keys to independent achievement.

The Hovercraft

These parents don't just stand there; they *do* something. And they are always nearby, rushing to the scene at the first sound of "I can't." They are the basket staplers, the premature rescuers, the crippling overhelpers. They see a daughter struggling with a zipper, a puzzle, a school paper, a fight with a friend, and they don't wait to be asked for help. They volunteer "Do you need help? Here, let me do it." "Do you want me to talk to her?"

Hovercraft parents undermine the independence of their daughters. Their lesson plan is a terrible twist on the tale of "The Little Engine That Could"; because their behavior says again and again: "I think she *can't* [well, not without my help]." These rescue missions erode a daughter's confidence in her problem-solving ability and diminish her capacity for independence.

There is so much she doesn't learn: how to tolerate frustration, how to take the initiative, how to learn from the consequences of her behavior. All these skills are essential to her self-reliance.

The Baby Boosters

These parent-teachers come in several varieties. The first are those who protest, *"But she's just a baby!"* (At the same time urging her young brother to "go for it, dude!") Grieving about the fact that their daughter is growing up, these parents talk baby talk beyond preschool; they still use her newborn nicknames, know what's best for her, and make few demands of her. For them, every step toward independence is a loss of their "baby."

Next, meet the parents who undermine independence with a battle cry: *"My poor baby!"* They are the overreacters, responding with drama and urgency to every bruise or common cold, disappointment, or playground tiff. They don't ask for much—only that their daughter stay forever young and in need of her parents.

Still other parents mourn, *"She's not a baby anymore!"* They explain, "She used to be so good and listen to her parents. Now she does and says what she wants; I have to worry about safety and strangers, and she insisted on telling me exactly how to make her birthday cake."

The lessons of dependence for daughters of baby boosters are powerful: to look to others for well-being, to expect help when you act helpless, and that you will or should always need help. (In some families, this includes the idea that the next round of help arrives in the form of a husband who does the heavy lifting of independence of her.)

Even worse, a daughter does not learn to comfort herself, to solve problems on her own, to develop a separate style. She may also sense a frightening cost of independence if the idea of thinking and acting on her own is seen as not being "good" in the eyes of a beloved parent. She wonders if being loved by a parent is linked to leaning on them.

Now, let's close the book on this curriculum and study the alternative. The first key is offering a model of your own independence.

DECLARE YOUR INDEPENDENCE

Lee, mother of a six-year-old, admits, "Since my daughter Molly was born, I have killed more spiders, opened more jars, and hammered more nails than in all of the years before she was born. I just feel it is so important for me to be a model of competence and independence instead of dialing the nearest man for help."

Lee's determination to declare her own independence is the first key in the competence curriculum for daughters. As a female model of independence, she shows her daughter the drill. Still, it seems essential that *both* parents model their own role-free competence and the independence of their thoughts and feelings.[15] Because daughters whose parents portray the importance of independent actions learn a larger lesson: *the value of self-reliance.* Try several strategies:

• *Don't let Dad or Mom do it.* Before you ask for help (especially in a potentially gender-typecast situation, such as reading a recipe or loosening a jar lid), make a genuine and vocal effort to do it yourself. This means dads stop asking moms, "Do we have any butter?"—and start looking. Moms stop believing that the ability to barbecue is linked to testosterone production.

• *Agree to disagree.* Openly argue with friends, family, and spouse about ideas and feelings in front of a daughter. Let her see the safety of offering her own independent ideas. Model fair fighting (sticking to your feelings without name-calling) and sound debating (sticking to the facts, attacking the other person's *argument* but not their personality or integrity).

• *Kiss and make up.* Be sure to joke and hug—and keep talking after you have publicly aired a disagreement with a friend or a partner in front of your daughter. Show her that talking in an independent voice can deepen, rather than destroy, the loving connection between people.

When parents declare their independence, they are perfectly poised to encourage a daughter's competence.

8

Encourage Her Competence

THE other night, Hannah left Jeremy and me in the dust during an extended game of Memory. After carefully putting the pieces away, she folded her arms and grinned from ear to ear. "Now *that* was skill!" she said. My smile was wider than Hannah's. We had been talking for weeks about the difference between games (Candyland and Chutes and Ladders are "luck"—it's the luck of the draw. Memory and tic-tac-toe are "skill" games—you have to plan and remember.).

The gleam in her eye told me she had begun to consider herself competent (although the word would never occur to her). How I hoped she would learn to rely on this view of herself.

In this chapter, let's take a closer look at six ways a daughter might learn to rely on her own competence and judgment.

CREATE CHOICES

Carol tells me, "Ever since Kelly (age eight) could nod, I have tried to offer her choices. Do you want peas or carrots? Do you want to go to the park or play in the yard? Do you want to wear pants or a skirt? And I have tried to accept the choices she made—although sometimes it's tough."

Parents like Carol, who champion a daughter's choices, counter the Cinderella Curriculum by teaching her an essential lesson: *how to trust her own judgment.* Yet the learning curve for both of you can be steep as you live with the consequences of her choices.

Choosing peas is a breeze, but how do you stop yourself from sending her to school with a sign that says, "She picked this outfit out herself"? Yet choosing her clothes is a snap—compared to maintaining radio silence about her choice of friends.

Here's the drill.

• *Offer choices only when you are prepared to accept her choice.* Kids can smell a fake process miles away. If you ask her to choose a camp and then say, "I thought you'd want to go to computer camp instead of tennis camp again," she sees the charade of the choice you offered.

• *Distinguish between limited choices ("Do you want to go to the movies or the game?") and unlimited choices ("What do you want to do?").* Being clear about the boundaries of the choice telegraphs your willingness to go along with her choice. Limited choices may work best for daughters of distractable temperament.

• *Join her to anticipate the consequences of a choice.* Introduce her to questions that are part of sound decision-making. For example, "What do you think will happen if you don't bring a coat? What will you be losing if you stop taking piano lessons?"

• *Find out the reasons behind her choices.* Get a daughter-sized view by asking, "Tell me what you like about that outfit [your friend Joey, etc.]; or, "How did you decide to write your paper about volcanoes?"; "How did you make your decision to spend all of your allowance at the video arcade?"

• *Let her know it is safe to disagree.* If you have offered a genuine choice, respect and confirm her decision—even when you don't agree. When you agree to disagree, you send the powerful message that she is *both* lovable *and* capable of trusting her own judgment.

• *Let her live with the consequences.* Learning from mistakes—from unforeseen consequences—is a key to smart choices. As long as she is safe from physical harm, why not let her get sweaty wearing tights in the summer, rub blisters from choosing not to wear socks, or find out that her new best friend is a snob? This process of self-correction is essential to her independence.

COACH INSTEAD OF RESCUE

Gary remembers, "When my daughter was thirteen, she and her mother moved to California. Every time Sonia called me, she would complain about the house they were renting—how far from the beach it was. And her mother told her she was too busy to find another one. I said, 'Well, why don't you find a real estate agent and look for one?' It turned out there was an agency in the neighborhood. We talked about what she should say to an agent, what she would do. She stopped in, talked to a real estate agent, and brought her mother to meet the agent, who eventually found them a new house near the beach."

Premature rescue is the Number 1 enemy of independence. How easy it would have been for Gary to rescue Sonia—to call his ex-wife or even call an agent himself. Instead, he coached her through a process of solving her problem and taught her a powerful lesson: *how to rely on her own ability.*

Do remember: Every time we rescue a daughter, we undermine her self-reliance. From zipping up her zipper to fixing a problem with a kid at school, to shadowing her so she doesn't fall, we discourage her independence. "Don't reward victimhood," said a workshop parent. Try these techniques instead.

• *Don't help unless she asks for it.* The best actions and advice are by invitation. If she asks for help immediately, challenge her by saying, "You try twice (or for five minutes), and if you *still* can't do it, I'll help."

• *Offer information and observations.* Walk her through the situation. ("You'll be able to climb down the rock if you bend your knees and stay close to the ground.") Make suggestions. ("Maybe you could try"; "I wonder what would happen if . . .")

• *Make her responsible for problem-solving.* Instead of offering your words of wisdom, ask her, "What do *you* think you will do?" "What do *you* think you should do next?"

• *Be a cheerleader*. Offer encouragement instead of rescue. ("I know it's not easy but stay with it! You can do it! You are almost there! I believe in you!") Remember, too, that a daughter whose temperament is "frustration-prone" may be less susceptible to being cheered on.

• *Help her bounce back*. Don't overreact to her falls—or failures. Acknowledge her feelings and help her move on. ("Ouch! That looks like it hurt—or like it was scary—but you look okay; you popped right back up.")

DEVELOP HER STRUGGLE MUSCLE

Hannah's teacher pulled me aside to tell me, "This morning I was trying to fix a broken music box; I was struggling and Hannah looked over at me and said, 'Stay with it, Renee, you can do it!' " We chuckled about her cheerleading—and I was delighted to learn that our resistance to rescuing had carried into Hannah's classroom. We hope that she is developing what child psychotherapist Stephanie Marston calls her "struggle muscle."[1]

Why is struggle so essential? "Mastery requires the ability to tolerate frustration," says psychologist Lois Hoffman. "If a parent responds too quickly with help, the child will not develop such tolerance."[2] Frustration is fertile ground for the growth of independence—a girl must learn to make mistakes and correct them. The larger lesson she learns is *how to depend on herself to succeed and meet challenges on her own.*

For every parent who has seen the glow when a girl shouts, "I did it!," here's how to set the stage.

• *Just stand there*. Avoid hovering to protect her from mistakes and mishaps. Let her struggle with decisions and frustrations in the comfort of her home. If she's not about to hurt herself—let her try and try again without your help.

• *Delegate*. I always ask the parents in my classes to make a list of everything they do for their daughters—and then cross off as many items as they can.[3] (For example: Can you teach her to pack her own lunch? Can you put her juice in a plastic pitcher so she can pour her own seconds? Can you teach her to find her "blankie"? Can you teach her to load or unload the dishwasher or washing machine? Can you get shoes that she can put on herself?) Like delegation on the job, you may get a better, faster outcome if you do it yourself. So brace yourself for spilled juice, lost pots, pink laundry, or a few extra minutes for her to don her shoes.

• *Celebrate her mistakes; and vary the pace.* Congratulate her on the struggles that don't succeed. ("Congratulations! You tried a tough back flip; I'll bet you get it next time!") Take one step at a time. For daughters whose temperament lacks persistence, break tough tasks into pieces.

• *Be a model of persistence.* Bring home stories of your own struggles—your own excitement when you finally succeed. Talk out loud when you are struggling: "This lid is tight. I better bang it on the counter or run it under hot water. . . . Ah, I got it!" Teach her the inner dialogue of successful struggle. One mother tells me she hears her daughter mimic the "Little Engine That Could" as she mutters, "I think I can, I think I can . . ."

ASSESS YOUR APPLAUSE

Your daughter has brought home a painting from school. Which sounds like you?

a. "What a beautiful picture! You are such a great artist!"
b. "I love the way you made the trees different shades of green. Isn't that the first time you have drawn a horse?"

The contrast between the two comments suggests the difference between praise and encouragement. As Stephanie Marston explains in her book *The Magic of Encouragement*, "Encouragement is descriptive praise, it focuses on *the deed and not the doer*."[4] Encouragement energizes independence because it highlights success, progress, or achievement—rather than vague global descriptions of the child or her work.

At this point, you may be wondering, "But doesn't lavish praise pave the path to self-esteem?" The answer lies in the experience of what a daughter may be learning from global praise. After all, she knows she's not a "great artist," and may feel the pressure of your expectations. She also may know that her picture is less than divine—or that you called her last drawing "beautiful" and she senses your insincerity.[5] In the process, she develops a pattern of investing in your approval rather than in her "achievement."

Yet the most important reason to assess your applause—and offer encouragement more than praise—is to offer her a lesson in self-reliance. You will be teaching her *to value her accomplishments for their own sake, and not for approval.* Let me explain how this might work.[6]

- *Avoid global evaluations and praise:* "You're a math whiz!" "You are going to waltz right into MIT!" They are tough to live up to. Substitute specifics: "You are really getting the hang of fractions." Or: "You'll be ready when algebra starts."
- *Focus on specifics such as improvement, newness, and persistence.* "You wrote your whole name this time!" "That's the first time you rode to the end of the block." "You just kept kicking till you reached the other side." "You got halfway down the mountain!"
- *Focus on her experience of her deeds.* "I'll bet you were thrilled when you saw the ball go over the fence!" "You must be proud of your high score on the science test."
- *Teach her "proud" talk.* One parent has a lovely bedtime ritual to encourage self-praise. When her daughters are tucked in bed, she asks, "Tell me something you did today that made you feel proud."

LET HER BE AUTHOR OF HER ACCOMPLISHMENTS

My ten-year-old niece, Chloe, played a winsome and funny Pinocchio at her drama camp's end-of-the-summer play. I sat in the audience, alternating between watching her parents glow in the dark and her delightful performance on stage. As we drove home after the cast party, my sister Cora commented on how comfortable

Chloe had seemed on the stage. Chloe's response was a mild denial, "Well, I've been doing this for five years!" Then Cora—determined that Chloe claim her compliment—added, "Well, it sure shows!"

For Chloe, and every girl on that stage, there are two elements of socialization that might keep her from embracing her accomplishments. And like Cora, parents must act to counter the culture. The first roadblock is a cultural taboo against bragging for girls.[7] Boys are expected to boast; but girls are told, "Nobody wants to play with a show-off."

Girls who think they are hot stuff may find themselves eating lunch alone. No wonder it becomes harder for girls to savor the sound of applause. This boycott against bragging is complicated by a second scenario: the tendency of adults to acknowledge girls for their *effort* rather than their *ability*.[8]

For these reasons, your daughter can develop a habit of thought that makes it hard for her to see herself as the author of her accomplishments. According to "attribution theory" (the study of what people see as the causes of events in their lives), this pattern of thinking ripens into a striking male-female difference in adulthood.

As psychologist Susan Bascow explains in her book *Gender Stereotypes*, "Females tend to attribute their success to external causes like luck or unstable causes, like effort. Failures tend to be attributed to lack of ability or another stable cause."[9]

Your daughter's independence rests on a foundation of wholehearted belief in her abilities. If she views her accomplishments as luck and her failures as lack of ability, she will walk the path in the direction of what Martin Seligman called "learned helplessness."[10] But when, as Cora did, we insist on showing a daughter her authorship, she learns the lesson of agency: *How to use her accomplishments—and the ability they display—to pave the road to independence.* You might take these steps with her.

- *Help her link her actions to the outcome.* Ask her how she did it. "How did you get those colors to blend?" "How did you get the idea for your paper?" "How did you decide it was time to steal third base?"
- *Argue with her attributions.* Help her take full credit for her accomplishments. If she wins the speech contest or the race, or gets

a ribbon at the science fair, she may tell you, "I was lucky," or "I worked harder than anyone." Remind her of her abilities (this is one of the times to talk in terms of global praise). For example, "You were always the fastest kid in the neighborhood [or the best storyteller]."

• *Show her how to take a compliment.*[11] Don't dismantle the compliments *you* receive from friends and family. Model comfort in acknowledging your authorship. Show her the difference between pride and boasting. If someone compliments you in front of her, you might say, "Thank you for noticing; I'm really proud of my garden."

• *Talk openly about your abilities and accomplishments.* Talk about your work on the job and in the community with specifics and with pride. "I finally got Evans to sign; I'm really getting good at resolving customers' problems without getting my boss."

SAFEKEEPING: THE FINAL FRONTIER OF INDEPENDENCE

Yet even with all these declarations of independence, it is our fear for her safety that ultimately undermines a daughter's independence. In a moving passage in her book *Necessary Losses,* Judith Viorst describes our longing to protect our children from danger.

> Our fantasy is that if we are good and loving parents, we can hold the tigers and thorns at bay . . . we can save our children. . . . Reality will find us late at night, when our children are out and the telephone rings. Reality will remind us—in that heart-stopping moment before we pick up the phone—that anything is possible. Yet, although the world is perilous . . . they must leave, we must let them go. Hoping we have equipped them for their journey. Hoping they will wear their boots in the snow. Hoping that when they fall down, they can get up. Hoping.[12]

Let's consider several more ways we can equip them for their journey.

9

Find Safety in Self-Reliance

WE rang in Hannah's fifth New Year at the Children's Hospital Emergency Room—stroking her forehead while the resident closed her chin with six stitches. As we drove to the hospital, I kept wondering if I could have prevented her fall. She had been joyfully imitating the ice skaters she had seen on television. On the first twirl, I glanced at her slippery socks and started to tell her to cool it. But I stopped myself, thinking, "Don't be such a careful captain!" On the second spin, she seemed to be picking up some technique, and by the third time—when I was convinced it was a safe move for her to make—she fell.

At the hospital, we were a brave bunch. We wore our party hats into the examining room, we made jokes (a nurse washes her hands with a soap-a-scope), we christened our resident Dr. K ("All the way with Dr. K"). We talked about what would hurt (the Xylocaine shot) and what wouldn't (the sewing of the stitches). But as she lay under the blinding overhead light, Hannah told the truth. "This is so scary," she said. Jeremy and I nodded. "Yes, it is," I told her. "That is why Dad and I will be here with you every second, holding you and talking to you."

Within days, Hannah was back to her usual rock-climbing self, but I was still scared. I knew that she would always be a leaping lizard; ever since she could belly up to the bureau, she had tried to use the open drawers to climb to the top. We used to spend a lot of time walking downtown, talking about which store ledges were "jumpers" (she could safely jump from them) and which were "danglers" (they were too high; she had to dangle her feet and ease slowly down).

We talked about what was safe and why, and of course, she had her share of bonks and black eyes. I was proud of my progress in reprogramming my genetic "Be Careful" code; we seemed to be raising a brave daughter. Yet for a time, after her fall, I lost my nerve. When Hannah would lean too far back in her chair, I would see her fierce half-moon scar and I would want to (but didn't) warn her, "You need to sit up, I don't want you to end up with more stitches!"

In this chapter, we will explore two questions that echo in my struggle to teach Hannah to be safe in ways that nurture her independence. How do we teach a daughter to be safe—without scaring her? And how do we emphasize safety, rather than danger—even when we feel scared?

Our strategies for safety cannot portray the world as a chamber of horrors—a place to "end up with more stitches." Nor should we detail the ways in which a daughters can become a victim. We must all find the courage to teach her to find safety in her own sure-footed competence.

A SAFE AND SOUND DAUGHTER:
FINDING SAFETY IN COMPETENCE

Three-and-a-half-year-old Hilary grabbed her mother Bonnie's hand the moment her mom entered the preschool room to walk her home. When Bonnie reached into her purse, Hilary immediately clutched her hand again. Bonnie asked her what was wrong, and she told her, "My teacher said that if we don't hold hands with a grown-up, we will get run over by a car." Bonnie hugged her and whispered, "Oh, Hilary, that's not going to happen!" And she recalled the many times she—and her husband, James—had asked each other: *"How can we teach her to be safe without scaring her?"*

A fuller story emerged the next day: One of the teacher's aides had been hit by a car and Hilary had unfortunately overheard the phone call to the preschool office from the hospital. Even worse, on a class outing, when some of the kids had strayed from the pack, they had been warned about "being run over." It took James and Bonnie several weeks to shift Hilary's focus from being scared to being what they called "safe and sound."

Nicky Marone, in her marvelous book *How to Father a Successful Daughter,* calls this an emphasis on "safety rather than danger." The lesson, says Marone, lies in "finding safety through competence."[1] Bonnie explains how they introduced Hilary to the idea of being "safe and sound."

> When we walked or drove down the street, James or I would offer a running commentary on the things we were doing to be "safe and sound" (in other words, the things we were doing to keep from being run over by a car).
>
> For example, we might say, "Look, the light is green, let's look both ways; now we are safe and sound, let's drive/walk through. After a few days, Hilary began to refer to a number of things as "safe and sound," or "not safe and sound." She began to hold my hand lightly on the way home from school.

Teaching a daughter about her own competence is essential to the growth of her independence. We must teach her to swim, not just how to keep from drowning. Then the lesson she learns is *to trust herself to make decisions about her safety, and how to take action in dangerous situations.* Try these strategies to emphasize safety and mastery, rather than danger and fear.

• *Emphasize safety as a way of being in charge.* Tell her how to be safe. Don't hand her the scissors and tell her how sharp they are. Try saying: "You always want to point the scissors away from you when you cut or walk with them." Or: "When you see the light or burner on the stove, stay away." "When you wear your bike helmet, you can fall without hitting your head so hard." "When you get ready to dive, check to see if anyone is swimming in your direction."

• *Teach her to calculate risks and anticipate consequences.* Avoid being a careful captain; be specific and give her the words that describe why she needs to be careful. For example, instead of hollering "Careful!" to a toddler, we must also include, "It's too *hot!*" "That is *sharp!*" "The floor is *slippery!*"

• *Tell her what to do to be safe:* "Move away!" or "Stand back!" or "Walk more slowly!" With older kids, tell them *what to take into account:* "When you sit on the edge of the chair, it can tip forward" "If you move much farther, you'll crash into the table" "That floor looks very slippery." Of course, you will interfere when danger is obvious to you, but not to her. Yet an occasional bonk may be worth the lesson of what it takes to be safe.

• *Model your own calculation of safety risks and consequences.* Show her how you make decisions about safety. Whether you are parallel parking, shoveling the sidewalk, or standing by the pool— think out loud. You might say, "I can't make it into that parking space without hitting that car," or "There are too many people in the pool to swim laps without bumping into someone," or "I better put on my snow boots."

• *Emphasize rules, rather than threats.*[2] Instead of always telling her the terrible things that will happen to her, state clear safety rules. So instead of "You are going to break your neck!" you might say, "The rule is no jumping on the bed." Instead of "You're going to fall," you say, "The rule is no leaning over the rail."

Next, consider this parent paradox: Although scaring her does not nurture self-reliance, insisting that she confront her fears can strengthen her independence.

BEFRIEND FEAR

Ann's five-year-old daughter Susan had a lot of anxiety about starting her swimming lessons. As she explained, "At first, I let Susan be fully afraid. I let her decide—and she sat at the shallow end of the pool. After a couple of weeks, I decided to push her a little. I told her, 'I want you to go ahead with your lesson—even if you are afraid. Let's see how it goes.' When she came home, I asked, 'How did it go?' and she said, 'Great! I jumped right off the edge; it was fun!' "

So many parents have told me stories about swimming lessons, they became emblematic of befriending fear as a way of nurturing safety through self-reliance. Am I suggesting that she can find strength in being scared? Yes, because the only way to learn to manage her fear in new situations is to have repeated exposure to them. Behavior psychologist Barclay Martin gives us the jargon: "The repeated arousal of the fear response in small controlled doses, eventually leads to the extinction of fear."[3]

Girls who have not learned to befriend fear become risk-aversive; their world shrinks. We must teach a daughter to let fear fuel her independence so she can learn a larger lesson: *how to rely on herself in new situations.*

Here's how to lead her to water—and get her to jump in.

• *Confirm her fears; but don't inflame them.* When she says, "I'm scared," let her *be* afraid by answering: "I know, it is scary at first." But don't match her intensity. (This is especially important with daughters of intense temperament.)

• *Share a similar fear (with your strategy for a happy ending).* Tell her, "I remember I was really nervous the first time I gave a speech; and I just pictured my best friend smiling in the audience. It really helped."

• *Remind her of past successes.* Tell her, "Remember how scared you were the first time you went hiking (went on the climber, or got on a horse)? And then you loved it!"

• *Rehearse.* One of the parents in my class practiced by riding the bus with her daughter between school and her office. Another role-played a confrontation with the daughter's friend. You can also rehearse by inviting her to visualize herself overcoming the fear (point to someone in the pool, saying, "That will be you next summer").

• *Lovingly coax her to take risks.*[4] On a skiing junket you might say, "Honey, I know you are scared. You are looking down a steep mountain. But just take your time. When you are ready, fix your eyes on your skis and not on the bottom. I'll be right here to coax you down."

• *Track with her temperament.* Temperament can shape her response to fear. For example, slow-to-adapt kids can seem scared when they are simply warming up. So take gradual steps. Before swimming lessons, let her put her face in the water in the bathtub, float in a rubber doughnut, or play in a plastic pool. Let her know what to expect at a swimming lesson.

Yet none of these strategies addresses the toughest issue of safekeeping and independence for parents and daughters: the danger of strangers.

THE DANGER OF STRANGERS:
RAISING A STREETWISE DAUGHTER

At a workshop, Julie tells a story from her own preteen memory bank. "I remember the summer evening that I wanted to ride a bike to my best friend's house five blocks away. It was getting dark and my parents both said no. I protested, saying, "Why not? I'm old enough to ride my bike by myself," and my dad answered, *"That's just the point!"* Julie's father has pointed to another paradox of independence. As parent educator Nicky Marone puts it, "How do we make our daughters aware of their vulnerability, without making them feel like victims?"

Marone asks, "But how do we socialize our female children? Due to the dreadful statistics of sexual abuse, kidnapping, rape and murder, we train girls to be aware of their victim status. Unfortunately, but predictably, individuals who feel like potential victims develop personalities that are fearful, timid, dependent, and overly cautious."[5]

As equalist parents, we wonder, "How do I teach a brave new daughter to emphasize her own safety as opposed to her vulnerability? How do I teach her to be streetwise instead of scared?" We must begin by understanding why scare tactics don't work.

TEACH HER, DON'T SCARE HER

Paula Statman's book, *On the Safe Side*, should be required reading for all parents. In it, she explains why scare tactics don't work. When we are scared about the dangers of the world, we scare and overprotect our kids. The result is that they don't develop the judgment or skill to recognize dangerous situations and cope with them. *Teach* kids about personal safety, don't *scare* them, says Statman.[6]

Her advice is fourfold: Separate your fears from what the child needs to learn, keep your own feelings in check, use nonalarming words, and emphasize safety rules. She gives the classic example of a frantic, relieved father who bellows, "I've been looking everywhere for you! You know you are not supposed to leave the yard without permission! You could have been kidnapped or killed! Haven't I told you there are lots of crazies out there, just looking for kids like you?"

This father would be wise to catch his breath, put his feelings aside, and think about what he wants to teach his child and wants his child to do the next time. Statman suggests he might say:

> "I was scared and worried when I couldn't find you. The safety rule is that you need to ask permission to leave the yard. You broke the rule, so you will have to come inside for the rest of the afternoon. Tomorrow, if you are willing to follow our safety rule, you can play again outside."

Avoid the words that create fear, use words that teach and reassure, and offer a safety rule. Instead of saying, "You can't go to the park by yourself, someone might kidnap you," try: "You will be safe if you . . ." or: "Our safety rule is that you stay with a buddy all the time if you go to the park."[7] In these ways, you begin to teach your daughter the final lesson in the independence curriculum: how to identify dangerous situations and be competent in them. Join her in these lessons.[8]

• *Establish safe boundaries.* Depending on the age of your daughter and the community you live in, set boundaries where you feel she can move safely on her own. Can she play in your unfenced backyard? Go next door? Walk two or ten blocks to a friend's house—calling when she arrives? Ride her bike to the playground?

• *Teach her the information she needs to be safe.* She needs to know: her full address, her phone number, how to dial 911, and her parents' first and last names.

• *Create a carpool code:* Establish a family code word like "stegosaurus" and suggest that she asks anyone who pretends to know her—and tries to get her to get into their car—what the code word is.

• *Teach her about touches.* Give her examples of "OK" touches (being hugged and kissed by family or friends when you want to be) and "Not-OK" touches (a hug that lasts too long, being tickled after you say stop, a grown-up touching your genitals or asking you to touch theirs). Teach her that people who don't know her should use *words,* not touches.

Model what you mean. If a stranger touches her, you can say, "I know you didn't mean any harm, but please don't touch my daughter." And by all means, teach her to be a tattletale when it comes to touches. Tell her to tell you right away if anyone tries to touch her in a way that is not OK.[9]

• *Teach her to be reasonably suspicious.* Remind her that adults don't ask kids for help; that no safe grown-up would ask her to keep a secret from her parents, and that kids don't always have to do what adults say. Teach her to trust her inner alarm system. Tell her that if she has a funny feeling about an adult—even one in uniform—that she should check it out with another adult whom she knows.

• *Role-play safety strategies.*[10] Depending on her age, offer a variety of "what if?" situations and ask her how she would respond: "What would you do if you had a flat tire on your bike and a stranger offered to help?" or "What would you do if you ran into the elevator and the door closed before I got on?" You can even pretend to be a stranger asking for directions, or an older kid she doesn't know inviting her to a movie.

• *Prepare a safe passage.* Plan definite safety strategies to get home safely if she is approached or followed by strangers. Depending on her age, you might identify spots between school and home and playground that might be safe havens. She also needs to know who helping adults are: security or police officers, store cashiers, etc. You can also teach her to call a helping adult's attention to the situation by yelling as loudly as possible, "You're not my mother/father!" "Help me, I'm being kidnapped," etc.

• *Emphasize an individual approach to safety.* Take your daughter's temperament into account when you provide information about potential dangers of strangers. For example, daughters of intense temperament easily overload—becoming anxious and clingy. Try to encourage her to be watchful and prepared without frightening her. For this daughter, read a safety book in several sittings, and talk out loud about your own precautions with strangers and dangers.

• *Read all about it.* Introduce streetwise books and videos to open discussion and provide strategies. Here are some of the best.

Youngest kids:

1. *The Berenstain Bears Learn About Strangers,* Stan and Jan Berenstain.
2. *Strangers Don't Look Like the Big Bad Wolf,* Janis Buschman. Abduction prevention. Available from Kids' Rights, 1-800-892-5437.

Older kids:

1. *Safety Zone,* Linda Meyer. Available from Kids' Rights, 1-800-892-5437. Scenarios and methods to prevent abduction. Parents read first and then introduce to kids.
2. *Playing It Smart: What to Do When You Are on Your Own,* Tova Navarra, Barron's Educational Series. Solutions to problem situations (such as getting separated from parents in a mall).
3. *Home Alone: A Kid's Guide.* Available from Anchor Bay Entertainment, 1-800-786-8777. Free to check out at Blockbuster video stores; shows ways kids can be safe at home.
4. *Stranger Danger,* Nickelodeon, Lucky Duck Productions.

Linda Ellerbee hosts a safety precautions special—helping to prevent abduction.

HOSTILE HALLWAYS: A SELF-RELIANT APPROACH TO SEXUAL HARASSMENT

On the school bus home, two six-year-old girls are called lewd names on a daily basis by six- and nine-year-old boys. A thirteen-year-old girl has her pants pulled down in class when the teacher leaves the room. An early-developing twelve-year-old girl dreads walking to the gym and passing by the boys who comment about her breasts—and one who grabs his crotch and moans when she walks by.

These stories are from two major surveys that offer parents disturbing data that sexual harassment is widespread (among both boys and girls) and that the impact of sexual harassment on girls is particularly devastating.[11] For example, girls saying they are afraid at school, or have difficulty concentrating on homework and during test time. One in three say they don't want to go to school or speak up in class; 40% of all girls who have been harassed say they feel less sure of themselves.[12]

Since your daughter can't quit school—as she might a job—we must join her in resisting situations that violate the integrity of her body and undermine her self-respect. We must be guided by the words of a fourteen-year-old Hispanic daughter who looked back on how little support she had gotten when she had been harassed. She wrote to the Wellesley study, saying, "I wish someone would have taken the time out to talk to me, and let me know that what was happening was not my fault and it sure as hell was not mindless flirting."[13]

When we take time to talk to our daughters about how they can respond to harassment, here are some steps we can take[14]:

• *Help her define harassment.* She needs to know that sexual harassment includes sexual comments, unwanted touches and gestures, sexual pictures or messages, writing sexual graffiti about her, spreading rumors, spying on her as she dresses or showers, saying she is lesbian or gay, bra-snapping, or pulling or brushing against her clothing in a sexual way.

• *Explore with empathy.* When your daughter brings home one or more incidents, listen for the impact. Reflect her feelings of anger, fear, guilt, or hurt, and let her know that she can trust her feelings. They are legitimate, and the situation (in all probability) was not provoked by her behavior—*it was not her fault.* Tell her that she is not a troublemaker to seek a strategy to deal with the situation.

• *Explain, don't excuse.* Explain that harassment happens when men and boys don't treat girls with respect and that (unfortunately) we live in a culture that encourages men to feel they are entitled to comment on girls' or women's bodies. She needs to know that some teachers still think that boys and girls are just "doing what comes naturally," who think that these disturbing behaviors are harmless "flirting."

Depending on her age, explain that harassment is not about feeling pretty, being sexy, or flirting. Instead, it is a way of making her feel less powerful than the boy or boys involved. But if she takes charge, she can feel strong in the situation.

• *Consider taking action.* Discuss what she will do if the harassment happens again. Can she role-play a way of stopping her harasser in his tracks? Would she feel comfortable reporting incidents to a trusted teacher? Might you join together to bring the harassment to the attention of school officials? (To take specific action, consult NOW's Legal Defense and Action Kit, "Sexual Harassment in the Schools." It costs $5.00, and is available from the NOW Legal Defense Fund, 99 Hudson Street, New York, New York 10013.)

THE DANGER OF INDEPENDENCE

I reread Louis Simpson's poem "The Goodnight" after Hannah's New Year's Eve fall. His words about a parent's fear of independence, as we allow a daughter to go out into the world, really hit home. He portrays a father tucking his daughter into bed and thinking about the dangerous world outside her room—as well as the dangers of keeping her there.

> The lives of children are
> dangerous to their parents
> with fire, water and air
> and other accidents;
> And some for the child's sake
> Anticipating doom,
> Empty the world to make
> The world safe as a room.
>
> A Man who cannot stand
> Children's perilous play,
> With lifted voice and hand
> Drives the children away.
> Out of sight, out of reach,
> The tumbling children pass;
> He sits on an empty bench,
> Holding an empty glass.[15]

We must choose to fill our glasses, and join our daughter in declaring her independence. We find strength in believing that her self-reliance will guide her on a safe and joyous journey beyond our doors.

KEY IDEAS

Strategy 3
Declare Her Independence

How to champion a daughter's self-reliance and teach her to be safe—without scaring her

- Females are not more fragile than males, so don't give a daughter more help or protection than she needs.
- Give her choices and let her learn about the consequences.
- Coach instead of rescue, so she'll rely on her own ability.
- Let her develop her struggle muscle—she will learn to tolerate frustration and fears.
- Praise her ability and specific successes (not just her effort).
- Emphasize safety rules, rather than potential dangers.
- Teach her; don't scare her. Give her information to take action in unsafe situations.

Strategy 4

BRING HOME HEROINES

*How to Find and Use Role
Models to Enrich a Daughter's
Sense of Self*

10

Review Role Models

"I was determined to surround my daughters with strong female role models," explains psychologist Laura Kastner. "I brought home stories and biographies. Our doctor was a woman; our dentist was a woman. When we remodeled our home, the architect and contractors were women. Toward the end of the remodeling time, as I was chatting with one of my daughters on her bed, I glanced up at a poster on her wall—one I had bought for her because it had three girls in swirling skirts sitting in a truck. 'What do you think is going on in that picture?' I asked. My daughter answered without hesitation, 'They are waiting for a man to come and rescue them.' "[1]

Kastner's funny and painful story reminds us how much hope we invest in the heroines we bring home—and how they can seem to be fighting a losing battle with the cultural messages that surround them. Our fourth strategy offer ways to counter our culture's narrow messages about what it means to be a woman.

The chapters in this section shine the spotlight on the heroines among us, asking: Who are these wonderful women and glorious girls? Where do we find them (in truth and in fiction)? How do they contribute to the strength and spirit of our daughters?

We begin by exploring whether strong role models help create stronger women.

DO FEMALE ROLE MODELS WORK?

Three-year-old Rebecca has two working parents. Rebecca's mother seldom cooks; her father makes dinner for the family. But when it's mealtime in her dollhouse, Rebecca grabs the mommy doll and gets her working in the kitchen.[2] Rebecca's story, like Laura Kastner's, alerts us to the fact that we don't quite know how (or whether) role models work.

If Rebecca has Mom making muffins for her dolls, does this mean she expects to be queen of the kitchen when she grows up? Similarly, when Laura's daughter fantasized about damsels in distress, does this mean that she can't envision herself becoming a doctor or a contractor (or that she will not become the author of her own active life)?

Still, these stories make us wonder: Is there evidence that role models "work"—data that confirms the connection between a girl's exposure to strong female role models and her strength and success as a woman? As usual, the experimental data offer mixed results.

In one fascinating study, college undergraduates and working women had vivid memories of heroines from childhood books.[3] In another, a low achievement orientation in girls was linked to a lack of nontraditional female role models in her life.[4] A survey of biographical literature of successful women is rich with references to both male and female models and mentors as a motivating force.[5]

Yet much of the research focuses only on working moms and reports like-mother-like-daughter data.[6] For example, studies suggest that the experience of having a mother who works strengthens a daughter's interest and pursuit of a career. Other data demonstrate women who have found a balance between work and family said they had more encouragement from their mothers than colleagues whose mothers didn't make balance a priority.

Studies also show us the power of a mother's mind-set. We find that daughters mirror working mothers' attitudes about sex roles; the less stereotyped the mother's view, the less stereotyped the daughter's. Also, mothers with more equal sex role ideas encouraged daughters to play more and be more active than mothers with nontraditional ideas about sex roles.

Still, not all equalist moms work, so perhaps the research most encouraging for our purposes is a study of children ages three to seven that found that brief presentations of picture books with egalitarian sex role models *reduced stereotypic thinking.*[7] Movie-loving parents will note with pleasure more equal sex-role models in movies produced a *more* enduring change than similar models in picture books.

HOW DAUGHTERS DEFINE ROLE MODELS

Even so, as you scan the videos to rent, remember that no study establishes a clear cause-and-effect role for female role models in building self-esteem or finding success in work or love. For this reason, our plans to bring home heroines is an informed leap of faith. Still, our intention is strengthened by what our daughters tell us. Just listen, and your daughter will tell you how role models work.

For every parent who wonders if s/he has overestimated the power of role models, we find the parent of a daughter like eleven-year-old Ellie, who defined the cause and effect of female role models with great joy. "I love to read biographies about women and learn what they have done. I feel like a door is opening. If they could do great things, maybe I can too."[8]

Or we talk to a parent like Christine, who named her twelve-year-old daughter Ana for her Aunt Ana Louise—a fiery-spirited woman who homesteaded solo in Montana and lived to be 104. "I documented Aunt Louise's life for my daughter and arranged for them to meet. After she died, my daughter told me that her aunt 'came to see her at night.' I remember once Ana referred to Louise's self-reliance, saying, 'Aunt Louise did what she thought she should do—even when other people thought it was a bad idea.' "

WHY WOMEN ONLY?

We hear the longing for heroines in our daughters' voices. The four-year-old who wonders, "Can girls be knights in shining armor?" The eight-year-old who complains, "This is the fourth book with no girls in it!" The twelve-year old who asks, "How come there aren't any women inventors?"

By now, we have learned that a girl's growing awareness of the lesser power and presence of women in our culture is a factor in the self-esteem slide of early adolescence. As equalist parents, we know the "invisible woman" litany by heart: the use of "he" as the pronoun of choice; boys featured as the action heroes in books, TV, and movies; women written out of history books, and missing in math and science.

For this reason, every piece of advice written for parents of daughters seems to begin with a lament for the invisible girl/woman and, next, complains about the quality who are visible (the tabloid queens for a day, or books like the hapless *Amelia Bedelia* and *The Baby-Sitters Club*). Such articles end urging us to offer our daughter strong female role models. In this chapter, we will echo that advice; but first, let's consider two caveats about female role models.

The first: Parents must be wary of creating an all-girl ghetto for your daughter. In our mission of finding strong models for our daughters to "wanna be," we can find ourselves pointing only to the experiences and qualities of females—barring heroes from our land. If you want your daughter's individuality to define her femininity, she and her heroines must meet brave and tender male friends, fathers, and grandfathers—and consider their choices as her options, too.

A second caution was suggested by Lucy W., mother of Kelsey, eight, who is not entirely convinced of the importance of bringing heroines home. "I don't think it matters what she sees on TV for a minute or reads in a book. The core of her experiences is the example of people around her—what matters is what *I* do."

Lucy's well-spoken point has been emphasized in every chapter of this book. We must continue to understand how every strategy suggested for our daughters might be modeled in our own lives and relationships. This includes a view of moms as heroines at home. But first, here's a ringside seat to watch role models in action.

WHAT IS THE ROLE OF A ROLE MODEL?

Hannah and I have a running joke about princesses. "How come you don't like princesses, Mom?" she asked after I declined to play Princess Jasmine for the tenth time in her puppet show. Here's how I explained: "Well, it seems they don't do too much—they don't work or have kids or hobbies. They just sit around the castle all day." For months after that conversation, Hannah would announce with a gleam in her eye, "Today I am going to be a princess and sit around all day."

Then I brought home an audiotape of *Free to Be . . . You and Me*[9] with the story of Princess Atalanta. In this wonderfully equalist fairy tale, Atalanta studies astronomy, "builds and fixes things" (we hear the sound of her hammering), and tells her father that she wants to see the world and then, "Perhaps then I will marry, perhaps not." Her father ignores her and offers her as a prize to the man who runs the fastest race.

In the happily ever after, Atalanta also runs the race and ties with young John—who has run the race for the privilege of becoming her friend. As the sun rises, Atalanta is traveling on horseback to new lands and John is sailing uncharted seas. Their marriage is possible; their friendship is certain.

Hannah was enchanted with Atalanta; she played the tape again and again. Within a week, she was role-playing. "I'm Atalanta; I'll race you," she'd announce, taking off in a mad dash down the street. Atalanta appeared in her puppet shows, and as we passed a group of contractors in an office building, she turned to me and asked, "Can I have a tool chest like Atalanta?"

Hannah's response to the fictional Atalanta and eleven-year-old Ellie's response to reading biographies of famous women both demonstrate three dynamics of a female role model as a tool for enhancing self-esteem at all ages.

• *Role models create a sense of identification.* ("I'm Atalanta; I'll race you.") They enhance her ability to picture herself as sharing the life experiences and qualities of a strong woman or girl. They encourage her to think, "I am like her."

• *Role models suggest a sense of possibility.* ("If they could do great things, maybe I could too.") They enliven her ability to imagine herself having new and different qualities and experiences. They encourage her to think, "I could be like her."

• *Role models offer her a sense of motivation.* ("Can I get a tool chest, like Atalanta has?") They mobilize her to "wanna be" and "do" the things she has discovered in the life experiences of her heroine. They encourage her to think, "I want to be like her, do what she does."

We see these three patterns in girls of all ages: the preschooler who points to a character in a picture book, saying, "I'm her"; the middle schooler who discovers Sally Ride and aims to be an astronaut; the high schooler who is studying photography "like my Aunt Kate." We understand how these heroines can help light the way for our strong and spirited daughters. But how can we get maximum mileage from these marvelous models? Consider two possibilities.

IS BARBIE BRAVE?: QUALITY ROLE MODELS

Hannah, Jeremy, and I are collecting brave girls. Whenever one of her friends or a character in a book or movie takes a risk, stares down a dragon, or stands up to a bully, we say, "That was a brave thing that Laura [her best friend] did." Then we add her name to a list that grew longer as Hannah grew taller: Sheila Rae (from a Kevin Henkes story), Fern *(Charlotte's Web),* Belle and Pocahontas (from the Disney store), Claudia Kincaid *(From the Mixed-up Files of Mrs. Basil E. Frankweiler).*

From time to time, Hannah will announce, "I'm brave, just like Belle and Fern and Sheila Rae." Last week she asked me, "Is Barbie brave?" Believe it or not, I answered, "She can be if she tries to be."

Our Brave Girls' Hall of Fame illustrates the principle of *quality role models.* We know that it is necessary—but not sufficient—to surround our daughters with competent and caring heroines. But if we want our daughters to identify with wonderful women and be motivated by them, we must *label* the qualities and experiences that describe our heroines.

We must point to what is brave, daring, inventive, tender, and wise about them. You might try these three ways.

• *Whenever you encounter a potential heroine who makes a smart, nurturing, or daring move, give it a name.* "Don't you love her curiosity?" "She really knows her numbers!" "What a loving mother she is!" "She never gives up, does she?" "What a great imagination!" "She must be very strong." "Dr. Shapiro is so smart; she figured out what was wrong immediately."

• *Discuss the history, decisions, and actions of real and imagined heroines.* "Why do you think Madeline wanted to teach Pepito how to be kind to animals?" "How did Harriet Tubman find the courage to lead so many people through the underground railroad?" "What do you think Amelia Earhart (or Ruth Laws) was thinking as she flew across the country/ocean?" "I remember when Aunt Kate got a camera for her tenth birthday; she had such an artistic eye."

• *Compare her experiences and qualities to those of her heroines.* "You are balancing on the rocks/climber/wall just like Mirette." "You have a memory like Cam Jansen." "You hopped on that horse like Annie Oakley." "Georgia O'Keeffe liked to paint in those desert colors too." "Did you know Rosalyn Yalow's parents also got her a microscope when she was eight?" "Your grandmother was a beautiful singer like you are." "Gwen and Jill are best friends like you and Laura."

Focusing on the qualities of strength and spirit in some of your daughter's heroines maximizes the impact of role models; but quantity counts too.

SEE HEROINES EVERYWHERE:
QUANTITY OF ROLE MODELS

Even the littlest angel will point out the absence of women in nontraditional roles. As Josh explains, "When Reva was two, she began to ask, 'Where are all the women truck drivers?' So we started scanning the highway—to no avail—to find one." It's not that you want your daughter to be a forklift operator (though she might be great in the job); it is that you don't want her to rule any options out. Here's where the numbers game counts.

If talking about the qualities of role models offers your daughter a sense of "I could be like *her*!" then frequent female finger-pointing can energize her sense of "I could be *anything*!" The use of *quantity role models* means pointing out powerful and interesting women out loud and on purpose. As you casually point to the heroines among us, you offer a daughter more and more options to define herself as a woman.

In this approach, the last thing you want to do is shriek, "Look! A woman truck driver!" This conveys the sense that seeing a woman in that role is as common as a UFO sighting. Consider, instead, several less boisterous ways of pointing to women in action.

• *When you encounter a woman in a nontraditional field, comment on her accomplishments or actions or skills—not her sex.* Avoid expressions like "lady architect" or "woman truckdriver," saying instead, "I'll bet she's a good map reader" or "Didn't she design that beautiful house for the Skinner family?" As you watch the news or read newspapers, casually point to newsworthy women's accomplishments.

• *Talk to your spouse and child about the contributions and triumphs of your female friends.* "Anne really pulled the school auction together—she's a great organizer." Or, "I'm so excited, Paula got promoted to manage her department." "Julie passed the bar exam with flying colors; she's going to be a great lawyer." Or, "I really admire the way Naomi spends so much time in Jane's classroom."

• *Put successful women in her path.* Visit a synagogue or church that has a female leader and explain, "I heard she gives a great sermon." When you join a medical group practice, greet the women by name in the hall. Take your daughter to galleries with one-woman shows. When her school is planning a field trip, suggest to her teacher that she or he might plan ahead and choose a date when women are visible on the site of the fire station, zoo, aquarium, etc.

• *Show her she is surrounded by strength.* Point to girls and women on the playgrounds, on the beach, on Rollerblades and bikes, who show strength and daring and risk-taking: "She's really working her muscles." "She is very coordinated." Celebrate the accomplishments of her pals (without comparing her): "Zoë must really be proud of her medal in the Science Fair." "Didn't you love Ella's singing in the play?" Talk about the triumphs of her baby-sitter.

WHEN DOES A ROLE MODEL BECOME A MENTOR?

Let's say that twelve-year-old Louise got a camera from her parents for her birthday, along with a biography of photojournalist Margaret Bourke White. They have offered her an opportunity for expression as well as a role model. Next, they arranged an hour lesson with Nina, an acquaintance who is a successful freelance photographer.

Whey they met, Nina was taken with Louise's exuberance and fresh approach; she invited her back to visit again. The next time Louise visited, she asked Nina about who bought her first camera, where she had studied, and what it was like to run a small business. In Nina, Louise had found a potential mentor.

If a role model—real or imagined—inspires your daughter to think, "I'm like *her*," "I *could* be like her," or "I *want* to be like her," then a mentor can take her one step further by recognizing her potential and showing her how. As Barbara Kerr explains in her book, *Smart Girls, Gifted Women*, "A mentor is not just a coach or tutor; but a person who takes an abiding and intense interest in the person as well as the talent."[10]

Hold the phone; we are not talking about precocious preteen networking here. Mentors of the youngest girls are the teachers and coaches and aunts and cousins and neighbors who have discovered your daughter and say, in effect, "I've noticed you; I see how special you are. Here's what you would have to learn to do what I do," or "I can help you chart your chosen path."

The parents I interviewed talked lovingly of such mentors: the violin teacher who became a spiritual and musical mentor, or the aunt in New York who invited her Northwestern nieces for a week of theater, museums, and music.

Mentors can join with parents in helping a daughter see her brightest future—help her develop what psychologist Daniel Levinson calls "The Dream."[11] As he defines it, "The Dream is a living, powerful future image of self that we have in our minds that begins and keeps us working toward the goal of success."

Let's consider ways you can introduce your daughter to the idea of connecting with strong female role models who are potential mentors.

• *Read and talk about books (fictional and biographical) where girls and women are nurtured in a mentor/protégé relationship.* Preschoolers will enjoy *Chrysanthemum* by Kevin Henkes; preteens will adore *Wise Child* by Monica Furlong. Biographies of Georgia O'Keeffe include the importance of her relationship with teacher/ mentor Elizabeth May Willis.

• *Both parents can talk about the women who have "shown you the ropes."* The teachers, coaches, camp counselors, and supervisors who took a strong interest in your gifts.

• *Offer to introduce her to women in your work or home community who excel in her areas of interest or strength.* Visit with an artist in her studio, a judge in her chambers, a carpenter in her shop, a day-care worker in the center. Expand on her interest in birds by connecting with women in the Audubon Society.

THE WISH AND THE WORK OF ROLE MODELS

Do role models work? Just ask Journalist Marilyn Webb, who has described her daughter Jennifer packing her role models off to college by buying a new audiocassette of *Free to Be . . . You and*

Me. "As she popped the new tape into her Walkman," remembers Webb, "she began singing loudly, remembering from her childhood every word."

> "Mommies are people," she bellowed. "People with children . . . Busy with children and things that they do; there are a lot of things a lot of mommies can do." This tape was traveling to college, she announced, *a reminder of what she intended to become. . . .* Jennifer is now twenty-two, among the first offspring of sixties feminists. "When I was growing up, I thought these were just old children's songs, that what they said about the world was really true," Jennifer said. Only as she grew older did she realize she was an experiment in nonsexist childrearing, *the songs were a wish, meant for her to make come true.*[12]

Today, the wish sounds resoundingly clear. Here's the job description.

> WANTED: A real or imagined girl or woman who has a strong body and mind—who is persistent and exuberant. She must be experienced in risk-taking, not afraid to be angry or messy, to be "the first," or to stand the village on its ear. She needs to be comfortable in her skin, able to speak her heart and find courage in her tenderness. She must see boys and men as potential allies.

Nice job if she can get it; but who should apply? Let's consider some qualified applicants.

11

Find Great Girls and Wonderful Women

WHEN Ann Ruething's daughter Elizabeth was born, she quit her airline marketing job to stay home. Ann recalls how her first efforts to bring home heroines grew into the marvelous, equalist Chinaberry Book Service. She describes her shock when she read a book of Mother Goose rhymes to her twelve-month-old daughter who "still had a song in her heart and was very innocent."

"I was taken aback by the violence and sexual stereotyping in those rhymes, and I didn't want to do that to her," says Ann. "So instead of the little old woman who lived in the shoe spanking them all soundly, I had her kissing them all soundly. I just changed negative words to positive words as I went along, but when the Peter Peter Pumpkin Eater (had a wife and couldn't keep her) page came up, I couldn't think how to ad-lib that one."[1]

Ann began to study the messages in books from "our itty bitty library" and wrote her impressions of them on notecards. These note cards eventually became the prototype for Ann's lively annotations of each book that appears in the Chinaberry catalog. She recalls, *I had to screen books; not censor them,* because I wasn't just looking for bad stuff I didn't want to read, but for good stuff I did want to read to her. Good role models and people being brave and kind and respectful to each other, and humorous stuff."[2]

Ann's determination to look for positive female portraits—rather than simply censoring negative ones—lights our path as we search for heroines in this chapter. Let's consider five directions that point to great girls and wonderful women.

THE BEST AND BRIGHTEST BOOKS:
FINDING THE GOOD STUFF

You have probably noticed that there is no Dewey decimal number for strong female role models at your local library. This leaves equalist parents blocking the aisles of libraries and bookstores "*tsk-tsk*ing" typecast books and searching for heroines to bring home. The picture books are a quick scan; but the older your daughter gets, the longer the books and the more difficult it becomes to read what she reads.

As she grows, so may her resistance—or indifference—to the heroines you bring home. As the mother of an eleven-year-old explained, "We can't keep her from reading teen romances or Stine's mysteries; but after the twentieth *Baby-Sitters Club* book, I will say, here, how about trying this?"

As you scan potential selections, here's what you might look for in her books:

- Are the females self-reliant (or do they avoid taking risks and end up being rescued by males)?
- Are the female characters focused on action—rather than appearance and weight?
- Do females hide accomplishments to keep male affection?
- Are boys viewed as friends and allies (or enemies and prom bait)?
- Does the heroine have friends she can be herself with?
- Are mother and father characters described as individuals or moldy sitcom stereotypes?
- Do the women and girls in the story speak their minds, get

messy, and take risks? (Or are they busy being neat and good girls?)

- Are the older women nurturing (or nagging crones)?

In a hurry? Speed-read the dialogue in quotes; find out who's talking and what they are saying. But don't plan to rely on your own childhood memories. You may be shocked—as Jeremy and I were—to revisit *Mrs. Piggle Wiggle,* and find the magical curses that delighted us as kids. But also to find a spanking on every other page, administered by the ditziest group of mothers and most distant set of fathers in fiction. Still, stereotypes can be instructive. As you will see in the next strategy section, typecast characters offer parents teachable moments; they give a daughter practice in skewering stereotypes.

Few books meet all of the criteria above—fewer still can pass the full typecast detector test. So let me share the work of twelve authors who celebrate women and girls. While you may quarrel with a character or two, each author evokes the voices of authentic, memorable girls.

TWELVE AUTHORS WHO CELEBRATE WOMEN AND GIRLS

1. Nancy Carlson
Carlson's heroines—Luanne Pig, Harriet the Dog, and Tina Beaver—are spunky, stereotype-skewering favorites among the toddler and preschool set. Recommended titles: *I Like Me, Luanne Pig Makes the Team, Luanne Pig and the Perfect Family, Harriet and the Roller Coaster, Harriet and the Garden, A Visit to Grandma, Take Time to Relax.* These were among Hannah's first and favorite books.

2. Kevin Henkes
Henkes consistently creates a girl with a gleam in her eye: Lily, Chrysanthemum, and Sheila Rae. He understands how complicated and passionate childhood friendships and adventures can be. Look for his books *Sheila Rae the Brave, Chrysanthemum,* and *Chester*

and Wilson. The audience includes ages 3–6+. Every child who gets a Chrysantheum book from us has fallen in love with her.

3. **Amy Schwartz**

Sometimes author, sometimes illustrator, Amy Schwartz fills her gallery with thoroughly original girls: From kindergarten Bea, who trades places with her working dad, to Gabriel, who convinces her tailor grandpa to make her a daring purple (not her usual navy blue) coat. Among the best for the 3–8 set: *Bea and Mr. Jones, Oma and Bobo, The Purple Coat.* I'm always delighted to rediscover these in the book basket.

4. **Sally Bingham**

Sally Bingham is the co-author of the widely used "Choice Series" personal journals and workbooks for vocational planning. In her children's books, she presents three meaningful "female" characters: Minou, the pampered Parisian cat who learns self-reliance, Sally, a fox hound who refuses to hunt her friend, and Berta Benz, who made the first cross-country drive in a gas-propelled automobile. Girls ages 5–8 will want to read: *Minou, My Way Sally,* and *Berta Benz and the Motorwagon.* These are fresh, feelingful stories.

5. **Faith Ringgold**

The brilliant quilt paintings of African-American artist Faith Ringgold have been transferred into several stunning books. From the fictional Aunt Connie and Cassie Louise Lightfoot to the heroic Harriet Tubman, the girls and women are unforgettable. Ages 5–12. Her richly detailed stories help bring the African-American experience home: *Tar Beach, Aunt Harriet's Underground Railroad in the Sky,* and *Dinner at Aunt Connie's.* I'm always moved by the beauty and pain in these books.

6. **Elizabeth Levy**

In her "Something Queer," mystery series—a cult among the 5–9 set—Levy introduces two whipsmart sleuths: Jill (a loyal best friend who lives with her single mom) and Gwen (who taps on her tinsel-topped teeth whenever she senses a mystery in the air). The illustrations by Mordicai Gerstein add sizzle to this series that includes: *Something Queer Is Going On, Something Queer in the Ballpark, Something Queer in Outer Space, Something Queer in Rock 'n' Roll, Something Queer at the Birthday Party, Something Queer in the Cafeteria.* Hannah likes to imitate Gwen; she has begun to tap her imaginary braces when something puzzles her.

7. David Adler

The "Cam Jansen" mystery series, written by David Adler, presents the wonderful red-headed Cam—nicknamed "the Camera"—for her photographic memory. Along with her sidekick, best friend Eric, Cam finds mysteries everywhere she goes. Along the way, Adler is careful to introduce readers to a balanced cast of men and women at work—avoiding gender typecasting in word and deed. Among the many to entice readers aged 5–10: *Cam Jansen and the Mystery of the Babe Ruth Baseball, Cam Jansen and the Mystery of the Dinosaur Bones, Cam Jansen and the Mystery of the Television Dog.* Cam is a terrific role model; she's thoughtful, observant, a boy for a best friend. I love it when Hannah solves the mystery before the last page.

8. Eleanor Cameron

In Cameron's "Julia Redfern" series, readers aged 7–12 will find a thoughtful, journal-writing heroine faced with a variety of challenges including her mother's remarriage. And don't miss Nina Harmsworth, who travels through time to nineteenth-century France to solve a mystery in *The Court of the Stone Children.* "Julia Redfern" books include: *That Julia Redfern, A Room Made of Windows, Julia's Magic,* and *The Private Worlds of Julia Redfern.* I'm looking forward to reading these as "goodnight books."

8. Constance Greene

"Why do they call it a period; why not an exclamation point or a question mark?" asks Al—one of the gallery of great girls in Greene's many books. From the feisty Isabelle to Kate and her sister, Jossey, readers aged 9 and older will want to take a look at titles that include: *A Girl Called Al; I Know You, Al; Isabelle; Isabelle the Itch; Isabelle Shows Her Stuff;* and *Beat the Turtle Drum.* I think Hannah will love the laughs in these books.

10. Scott O'Dell

Newbery award winner Scott O'Dell is best known for creating the character of Karana, the haunting Indian heroine who lives alone in the book *Island of the Blue Dolphins.* I can't wait till Hannah approaches 8, so she can meet 14-year-old Bright Morning, the Navaho heroine of *Sing Down the Moon,* and Raisha, a 16-

year-old African woman—a slave on the island of St. John—who risks her life to join the Great Slave Rebellion of 1733 in *My Name Is Not Angelica*. And in a sequel to *Island of the Blue Dolphins*, called *Zia*, a young woman sets off to rescue her Aunt Karana, left behind eighteen years before.

11. Lois Lowry

Lowry has a gift for creating memorable original heroines, especially Annemarie Johansen in *Number the Stars*. In this story, set in Denmark during World War II, Annemarie hides her Jewish best friend, Ellen Rosen, and embarks on a heroic mission to save her life. Lowry also created the unforgettable Anastasia Krupnik, the headstrong, inventive character who is a favorite of 8- to 12-year-olds. Her stories include *Anastasia Krupnik, Anastasia Again!, Anastasia at Your Service, Anastasia Has the Answers,* and *Anastasia's Chosen Career*.

12. Elaine Konigsburg

In *From the Mixed-up Files of Mrs. Basil E. Frankweiler*, Elaine (E. L.) Konigsburg has created two of the most original females in print: eleven-year-old Claudia Kincaid, who talks her brother into running away to hide in New York's Metropolitan Museum, and 70-something Mrs. Frankweiler, a wonderfully eccentric zillionaire who owns a statue that just may be the work of Michelangelo. After we listened to the audiotape (Listening Library) and read the book, Hannah wanted to practice "hiding" in various museums. Find other great girls for readers aged 7–12 in Konigsburg's other books: *Jennifer, Hecate, Macbeth, William McKinley and Me, Elizabeth*; and *Father's Arcane Daughter*.

MOVE OVER, BOY'S LIFE

Consider two fresh and original magazines for young girls; both avoid the dating-clothes-rockstar triumvirate of magazines for their older sisters. Each one has a particular twist on the role of heroines in the lives of young women; each speaks in a distinctive, compelling voice.

HOPSCOTCH: *The Magazine for Girls*

Editors Donald and Jane Evans seem to be seeking a balance between hurrying girls to grow up and helping them find a sense of purpose. As they explain, *"Hopscotch* was created to challenge young girls . . . we want them to grow up and be all they can be, while still enjoying their childhood." *Hopscotch* emphasizes girls' involvement in "subjects that have interested youngsters for decades": pets, nature, sports, hobbies, games, crafts, biographies, science, and careers.

Girls are center stage, yet the political and psychological posturing is at a minimum. A recent issue emphasized stories about "girls who have done something original and succeeded" (e.g., Lillie Hitchcock, who fought fires at age 8, and ballplayer Lou Colacito), rather than talking about role models or nontraditional roles.

Hopscotch's best moves are lot of stories with girls in challenging, exciting tales and the deliberate avoidance of political correctness. My complaints are occasionally whiny "why can't girls" poems, and a less-than-consistent commitment to diversity.

Spend some time in the library leafing through back issues or contact the magazine for a sample issue: Call 415-358-4610, or write P.O. Box 164, Bluffton, OH 45817-0164. Although *Hopscotch* is geared toward preteens, you'll find some stories and poems suitable for preschoolers.

NEW MOON: *The Magazine for Girls and Their Dreams*

New Moon is another constellation entirely. Here's a description from the editorial board in the premier issue: "This is not a magazine where grown-ups are in charge and come up with the ideas. *New Moon* depends on you and your ideas. We want this magazine to inspire and empower girls between the ages of 8–14. We want girls like us to stick up for themselves in the face of discrimination. Why can't a girl grow up to be a construction worker, engineer, surgeon, or president?"

New Moon began to address Duluth, Minnesota, mother Nancy Gruver's concerns as her 12-year-old twin daughters approached adolescence. It has blossomed into a companion magazine for parents edited by Gruver and husband, Joe Kelly, *New Moon Network*. She describes *New Moon* as a place "that doesn't tell girls where they should be—but where they can tell the world where they are—without adults or advertisers as interpreters."

The magazine is packed with regular features, including "When I was a girl" (stories from wise elderly women), "She did it!" (a girl who excelled), "Her Story" (history of girls and women), "I can fly" (a girl who has acquired a physical skill), "The Experiment" (a science investigation), and "How Aggravating!" (girls write about inequities in girls' experience).

As you can see, this is an exuberant, frankly feminist enterprise—one that talks back to gender typecasting, and celebrates and nurtures the spirit and strength of its readers. I find the heroines we meet on the pages of *New Moon* (including the young editors) to be zestful, brave, smart, and sassy—just the kind of girls you hope your daughter brings home from school. Available by calling 218-728-5507, or writing to New Moon, P.O. Box 3587, Duluth, Minnesota 55803-3587.

WOMEN HISTORY FORGOT

No one does a better job of writing women back into history—and inspiring girls to dream of heroines—than the Women's History Project. From their office in rural Northern California, they offer teacher training, publish a quarterly newsletter, create curriculum materials and games, publish posters, and produce videos, coloring books, and card games.

For parents short on time and long on commitment to finding strong heroines in history, I cannot recommend their catalog strongly enough (available by calling 707-838-6000). The last catalog listed over 400 items including biographies of historical heroines such as architect and engineer Julia Morgan, Dr. Elizabeth Blackwell, Mexican poet Juan Inés de la Cruz, sharecropper and civil rights leader Fannie Lou Hamer, and computer pioneer Grace Hopper. An additional resource is the *Book of Women: 300 Notable Women History Forgot,* published by Bob Adams.

DISCOVERING WOMEN IN MATH AND SCIENCE

In my fantasy of the best of all possible worlds, the woman next door is an astronomer, a chemist, or a mathematician. You and your daughter find adventure in frequent visits to her observatory or lab. Perhaps she buys your daughter an inexpensive telescope or microscope or a Boggle Junior math game for her birthday. She talks about when she first knew she wanted to be a scientist and about how she—like your daughter—was fascinated by Saturn or long division or growing crystals.

Sadly, for many of us, the models and mentors of women in the nontraditional fields of math and science do not live in our neighborhoods. Yet we can begin, at an early age, to link a daughter's joyous curiosity about the world to women and girls who study math and science.

Start by bringing home fictional heroines who are fascinated with the moon, stars, plants, animals, and outer space; who love to get messy, take things apart, solve mysteries, and figure out how things work.

Examples include *Nicky the Nature Detective,* by Ulf Svedberg; *The Universe Is My Home,* by Bill and Sally Fletcher; *Aunt Eater Loves a Mystery,* by Doug Cushman; and *Junie B. Jones & Some Sneaky Peeky Spying,* by Barbara Park.

Set the stage for her adventures and accomplishment in math by choosing preschool picture math books that have girl characters: *Eating Fractions,* by Bruce McMillan, and *Who Wants One?,* by Mary Serfozo.

For older girls, bring home biographies of women in math and science—especially ones that help her to see how the childhood interests of many women led to their careers in math or science. Sample these sources (all available from the Women's History Project):

- *You Can Be a Scientist Too.* Video by Equity Institute. Grades 1–4.
- *American Women in Science Biographies.* Multicultural examples of women in science. Equity Institute. Grades 1–4.

- *Science Is Women's Work*. Photos and biographies of American women in the sciences. Nancy Gallop. Grades 4–8.
- *Women and Numbers*. Terry Perl. Grades 5–8.
- *Equals: Biographies of Women Mathematicians*. Terry Perl. Grades 7–12.

FAMILY HISTORY: FINDING HEROINES IN THE FAMILY

One of Hannah's foremothers was a Russian revolutionary; one was a pediatric nurse who raised four daughters; another was a ballerina with the New York City Ballet; yet another was an ardent Zionist—Israeli Prime Minister Golda Meir was her houseguest. They are my grandmother Rachel, my mother Selma, Jeremy's mother Natalie, and his grandmother Paula.

Hannah asks about Grandma Selma's picture in her nursing cap and Grandma Natalie's picture dancing in *The Nutcracker*. When she saw the movie *An American Tale,* we explained how her great-grandmother Rachel had come to North America from Russia on a boat. As she gets older, Hannah will appreciate the revolutionary part—especially the times when Rachel slipped out of her bedroom window to meet her boyfriend in the forest. When she studies about the birth of Israel, we will tell her about how Paula met Golda.

To find heroines close to home, spend some time with your partner and siblings to recall some of the qualities and experiences of women in your family tree: the great-aunt who was an artist, or a veterinarian; the cousin who was a community organizer, a teacher, a marathon runner; the grandma who gave the best advice. Use them as both "quality" and "quantity" role models—casually pointing to their triumphs, traits, and interests: "You know, your grandmother loved to play chess; your aunt had a beautiful singing voice, like you do; your cousin Simone adored animals."

Invite interested daughters to do a more deliberate search for family stories with two resources: *The Great Ancestor Hunt: The Fun of Finding Out Who You Are,* by Lila Perl, and *How to Tape Instant Oral Biographies,* by William Zimmerman.

When we encourage daughters to climb the female family tree, we are inviting them to explore the future choices they will have as women. Next, we must ask what our daughters learn as they consider the choices that their mothers have made in their lives.

12

⮜—⬧—⮞

Model Choices

SEVERAL years ago, twenty-something Sally watched me speed-dress after a swim at the gym. "Where are you always hurrying off to?" she asked. "Well, Hannah is only two, so I try to pack eight hours of work into five, and jump in for a swim so that Jeremy or I can get home before she wakes up from her afternoon nap." Sally sighed, "Is *that* what I have to look forward to?"

For weeks I was haunted by her question, wondering about the kind of model Hannah would see in me. When I told my friend Carol, she had a story of her own: Her three-year-old daughter, Reva, coming home from daycare and announcing (like Carol), "I can't wait to get out of these clothes!"

Carol worried, "What am I teaching her about how I feel about my work? Then, I talked to a client of mine—a human resource manager from IBM—who reported, "My eleven-year-old daughter and her friends tell me they have no intention of working as hard as I do."

All these experiences point to the most complicated question about role models. In this chapter, we ask, What are women (and men) teaching their daughter about the choices she will have as a woman?

WHAT MOTHERS MODEL

As you know, the question of mother as role model has been the subject of millions of words in print. Unfortunately, since neither the journalism nor the social science communities can resist a fight, such discussions are inevitably framed in terms of pitting the model of the working mom with the model of the stay-home mom. The variable of judging the models: how the kids "turn out."

If you are interested, I can point you to piles of contradictory studies.[1] Which do you prefer: the ones that suggest the children of working moms are *more independent and academically successful*? Or the ones that show working moms' kids are *more anxious and depressed* than kids of stay-home moms? How about the studies that suggest that working moms spend more time with their kids than stay-home moms?

Did you want to see the statistics about the numbers of women who have "abandoned" careers to stay home?[2] Or would you rather read the studies that compare the kids of single, working moms with kids who have married moms?[3] By the way, did I mention that Dad wasn't part of any of these studies?

The Mommy Wars

I propose we skip the studies. Instead, I suggest that equalist parents become conscientious objectors in the Mommy Wars. We must object to the politically correct assumption that only working moms can be strong models for daughters. This leads us to the devaluation of caring. It also creates a self-defeating model in the words of a mother who describes herself as "only a housewife."

We must also object to "maternal correctness"—where status is defined by a bread-winning papa and having time to bake (not buy!) cookies for your daughter's class picnic.[4] We must understand, too, that the combination of maternal and political correctness is a recipe for female flame-out. I suggest that Wonder Moms—who dash home from work to decorate a three-tier birthday cake—must enroll in a Martha Stewart Recovery Program.

We must also note that Mommy Wars are a white, middle-class battle. As poet and educator Beverly Smith notes, "In the black community I grew up in, being a mother held status, so whether women worked or did not work, if they were mothers, they were still valued. Women's work contributed to the well-being of the family unit."[5]

LIKE MOTHER, LIKE DAUGHTER

Here's the drill: Instead of fighting the who-works wars, why not assume that mothers, like daughters, can model femininity through their individuality? Moms, I invite you to explore a variety of ways you model your choices as a woman.

• *A model of mastery.* Every mom must step outside the family and strut her stuff—express her smarts, spirit, and special gifts. Parents who need their kids to be the best—in order to have a sense of accomplishment—are vulnerable to lessened self-esteem. So take your daughter to work (whether you work in a high-rise office building or as a volunteer in a nursing home). In your expression of excellence, your daughter sees a model of achievement.

• *A model of expression.* Each mom can find a means to speak her mind, and express anger, good humor, and strong opinions. She can show her daughter how to agree to disagree (without fearing the loss of loved ones). In your comfortable communication, your daughter finds a model of authenticity.

• *A model of connection.* Every mom finds ways to express caring and tenderness that are uniquely her own: Are you a foot massager? Lunchbox note-writer? Snuggler? Sender of valentines? Consider how showing your affection with family and friends offers her a model of connectedness.

• *A model of self-acceptance.* Each mom can find pleasure and comfort in expressing her own style—accepting her body, and beauty, rather than being a fashion victim or dwelling on bad hair days and cellulite. She can talk about what she has learned, rather than dwell on her mistakes. In these ways, you model self-acceptance to a daughter.

• *A model of self-reliance.* Every mom can declare her independence by taking risks, trying new experiences, asking for help only when she needs it. As she watches, a daughter sees a model of autonomy.

• *A model of choice.* Each mom can share her struggle to find a balance between working and caring. Talk to your daughter about the choices you have made. Can you show her that she can work with pleasure—and without obsessive guilt—or truly savor the satisfaction of managing a home? As you convey your choices, you offer a model of decision making and comfort in your own skin.

TWO ROLE MODEL ROADBLOCKS

Despite all of your best efforts to convey positive choices and bring home brave, self-reliant, and tender heroines, you may feel defeated by the Disney divas—outmarketed and outspent by the people who love to bring us damsels in distress. Or your search for women who choose action—cowgirls and pirates to counter passive princesses—may raise the tough question of equal access to violent role models. Let's take a closer look at each of these roadblocks.

Roadblock 1. *Guns and Daggers*

Hannah received a box of dozens of Mardi Gras necklaces when her cousin Adam was living in New Orleans. After a few days of decorating her room and herself, she and her friend Laura invented a game called "Pirate"—where the necklaces were stolen and became hidden treasures. In the spirit of her play, I bought her a book on pirates and I read it with increasingly mixed feelings.

On the one hand, I was delighted to find pirates Mary Read and Annie Bonney listed along with Bluebeard. But did I really want Hannah to consider these robbing, ransoming, kidnapping women as role models? Yet Mary and Annie's more dicey adventures didn't seem to faze Hannah. She would shinny up the monkey bars yelling, "I'm Annie Bonney!"

So I scanned the aisles of a costume supply store, and found that the pirate kit came with a three-foot plastic sword. The sword stopped me in my tracks. Did I really want to arm Hannah to encourage her to identify with adventurous women?

To understand how you might answer the same questions, stand in the "action" section of a toy store, where you see: torch swords, warrior daggers, sheriff clickers guns, soft zap guns, and assault force weapons. You will not see a single female face pictured on the packaging. Before you raise your eyebrows, ask yourself: Do you really *want* your daughter to have equal opportunity to see herself pictured on the packages of guns and swords? (You probably don't want to see your son either.)

In our rush to fuel a daughter's imagination, I would ask you to read a recent study that found that girls raised watching more violent female role models on television imitated them. In other words: A violent superhero who looks pretty in pink is not a heroine to bring home to supper.

Yes, your daughter and mine will play pirates, but to enrich her imagination with models of active girls and women, here are some additional parent choices:

• *Show her women in sports.* Attend the local high school or college all-girl basketball league. Watch the Olympics on TV. Show her pictures and stories from the Sports page. Check out biographies of sportswomen: *Bonnie Blair: Golden Streak* by Cathy Breitenbucher, or *Jackie Joyner-Kersee Super Woman* by Margaret Goldstein (available from the Women's History Project).

• *Introduce her to real heroines in action.* Tell her tales of the Old West: *The Story of Women Who Shaped the West* by Mary Virginia Fox; or about women at war, *Civil War Heroines* by Jill Canon; for women as explorers, see *Women of the World,* by Rebecca Stefoff; or in the air, *Ladybirds: The Untold Story of Women Pilots in America,* by Henry Holden, or *Mae Jemison, Astronaut* (from the Women's History Project).

• *Tell her a story.* Choose among many brave, feisty females in books and on tape:

Maggie the Pirate. Ezra Jack Keats's kids play backyard pirates. Ages 2–4.

Emily and the Golden Acorn, by Ian Beck. Emily and her brother's treehouse turn into a pirate ship. Ages 4–8.

Quest for a Maid, by Frances Mary Hendry. A thirteenth-century adventure story. "Only Meg can save the Queen." Ages 10+.

The True Confessions of Charlotte Doyle, by Avi. Adventure on the high seas with thirteen-year-old Charlotte. Ages 10+.

Emily Eyefinger series, by Duncan Ball. A girl with an extra eye at end of her fingers has daring and dangerous adventures. Ages 6+.

Heartlight, by T. A. Bacon. Kate and her astrophysicist grandfather journey into space to save our galaxy. Ages 10+.

Girls to the Rescue, by Bruce Chatwin. Ten nontraditional fun tales where girls use wit and wisdom to rescue themselves and others. Ages 6–12.

Annie Oakley: Little Miss Sure Shot, Rabbit Ears Productions, video and book. Ages 3–12.

Roadblock 2: The Disney Divas

You daughter would have to be living in Antarctica to avoid meeting Cinderella, Snow White, Sleeping Beauty, Ariel, Jasmine, Belle, Pocahontas and Esmeralda. Some parents have compared the Walt Disney Company's influence on our cultural fantasies to that of Hans Christian Andersen or the Brothers Grimm.

Here's the big difference: There was never a Brothers Grimm Boutique—filled with Hansel and Gretel pajamas and underwear, videos, laser disks, board games, and coloring books. The mass marketing of the Disney divas creates a "they are everywhere" feeling; I dare you to find a lunch box without a once or future princess.

Over the last few years, dissing Disney has become a parent parlor game: For a time Ariel *(The Little Mermaid)* replaced Aurora *(Sleeping Beauty)* as the object of understandable feminist fury. Sleeping Beauty's prince-dreaming snooze paled next to Ariel's decision: to trade her voice for a chance to win Prince Eric.[6]

In recent Disney discussions, I've heard parents agree: Belle was the best, Princess Jasmine was positively retro, Nala was the token female in *The Lion King*'s male bonding rituals, "Princess" Pocahontas—an otherwise plucky heroine—didn't need that deerskin décolletage. And that Esmeralda was too smart to dress like such a tart.

Frankly, I find Disney's preoccupation with princesses to be boring—worse than the British tabloids. I am much more concerned about choice implied by the equal opportunity villains—for example, Cruella de Vil *(101 Dalmatians)*, Medusa *(The Rescuers)*, and Ursula *(The Little Mermaid)*—who offer ugly models of powerful women. They are, without exception: unmarried and childless, the jealous, bitter destroyers of young women.

I don't think you can banish these potential princesses or their female tormentors from your home. But you can avoid multiple viewings by *renting, not buying,* the videos. You can include the Disney books among many, many others. You can also offer a commentary or ask questions about the characters: "Do you think Ariel should have traded her voice? It was the most important part of her." (For complete instructions on "second opinions," see Chapter 14.)

Best of all, you can offer your daughter some princesses both of you can be proud of.

- *Tumble Tower,* by Anne Tyler. Princess Molly and her wonderfully messy room. Ages 3–6.
- *The Paper Princess,* by Elisa Kleven. The freshly cut paper princess blows away with the wind calling "I'll finish myself." Ages 3–8.
- "Atalanta," from *Free to Be . . . You and Me,* by Marlo Thomas et al. Atalanta cleverly thwarts her father's demand for her marriage and sets off to see the world. Ages 3–10. Available in book, audiocassette, and videocassette form.
- *The Princess and the Lord of the Night,* by Emma Bull. Self-

reliant Princess Ella sets herself free from a terrible curse. Ages 5–10.

- *The Princess and the Admiral,* by Charlotte Pomerantz. Vietnamese Princess Mat defends her kingdom with nothing but a supply of firecrackers. Ages 7–12.
- *Young Guinevere,* by Robert San Souci. Long before becoming Queen, Guinevere takes a perilous journey to aid her people. Ages 5–8.
- *Tatterhood and Other Tales,* edited by Ethel Phelps. Twenty-seven folk and fairy tales about women of bravery and kindness. Ages 4–10.
- *Maids of the North,* edited by Ethel Phelps. Feminist folktales from around the world. Ages 4–12.

Just as important, give your daughter tales of wise and loving older women who offer nurturance and guidance to our heroines.

- *Miss Rumphius,* by Barbara Cooper. A great-aunt gives the advice she heard from her grandfather, "You must do something to make the world more beautiful." Ages 3–7.
- *Gwinna,* by Barbara Helen Berger. A twelve-year-old who sprouts wings is given guidance by the kindly "Mother of Owls." Ages 8–12.
- *Wise Child,* by Monica Furlong. A young girl in a Scottish village is adopted by Juniper, a local wise woman. Ages 10+.

LAUGHING ALL THE WAY

Remember to bring a sense of humor to your search and choice of heroines. Consider the experience of Brenda, who took her eight-year-old niece Andrea and best friend to see the rerelease of *Snow White.* As she explained, "The adults in the audience were hissing, and I was fuming. How could I be exposing her to this: A mother poisoning her more beautiful daughter, a snoozing Snow White, and only a prince could help? Then I looked over, and Andrea and her friend had fallen asleep."

KEY IDEAS

Strategy 4
Bring Home Heroines

How to find and use role models to enrich a daughter's sense of self

- Be specific. Name the actions, accomplishments, and values of girls and women you admire.
- See heroines everywhere. Point to powerful wonderful women often, out loud, and on purpose.
- Balance her books. Skim for stereotypes, read dialogue in quotes, choose characters who let their true colors shine.
- Let truth be as strong as fiction. Give her books about women in math, science, and history. Find heroines in your family's history.
- Model choices for women. Mothers can model their own style of accomplishment, opinion, tenderness, self-acceptance, and independence.
- Resist violent—though adventurous—role models. But enrich her imagination with girls and women in action.

Strategy 5

WEAR GENDER GLASSES

*How to Show and Tell the Story of
Sexism—and Counter our Culture's
Narrow Views of Women and Men*

13

Show and Tell Her About Sexism

SEVEN-YEAR-OLD Raeya came home from a meeting at school and asked her mother, Paula, what seemed to be a simple question. "Today, Mr. Eliot asked for two strong boys to move some chairs. A few of the older girls got really angry at him and jumped up to move the chairs themselves. *I don't understand; why were they so angry?*" Paula—deciding to make the long story of sexism short— answered, "I think the girls were angry because Mr. Eliot seems to be one of those people who assume that girls aren't as strong as boys."

In the fifth strategy, we will be inspired by Raeya's question and Paula's answer as we guide a daughter's discovery of (and resistance to) gender prejudice. As equalist parents, we wear gender glasses. When we look through them, we see the way sexism is linked to lowered self-esteem. For us, gazing at gender is what psychologist Bob Kegan calls a "meaning-making activity."[1] Like Paula, we wonder, How do I explain the meaning of the sexist situations that my daughter brings to me—or that I see?

In this chapter, we prepare to show and tell our daughters about sexism. But first, we must ask a quartet of prickly questions: Do growing girls *need* gender glasses in order to trust and find meaning in their unique experiences in the world? If so, do we offer to share our own gender glasses—inviting our daughter into our room, with its view of how gender typecasting can devalue and limit girls and boys—*or do we wait to be asked?*

In other words, if gender glasses didn't exist, would parents need to invent them? Or, as Aretha Franklin once asked, "Who is zooming who?"

GENDER GLASSES: WEARING THEM, SHARING THEM

Robert, whose daughters, Sarah and Eliza, are eleven and thirteen, portrays the power of sharing gender glasses with a daughter. "Once you show daughters [how women can be limited, left out, or victimized], they catch on quickly. In a way, they lose their innocence and will never see the world in the same way again." Robert's comment evokes the key issue for equalist parents: Do we show (and tell) them what we see? Do we share the meaning that we have made about gender prejudice in our culture?

Joe, whose twin daughters, Mavis and Nia, are thirteen, is adamant in the affirmative. "This sexism stuff is real. My job isn't to protect my children from reality, but rather to support them in creating a personal reality that nurtures them. From the very beginning, when we sat around the dinner table, talking about politics and current events, the recurrent refrain about many issues has been, 'It's not fair.' In our family, we view sexism as a matter of fairness."

Yet according to parents in my classes and interviews, we don't need to point, because even the littlest girls have noticed how boys and girls are treated differently and have different experiences. Countless parents have shared stories of three- and four-year-old daughters (remember our concrete-thinking preschoolers and their passion for classifying?) who demanded to know the following:

Why are all truck drivers men/baby-sitters women? Why isn't a woman President? Why are boys allowed to get dirty and do more things? Why won't boys let me play? Why does everybody talk about my curly hair? Such questions suggest that girls may encounter what Carol Gilligan calls the "wall of Western culture" brick by brick.

DAUGHTERS EXAMINE THE EVIDENCE

Many older daughters, like eight-year-old Rebecca, present parents with their view of our culture. Rebecca wanted to know more about the Pro-Choice rally she was attending with her parents. Her mother explained the meaning of the march as being about increased opportunity and control for women; she compared it to film clips of marches led by Martin Luther King, Jr. that Rebecca had seen on television. After listening to this explanation, Rebecca's question revealed the meaning she had made: "How come white men have all the stuff?" she asked.[2]

Daughters like Rebecca, explains Carol Gilligan, study the evidence around them: "Like anthropologists, they pick up the culture; like sociologists, they observe race, class and sex differences. Like psychologists, they come to know what is happening beneath the surface. Like naturalists, they collect their observations, laying them out, sorting them out, discussing them between themselves."[3]

As we listen to nine- and ten-year-old girls, we observe a mix of evidence, explanation, and exclamation.[4]

Meike: Last year in my gym class, my teacher said, "Now it's time to learn to play basketball, *but I am sure the boys know how to play.*" That really got on my nerves.

Julie: I can't stand it when people think that boys are better than girls. What I hate even more is the words like snowman, fireman, postman, and policeman.

Amanda: When I go to McDonald's and order a Happy meal, they always ask me if the meal is for a boy or a girl. This is so they can choose the toy. The girl toy is always a Barbie, and the boy toy is usually something more interesting, like a race car. Why don't they just ask me what toy I want, *instead of assuming that all girls want Barbies*? I think this is unfair.

DO THEY NEED GLASSES?

Meike, Julie, and Amanda have shared their gender gaze in an ongoing column in *New Moon* magazine, called "How Aggravating." In this column, girls write about their encounters with gender unfairness. According to publisher Joe Kelly, the column receives more parent mail than any other feature. When we compare the views in two parent letters, we see both the power and the danger of inviting daughters to try on our gender glasses.[5]

One parent wrote, *"I wonder if these girls would be so conscious of gender bias in school if we adults had not pointed it out to them.* Wouldn't it be better to teach our girls what they can accomplish rather than what they can't? The victim attitude is to me as destructive as the original discrimination."

Another parent expressed a polar opposite view: *"Girls do see, feel and understand sexism regardless of whether adults name these actions.* The pain, humiliation and frustration are real, regardless of whether a girl says, 'Why can boys get away with that?' or whether she can put a name on the actions and say, 'That's sexism.' "

Both parents' arguments light our path as we join our daughters in the meaning-making activity of understanding and challenging gender prejudice. Listening to the two parents, we are reminded of Aldous Huxley's comment, "Experience is not what happens to you; it is what you *do* with what happens to you."[6]

If we want to collaborate with our daughters (rather than control them) in what they "do" with gender prejudice, we must help them see the gender expectations that can limit their choices. We must join them in naming sexist situations.

THE GAZE OF GENDER: A GIRL IS WATCHING

The idea of a girl's gender gaze can be smartly summarized in a question asked as part of a "Take Our Daughters to Work Day" curriculum, created by the Ms. Foundation.[7] It is a question that wonders how girls make sense of what our culture teaches them about women. To wit: *"A girl is watching: What is she learning?"*

Consider several directions where your daughter may have a clear view to learn the limitations of gender typecasting.

Not-So-Great Expectations for Girls

Oh say, does she see: the picture on the preschool doctor's kit (boy as doctor, girl as helper), the dozens of books with damsels in distress, the school counselor who assures her that she will "never need physics"? From the teacher who asks for "three strong boys," to the relative who asks, "How will you ever have a family if you go to law school?," your daughter may struggle to make sense of the images and experiences that telegraph low expectations for girls—as compared to boys.

The Perfect Woman

Has she shared her view of the images and expectations that pressure her to become a perfect woman? Has she noticed the number of people coaching her to "be nice"—even if this means a charade of hiding the truth of her anger, confusion, pain, or joy?

Does she see the crazy-making media images of razor-thin maternity models or the impossibly beautiful women who bring home the bacon; fry it up in the pan (and never let him forget he's a man)? What do these stifling standards mean to her?

The Invisible Woman

Thumbing through her toddler picture books, she may begin asking, "Where are the girls?" As she grows taller, her list of queries may grow longer. "Why aren't there women in my science and history books, behind the wheels of forklifts, at the fire station, on the pulpit, in the outfield, on the executive floor, and in the White House? Why are most of the women white?" What does she learn from the answers?

The Words Without Women

It won't take long before she understands the meaning of the phrase "the King's English." Has she noticed, for example, the use of "man" for "person," "he" and "his" as preferred pronouns, male-only job titles ("foreman"), or trumpeted exceptions to the rule ("woman doctor"); and gender-loaded parallel words like "bachelor/spinster?"[7] What does she read between the lines?

A Women's Worth

Has she noticed the words that can be used to describe women (tarts, chicks, broads, bitches, and unprintables); the ways boys are taught that it's not so great to "be a girl"; the premium placed on having a son; the low value placed on traditional nurturing and caretaking (as in "I'm *just* a stay-home mom"); women's smaller paycheck for the same work as a man; the high visibility of women in low-paying jobs? How does she see herself and her potential in this harsh light?

Girl Watching

From the super-skinny, overdressed supermodels to the air-brushed bodies in the *Playboy* centerfold, to the nasty nicknames for her body parts, is your daughter confused by images of both admiration and contempt for female beauty and by our culture's concern with sexy, slender bodies? Has she noticed our culture's contempt for older women? How does she see the media images that emphasize a woman's youth, sexuality, and attractiveness, rather than her achievements?

"IT'S NOT FAIR"

As we gaze in these directions with her, we see a deeply disturbing vision of what our daughter may be learning: that women in our culture can be diminished, pressured to be polite and perfect, devalued, ignored, or treated like objects.

Yet a daughter may sum up her view in a simple sentence (the same one she used to describe your unwillingness to buy her a horse, let her stay up to watch David Letterman, or pierce her nose): "It's not fair," says she.

One dad reminds us of the importance of validating this meaning-making. "We have to offer her a confirming response; we have to say, 'Yes, you are right, it isn't fair. It's not you; it's not your fault, and you are not crazy.'"

Writer Anita Diamant's explanation of gender prejudice to eight-year-old Emilia includes "a lot of straight talk about fairness." She has explained, "Racism is an evil belief system that permits some people to mistreat others on the basis of skin color," and showed Emilia that sexism is just as real as racism, and a potential threat to her.

Diamant's point: "Now Emilia will at least know that if the boys won't let her play basketball at recess, or if men make lewd comments on the street, *the problem does not lie with her, but with antiquated and poisonous notions about gender.*"[8]

Do remember: Straight talk about fairness must also include our sons.

SCHOOL FOR BOYS

I remember the day I walked into Hannah's preschool class and spotted her friend Ben. He was pushing a baby carriage into the "homecenter" with a pink patent-leather purse perched on his shoulder. He, Hannah, and Laura were playing "family" (their favorite game besides "pirates"). I watched this scene with a wistful eye, wondering if Hannah and Ben's friendship would continue to flourish on this lovely, level playing field.

Sadly, within several months, I began to see them learning the limits of the double edge of gender typecasting: I heard Ben had been told, "Boys don't take care of babies." And Hannah had been told (by Ben) that she couldn't play a certain "boys only" game. So, Ben was already being encouraged to cast off his tenderness, and Hannah was encountering the idea that boys don't think it is so great to be a girl. How can we help Hannah and Ben make sense of this nonsense?

Educator Raphael Best might label Ben's new behavior toward Hannah as a result of beginning to learn "the second curriculum"— a social learning where boys are pressured to distance themselves from mothers, female teachers, and girls.

With heartbreaking accuracy, Best's book, *We've All Got Scars,* describes the playground politics of boys sneering at anything female. By age six, says Best, the ultimate insult is to call someone a "girl!" She details the "Negative Canon" of learning to be a man. It is based on the idea that whatever females do, that is what boys must *not do.* For boys, this brings a long list of taboos: no playing with girls, no displays of affection, no weakness, no cleaning the classroom, and no playing with babies.[9]

My neighbor John tells me hopefully, "I remember that stage; but Graham is starting to be interested in girls again." We notice that most boys move out of the "no girls in the clubhouse" phase so they can flirt and date and mate. I wonder: Does the contempt for girls resurface in reports of sexual harassment of grade school girls? What happens to the voice of feeling that boys send underground?

A Boys' Relationship Crisis

Carol Gilligan makes a convincing argument that for boys, this kind of early childhood education creates a "relationship crisis" that compares with what happens to girls in early adolescence. Viewed from this perspective, the "He-Man Woman Hater's Club" is not just about boys devaluing femininity—it is also an experience of boys distancing themselves from their deepest feelings. Gilligan reminds us how much boys lose when they learn it is not good to be a girl—or act in a nurturing, so-called feminine fashion.[10]

For boys in early childhood, the pressure is to identify with the ideal of emotionally empty superheroes as a route to manhood. For girls in early adolescence, the pressure is to identify with the ideal of the perfectly good and impossibly beautiful woman. In both ideals, our sons and daughters are encouraged to disconnect from their genuine feelings.

I thought about the unfairness to Hannah's friend Ben—his

forced flight from things feminine—with a bittersweet memory of my arguments with my friend Ray about the losses of men and women. I wondered whether Ben would learn to silence his sensitivity—to narrow his emotional range as he learned to be a man. I thought, too, about how Hannah might lose a friend—and of her painful puzzle of trying to understand a friend's contempt for her femininity.

I wonder: Can Ben and Hannah cut these shortchanging stereotypes down to size—and define themselves apart from the limits of gender? If we want to help them, we must understand how both sons and daughters are diminished by the idea that girls and boys are opposites (or that one sex is superior). We can begin by treating our children as individuals, not members of a gender group.

We must also remember that when boys are socialized to "be boys"—to separate from the world of women, they (like adolescent girls) lose potential and silence their feelings. When boys are asked to disconnect from their vulnerability and sensitivity, they are reduced to doing the heavy lifting; and that's not fair, either.

Still, you must be ready to remind me of a promise I made earlier—that we can tell the story of sexism without snarling. Allow me to tell you how parents might explain why a woman has never been President.

HOW COME A WOMAN HAS NEVER BEEN PRESIDENT? (AND OTHER QUESTIONS DAUGHTERS ASK ABOUT SEXISM)

When I ask parents how they answer a daughter's gender-busting questions, I hear them answer in terms of the past, the person, the culture, and the facts. Here's a sample.

The Past.   *Put the meaning of prejudice in a hopeful historical frame: that was then, this is now.* In this approach, when your daughter asks, "How come we have never had a woman President?" you would stifle the urge to say, "That's because men are scared of a strong woman." Instead you could answer, "For a long time, women did not have as many opportunities as men—they have only voted and owned property for a very short time. But things are changing: Shirley Chisholm and Pat Schroeder have run for President, and Geraldine Ferraro has run for Vice President. I'll bet you or one of your friends will be the first woman to be President."

The Person.   *Stick to the person's typecasting behavior*—and avoid name calling and patriarchy bashing. When a daughter asks, "Why did my counselor tell me I don't need science?" you wouldn't curse, "That chauvinist Cow!" You could say, "He is one of those people who doesn't believe that both boys and girls are interested in or good at science. But you have always loved learning about the way the world works. Besides, science is a part of many jobs you might want when you grow up. So we need to let him know that you *do* need science."

The Culture.   *Explain sexism by looking at the big picture.* They invite a daughter to look at how ideas in our culture can limit girls, and then they encourage her to counter the culture. When Hannah asks me, "Nobody talks about Dad's hair; how come everybody is always talking about my curly hair?" I can stop myself from saying, "Doesn't it make you want to pull your hair out by the roots?" and answer, "I know, people talk about my curly hair too. I wish they would ask me about the book I'm writing. But we live in a world where lots of people care too much about the way girls and women look. When people talk too much about your hair or clothes, you can do what I do—start talking about something else."

The Facts.   *Skewer sexism by citing specifics*—try a reality-testing approach. For example, when a daughter is steamed because her teacher asks for "four strong boys" to move chairs, you can refrain from hissing by sticking to the facts. You might say, "Ella is on the basketball team; she's certainly strong enough to move chairs," or "You could have helped. Remember the time you carried all of our suitcases when we went to Hawaii?"

THE TOUGHER QUESTIONS

Equalist parents understand how each question about gender prejudice that a daughter asks (depending on the situation and her age) calls for a creative and *brief* combination of one or two of the meanings above. Yet none of the four approaches can answer the toughest question, *The Question of Why.*

As Joe explained, "I can't explain *why* gender prejudice happens—any more than I can explain why there was slavery and why white Europeans treated Africans like animals. Sometimes I can only ask, Why is it important to do something? And what can I do about it?"

When parents consider "what to do" about gender prejudice, we encounter even thornier questions: How do you explain the puzzle of women's inequality without lowering a daughter's self-regard? Yet if we ignore inequities (saying, "You have the same shot as a man"), won't that answer fly in the face of what girls see? And then, if we insist that equal opportunity exists, how do we prepare her to do battle with gender prejudice?

Journalist Judy Mann has written about discussing these tough questions over lunch with psychologist Carol Gilligan. First, Mann talked about her twelve-year-old daughter Katherine's teachers—"who teach that everyone is equal in democracy, when the girls know perfectly well that they are not equal." Then, she explained her dilemma—if she told her daughter that things were not equal for women, would her daughter begin to think that something was wrong with women? Yet if she told her that women had equal opportunity, they would both know that she was lying.

Gilligan told Mann, "Tell her that she is right; things are not all that great for women, but that together, you and she will make a difference."[11] As parents who want to join our daughters to make a difference, we must be prepared to share our gender glasses. Together, we can find the courage to counter the culture.

14

Counter the Culture

HANNAH was quite curious about the *Beezus and Ramona* audiotape she received at a Chanukah Party; she wanted to play it as soon as we got home. And so I—who often screen and scan books and tapes—agreed and held my breath, waiting for the first stereotype to drop. We didn't have to wait long. In the very first story, older sister Beezus, exasperated by (Hannah-aged) sister Ramona's passion for a book called *Scoopie the Steam Shovel*, whined, "Why did she have to like a book about steam shovels? *Girls aren't supposed to like machines!*"

Imagine my dilemma: I've just written a chapter about how girls avoid computers because they think of them as "male machines." Yet here I am—Hannah's head in my lap—knowing that she is listening to the kind of stereotype (gender prejudice) that contributes to computer avoidance. I fantasize about pressing the erase button, or "losing" the tape on the way to Grandpa's. But I can see she is hooked on this otherwise wonderful, sisterly tale. I need to find a way to share what I see through my gender glasses.

After she had listened to the tape for several nights, I finally told her, "I can see why you like these stories, but I think Beezus some-

times says things that aren't true; like remember when she said that
girls don't like machines? Well, you like the VCR and your
tapeplayer and the computer at school." Hannah nodded and
named some other machines she liked, and she continued to play
and replay the tape.

Then one night, after listening to Ramona say, "Mothers are
more interested in how their kids act than fathers," Hannah told
me, "That reminds me of when Beezus said, 'Girls don't like machines.' Because it's not true; Dad cares about how I act." I was
stunned by her surmise and decided to take a giant step and share
my gender glasses.

I applauded her observation and answered, "You are right. *Both
of those ideas are called stereotypes.* A stereotype is when you talk
about everyone in a group as if they were the same—like all girls do
this or all dads to this, or all African Americans are like this. . . ."

From that day on, whenever Hannah or I hear a generalization
about boys or girls, we nudge each other and say, "Stereotype!" I
can't help but wonder how much we would have missed if I had
used my gender glasses to eliminate Beezus and Ramona from Hannah's library.

In this chapter, we join our daughters to discover—and stand up
to—sexism. We can teach them about the tools they need to counter
our culture's stereotyped ideas about men and women.[1] But first,
we must study our own feelings about gender prejudice.

FEAR: WILL SHE BE CAPTURED BY CULTURE?

Anita sees her nine-year-old daughter Emilia as a leader. "She's
capable, smart, and strong; her karate kicks are awesome, and she
doesn't care who knows it. She seems poised for a takeoff into a
bright future. But still, *I am afraid for her.*"[2] Parents like Anita,
who understand how our culture's narrow view of girls can direct a
daughter to the Glass Mezzanine, describe their feelings in a word:
fear.

As psychologist Dana Crowley Jack explains, "We fear so much
for our daughter's safety. We are so worried that she will be captured by culture—be silenced and forgo her creativity and unique-

ness. We are so concerned that she will be whisked off for ten years and re-emerge as a damaged woman, that we forget that children must find their own way."[3]

For many parents, the anxiety of being on red alert may create a stifling marriage of political correctness and overprotection. This involves parents in all kinds of family fun: outlawing lipstick and nail polish, scanning for sexist slights, burning books, and the microanalysis of every role model.

Dana Jack explains this pitfall for parents. "We have to remember that every girl experiments with traditional (and stereotyped) femininity. We can't be too controlling or fundamentalist—or what we get will be what we forbid." The difference between panic and preparing daughters to face prejudice, says Jack, "lies in providing alternative models in the way we live; in telling stories of strength and courage in women's lives."

We must manage both our anxiety and our anger as we prepare our daughters.

RESENTMENT OR RIGHTEOUS ANGER?

Six-year-old Jemma asked her mother:

"Mom, how come you always refer to God as a she?" Said Nancy, "That's to make up for all of the people who call God he."[4]

We all identify with Nancy's frustration in trying to roll a rock uphill as we try to reshape cultural images of power in our daughter's image. On second look, we see that Nancy has managed to draw a graceful line between expressing her feelings of what Christina Hoff Sommers has called "righteous anger" and "resentment."[5]

Let's put a parental spin on this distinction. "Resentment" is the problem that has too many names; it's free-floating anger and male bashing. The expression of resentment casts men as all-powerful, women as victims, and parents as policers of patriarchy. It's a full-time job that includes angry generalizations about men and being hyperalert for sexist slights.

In contrast, "righteous anger," like Nancy's, is a powerful tool for equalist parents. It mobilizes us to act as agents of a counterculture. We are motivated to bring home heroines and provide alternative ideas and images so our daughter can look in the mirror of our culture and still see her vibrant reflection.

PAIN: REMEMBERING THE GIRL INSIDE OR LISTENING TO THE GIRL BESIDE US?

Jane O'Reilly has written a marvelous essay, "The Lost Girls," about the pain of identification that women can feel as they watch a daughter approach the age of the glass mezzanine. She describes a gang of girls swimming, and easily guesses which one is almost eleven ("ardent, vital and confident") and which one is fourteen ("mannered, anxious and doubtful").

> How did I know? It happened to me. It happened to all of my friends. We remember our eleventh year as the last time we felt truly ourselves. We were brave and eager. And then we discovered that these were not the required traits for girls. Only boys could be expected to inherit the earth. That's why we became feminists. We wanted ourselves back. We wanted a straight path for our daughters. I wish someone had talked to me when I was eleven . . . recognized my "bad" and "dangerous" behavior as curiosity and courage. I want to *intervene,* to use my experience so another girl doesn't have to repeat it.[6]

Like O'Reilly, parents who watch girls collide with culture can feel the pain of their own past. Mothers grieve for the braver girl within and fathers mourn for the more tenderhearted boy left behind in becoming a man. When we identify with our daughters, we create a bond of empathy; but we can also become intrusive—insistent in our interpretation.

Jane O'Reilly discovered this dynamic when she decided to share her gender glasses with her ten-year-old goddaughter, Zoe. When she tells Zoe that "men are considered more valuable than women in most cultures," her goddaughter glared at her and roared, "That is absolutely not true!" "Yes, it is true!" O'Reilly roared back. Then Zoe spoke from her own experience, "I do not know a single father of any of my friends who thinks less of his daughter than of his sons." While O'Reilly paused to respect Zoe's opinion, Zoe flew out the door with her dog.

We cannot let our feelings or the view through our gender glasses keep us from believing her story. Yet how do we show a daughter sexism we see—and still honor her view? Consider four ways to point out sexism.

STATE A SECOND OPINION

Let's study the technique Myra uses to teach her children about the stereotypes they see on television. "I realized that every time a commercial came on, the children looked at me. I hadn't even been aware of it, but I was continually irreverent about commercials showing women dressed up, doing housework and smiling, selling cars, modeling clothes in positions that would have broken a normal woman's back. I think they began to look forward as much to my version of the commercials as any produced by the products. I never considered that I was instructing my children in sexism—but I was."[7]

Note the humor and the power of Myra's second opinion. As she makes fun of commercials, she invites her kids not to believe what they see. We'll never know if Myra's commentary motivated her daughter to come home one day complaining about stereotypes in a classroom poem. Yet we can make sure that we offer cultural critiques to a daughter without insisting on being her eyes and ears.

Myra's humorous approach to countering cultural images reminds us that *tone is everything*. Sometimes we lose our sense of humor when we see limited images of women reflected on the wall of culture. We snarl, "No one is going to talk to my daughter like that! Or fill her head with those empty ideas!"

Yet to grimly insist on our ideas is to offer an invitation for her to close her eyes. She thinks you are mad at her; she feels like "a bug under a microscope." And worse, she thinks you are nagging: "Oh Dad/Mom, not that *stereotypes stuff* again!"

I suggest these scenarios to offer a second opinion.

• *Try thinking out loud.* When looking at a book about artists or inventors, you might muse, "That's odd, I don't see any women in these pictures." Flipping through a magazine of teeny-weeny-bikini-wearing models, you might comment, "We sure don't know anyone who looks like that."

• *Invite her to share your amazement.*[8] *"Can you believe* that in almost every movie we see the women depend on the men to figure things out?" *"Isn't it incredible* that even though so many women are police officers, they are still called policemen?" *"Isn't it amazing* that when your Aunt Susan was a little girl, people tried to discourage her from studying architecture?"

• *Repackage and revise.*[9] Rewrap typecast toys (the ones with one sex pictured) in your own box with stickers, stars, ink pad prints, or pictures cut from equalist catalogs such as *Toys to Grow On.* Explain your actions, inviting a daughter to help. ("This toy only has a picture of boys on it and it's for Jenny. Let's find another way to wrap it.") Revise stories for younger kids by adding pronouns or adding a female character. Invite older kids to join the fun of adding a feminine voice to the story.

• *Offer an opposite view.* After listening to a blow-by-blow description of an incident, mirror her feelings first. After joining her in empathy, offer a contrasting opinion. "You must have been furious when he/she said that." And then: "But he/she is wrong. Anyone who thinks that isn't seeing you for the person you are."

After a family Thanksgiving, let her know that *you* know Uncle Barry was off base: "Imagine Barry thinking you can't work and have a happy family. Just look at us—and your friends Sarah and Laura's families."

• *Let humor help.* Like Myra, you will learn that lampooning the limits of stereotyping works best with older kids. Still the funniest is the book or tape of *Free to Be You and Me,* with one caveat: The youngest kids (preschoolers, busy classifying) can take the satire *literally.* They may repeat sexist satire as fact.

OFFER HER AN ALTERNATIVE

Since his daughter Molly could toddle, Herb had been trying to show her an alternative to stereotyped views of men and women. He remembers a time when she was fifteen, and he was returning from a trip where he had performed his first wedding ceremony.

> Molly met me at the door: "Dad, drop your suitcases right there; you've got to hear this message." She marched me up to the answering machine and played a thank-you call from Allison, the bride. Allison talked about how grateful she was for what I had said about love, marriage, and commitment and *how valued she had felt as a woman.* Molly said, "I would love for someone to leave me a message like that!"

Like Herb, parents can challenge stereotypes without an argument or interpretation. Instead, we can offer our young daughters an eyewitness alternative to stereotypes about the sexes. In this way, parents can share a meaning of gender roles that runs counter to cultural norms.

Depending on the age of your daughter, you can direct her gaze toward men and women of tenderness, courage, and conviction, including yourself. Here's a starter sample:

- Women who have pursued family life without sacrificing their sense of self.
- Boys and men who respect, value, and adore women—and who prize their own nurturing qualities.
- Families who evenhandedly share domestic chores and the responsibility of caretaking.
- Fictional heroes (such as Sam Beaver in E. B. White's *The Trumpet of the Swans)* who are bold, bright, and tender.
- Women in art, science, and sports whose achievements skewer stereotypes.
- Men who nurture close relationships with other men.
- Your own successful struggles in challenging gender prejudice.

- Your own acts of protest—organizing, letter writing, dialoguing, demonstrating.

GIVE HER THE WORDS

Hannah was describing a duck she had seen at the aquarium in great detail. She paused for a moment and wondered, "Do you think he *or she* ever leaves the aquarium?" Jeremy and I (who have added "she" pronouns since before Hannah could talk) flashed each other one of our "maybe it's working" smiles. But later, we talked about how daffy the dual pronouns sounded coming from Hannah rather than us.

We cringed, wondering: Are we raising a politically precocious child? Is she simply imitating our pronoun bean-counting? Or as linguist Robin Lakoff has suggested, is her language shaping her ideas?[10] When Hannah adds a "she," does it make her feel like more of a player?

After the duck description, I began to notice how often Hannah added "she"—and how often she asked where the girls were. For example (when a policeman showed up in a story she asked "What about a police*woman*?"). As I listened to her, I became convinced that talking back to the male bias in our language was an essential tool for parents. At first, you can expect to feel as if you had marbles in your mouth. But remember that you are giving her the words to see herself in the action.[11] Walk the talk in these ways.[11]

- Avoid the generic male pronoun; it doesn't mean both sexes. Alternate "he" and "she" or just include both in the sentence.
- Avoid "man" words. Select some substitutes.

MAN WORD	ALTERNATIVE WORD
mankind	humanity, human race, people
primitive man	primitive people or peoples
man's achievements	human achievements
"If a man drove fifty miles . . ."	"If a person (or driver) drove fifty . . ."

the best man for the job	the best person (or candidate)
man-made	synthetic, artificial, manufactured
manpower	human energy, workforce
grow to manhood	grow to adulthood, manhood, or womanhood

• Change job labels to fit employees of both sexes.

SEX-LINKED LABEL	ALTERNATIVE LABEL
policeman	police officer
fireman	firefighter
workman	worker
repairman	plumber, electrician, etc.
chairman	chairperson or chair
caveman	cave dweller
congressman, congresswoman	Member of Congress
businessman	businessperson
mailman	postal worker, letter carrier, mail carrier
insurance man	insurance agent

CREATE A PARENT-DAUGHTER DIALOGUE

Psychologist Maria Root explains how to draw a daughter into a dialogue of meaning about what she sees.[12] If your daughter comes home complaining, "My teacher let two boys be captain of the math game," don't immediately assume this is a case of gender bias. Begin the dialogue by asking, "Why? What does this mean? Was this sexism or did they draw names out of a hat? Or were two girls captain last time?"

Root's suggestion—that we seek the reasoning behind the situation—offers a path to join a daughter in looking at gender prejudice from her point of view. Says Root, "We explain sexism in the same way we might explain racism. We ask: 'Does it ever happen in your class that the boys get special—or different treatment than girls?' "

She suggests that when a daughter announces, "I hate all boys," we don't argue with her or silence her feeling but, instead, begin a dialogue of reflection. We can ask, "Every single one? I know you like Kevin. What has happened to make you hate all boys?"

Psychologist Dana Jack is eloquent about the folly of forcing a daughter to look through our gender glasses. "I don't want to be the authority. I want to show her a way of questioning and understanding so that she can learn to trust her own mind and perceptions." Gender glasses are a collaboration, emphasizes Jack. "Go find out what she thinks about it."[13]

To share her vision, ask your daughter these questions:

- What do you see?
- What do you think about it?
- Is this true in your life?
- Why do you think she/he did or said that?
- Why do you think this happened?
- Has this ever happened to you before?
- What did you (or your friends) think of what she/he did?
- What do you think you might do (or say) if this happens again?
- How can you tell that person how *you* see this situation?

Now, let's imagine how these questions suit various situations.

- *You are reading a book where a female character acts dumb or doesn't do her best around boys.* You can ask, "Why do you think she let Alex win the race?" or "Why do you think she pretended to need help?" "Has this ever happened to you?" "What would you do in the same situation?"
- *You are watching MTV, a commercial with snazzy supermodels, or flipping through a no-flab fashion magazine.* Ask her, "Do you think she looks attractive?" "What do you think about the way she dresses, or dances?" "Do you know anyone who looks like that?"
- *A not-so-favorite relative has just unloaded an old warhorse about working women.* Take your daughter aside and ask, "What did you think of David's (or Dina's) comments about women who

work?" "Do you think our family is like that?" "Do you see that happening in your friends' families?"

• *An older daughter has grown quieter, tentative.* You might begin, "I have just read an article about how girls feel less confident when they reach your age. Let me read a piece to you." Then: "Do you think this is true? Do you and your friends ever talk about feeling this way?"

When you join your daughter to explore the meaning of what she sees, your discussion can lead her to stand up to—sexism. For example, you might rehearse a "next time." Once you've asked, "What do you think of what happened?" you can increase her sense of mastery by asking, "What do you think you might do or say next time?" (Or even, "I'll be your teacher, try it out on me.")

Encourage her to protest. When you have discovered how she has made sense of the sexism situation, you can invite her to take action. Ask her, "How could you let that company (that teacher) know how you feel about the way women look (or act) in their advertisements?" Or, "Do you think you might call or write, or set up a meeting?"

TEACH YOUR CHILDREN WELL

You can learn to share your gender glasses without blocking her view. Still, you may need to brace yourself for the consequence of what she has learned: Her gender gaze will also include your behavior. "She's our inspector; she keeps us clean," explains one father. But here's the best part: When parents teach (and learn from) their daughters to resist our culture's limited view of women, we create a loving bond of trust. Just listen to this mom.[14]

"At five, my daughter Sarah is no longer an innocent feminist, no longer naive. She has had some experiences with sexual prejudice. We talk about *we* and *they*. When she sees something on TV, or someone says something that is degrading to women, Sarah will comment, 'Mama, *they* think girls are afraid. But *we* know better.' We certainly do."

KEY IDEAS

Strategy 5
Wear Gender Glasses

How to show and tell the story of sexism—and counter our culture's narrow views of women and men

- Share your gender glasses. Show her the limits of sexism, but don't block her view.
- Remember that stereotypes diminish both daughters and sons.
- Tell the story about sexism. Explain gender prejudice in terms of the past, the person, the culture, and the facts.
- Probe your own feelings. Fear, resentment, and past pain can cloud your vision.
- Point out prejudice. Offer a second opinion on stereotypes. Suggest alternative role models.
- Argue with the King's English. Avoid male pronouns, adjectives, and job labels.
- Open a dialogue with your daughter. Ask leading questions to see the view from her room.

Strategy 6

TELL THE TRUTH
ABOUT BEAUTY

*How to Teach Your Daughter to
See Beyond Ideals of Perfect
Beauty—and Celebrate Her
Beautiful Self*

15

Beware of Beauty Bias

JEAN recalls meeting Deborah's nine-year-old daughter, Rachel, for the first time. "Rachel was a stunning young girl, with gorgeous coloring and luxurious hair. She was so striking that I waited until she had left the room to tell Deborah how gorgeous I thought Rachel was. Deborah answered, 'Thank you for not saying anything when Rachel was in the room. *Everybody* talks about how beautiful she is, and we want her to grow up thinking there is more to her than being beautiful.'"

Parents of daughters understand why Deborah was so grateful not to discuss Rachel's beauty. We have all struggled to focus a daughter on her strengths and spirit—to keep her from judging her worth by her appearance. In the sixth strategy, we will explore the challenges of raising a daughter in a culture that defines femininity in terms of beauty. We will learn how to tell our daughters the truth about beauty.

BEAUTY SCHOOL

Yet we won't spend all of our time throwing darts at poster girls for *Playboy, Vogue,* Estée Lauder, and Ultra-Slimfast. In this chapter, we begin by learning the crippling cultural lessons that prevent a daughter from seeing her own beauty. Each of these lessons creates a potential problem in her adolescent years, because of her newfound ability to observe herself.

When parents study these lessons of beauty bias, we see that we have learned them too—they affect our own self-images. Before we can teach a daughter to counter the culture, parents must finish their own beauty business. Then, we can teach our daughter to be "beauty wise"—to move beyond the cultural ideals blocking her view of her splendid beauty and feminine body.

As usual, we will start on her birthday—her first day in beauty school.

LESSON 1. BEAUTY BELONGS TO WOMEN

A baby girl is born into a world that immediately shows a bias toward her feminine "beauty." Consider, for example, the study where parents of (physically similar) day-old infants described their daughters in terms of appearance: "beautiful," "soft," and "cute." Sons were characterized in terms of actions: they were "firm," "strong," and "well-coordinated."[1]

Remember how Baby X—when dressed in blue—was described as "strong," "bouncy," and "active"? When swathed in pink, she was "lovely" and "sweet."[2] As sociologist Jessie Bernard has tartly suggested how girls are encouraged to be pretty in pink, "Early in life, the pink world starts to process girls to value it."[3]

Thus begins a well-documented pattern. Throughout childhood, girls receive more attention for their appearance than their accomplishments. To her, we say, "What pretty shoes!" To him: "I'll bet you can really run fast in those."

As a growing girl looks around her, she sees the beautiful models who sell everything from deodorant to cars, the pretty women in movies and on television who win men with their beauty, the gorgeous women who grace magazine and book covers and paper bill-boards, the nude beauty of women in museums—captured by paint or stone.[4]

Psychologist Rita Freedman, in her provocative book *Beauty Bound*, talks about how girls apply this lesson of being beautiful. When a girl lives surrounded by images of beautiful women, and hears constant comments about *her* appearance, she begins to think, "I'm a girl and girls are pretty, so I must be pretty."[5] But imagine her confusion. First, she has learned how important it is to be beautiful—yet why don't movie and magazine beauties look like her or anyone she knows?

Then, she is told that she *is* beautiful (or will be when she grows up), but why do all the advertisements tell her to doubt her beauty? If she is so beautiful, why does she need makeup, makeovers, mois-turizers, pushup bras, hot rollers, hair color, razors, and thighmas-ters to be truly beautiful?[6] And why doesn't beauty last? She is told she will "always be beautiful," but where are the pictures of "older beauties"?

The future danger of teaching a daughter to define herself by beauty—in a culture consumed by images of impossibly beautiful women—is best summed up in a study of 20,000 teenage girls. Nearly half of the girls reported that they frequently felt ugly.[7] The lesson that beauty belongs to women launches a lifetime of pain expressed in consumerism ("It's not me that looks radiant, it's my new moisturizer"); terror of aging ("I'll lose my looks"); and worse, seeing herself as an object ("Does *he* think my thighs are too big?").

Even before adolescence, a girl begins to make crippling connec-tions: Not only is she expected to become a beautiful woman, but her beauty will define her goodness—her ability to be loved.

LESSON 2. BEAUTY BRINGS GOODNESS AND LOVE

Picture your six-year-old daughter, planning her birthday party. You ask, "What about Leslie? Are you inviting her?" Your dear one answers, *"I don't like her—she's not very pretty."* Where, you won-der, did she learn to dislike the less beauteous among us?

It is stunning to discover how early children learn the beauty-brings-goodness-and-love lesson. Studies suggest that children as young as four years old held the "attractiveness stereotype"[8]—they showed a distinct preference for attractive children. They expected better behavior from good-lookers (to be friendly and helpful) and they expected to like them. Unattractive children were seen as "scarier"—the boys more likely to act out (hitting, fighting, hurtful words).

It is clear that they have learned this stereotype from us. These children's judgment of attractiveness closely matched those of adults in the study. Clearly, children notice adults' affection for attractive children. Listen to this seven-year-old's description of how girls and boys are different: "Girls do not get hit by their mothers because they are more beautiful."[9]

We wince and yet this youthful scribe is not far from the truth—because data from studies suggest how adult judgment is affected by physical appearance.[10] Researchers have found the following: Baby nurses attribute higher intelligence to cuter babies; mothers snuggle and kiss attractive babies more; good-looking toddlers are punished less often.

In one study, adults evaluated attractive children who had committed harmful acts (throwing stones at dogs, aiming a snowball at another child's head). The attractive children were less likely to be seen as antisocial and the harmful act itself was judged less negatively than the acts of their unattractive peers. In another study, teachers perceived attractive children as being more intelligent, more likely to continue with advanced education.

Do both girls and boys suffer from the beauty-brings-goodness-and-love stereotype? Yes, but it operates differently for each sex. Because our culture emphasizes a woman's appearance and a man's achievement, young women learn to look to beauty to flag their success at being feminine—and lovable.[11] A girl is trained to *define her potential in her physical self,* rather than in terms of her originality, energy, kindness, or accomplishments.

The lesson that love comes with being lovely surrounds her. Just look at her storybooks. Virtually all the evil females are snaggle-toothed, sallow, and wart-covered (ugly!). The bravest heroines are always beautiful—even relying on beautiful body parts to save the day (Cinderella's dainty foot, Rapunzel's mane of hair).[12]

A daughter turns from her books to observe adult adulation of good-lookers (and disdain for the beauty-impaired). Magazines and movies are populated by girls and women whose beauty is beloved, admired, and imitated. Think how often she meets someone who underlines this lesson by saying, "You are so pretty—you *must* have a boyfriend!"

This link of love, goodness, and beauty stunts the growth and self-regard of our daughters. If she learns that beauty is a scarce and powerful resource for being good and winning love, she begins training for a lifelong, envious competition with other women ("Am I the prettiest?"). If she believes that beauty brings love, she begins to equate her ability to love and be loved with how she looks.

I'm afraid there is more: She will soon learn that having a beautiful face is not enough; she must also seek love with her never-too-thin body.

LESSON 3: BEAUTY IS THIN

In her deeply moving book, *Reviving Ophelia,* psychotherapist Mary Pipher writes about Geena, a bright and chubby clarinet player who loved to read, compute, and play chess—who showed no interest in makeup or clothes. Pipher describes her painful awakening on her first day of junior high.

> She walked to her first day of junior high with her pencils sharpened and her notebooks neatly labeled. She was ready to learn Spanish and Algebra and to audition for the school orchestra. She came home sullen and shaken. The boy who had the locker next to hers had smashed into her with his locker door and sneered, "Move your fat ass!"
>
> That night she told her mother, "I hate my looks. I need to go on a diet." Her mother thought, "Is that what this boy saw? When he looked at my musical idealistic Geena, did he see only her behind?"[13]

My eyes filled with tears when I read about Geena. I was thinking about how many girls are devastated by the lesson she learned: *to determine her worth in terms of her size.* Even worse, to evaluate herself from the outside. Even if Geena hadn't bumped into the nasty boy next door, she, like your daughter, will be bombarded with our society's beauty-is-thin, fat-phobic messages.

Everywhere, she encounters tauntingly thin models and actresses, fashions that look best on the thinnest, magazines packed with self-loathing/exercise articles, thin celebrities slurping chocolate diet drinks. Add parents and teachers offering a constant commentary on their *own* weight, diets, or less-than-thin thighs.

The worst news for our daughters is that the scale is tipping lower for thin beauty. One study of slimness reports that our culture's ideal standards (as determined by Miss America's weight) grew even skinnier between 1979 and 1988. By 1992, Miss America's weight was 13–18% *below* the average expected weight of women.

Just to put this in perspective: Body weights below 15% of the average expected weight are one of the diagnostic criteria for the eating disorder anorexia nervosa. I would say that this study gives a new—and sad—meaning to Miss America's signature song. Try singing "There she is, your ideal . . ." when you know that these "ideal" women display one of the main symptoms of an eating disorder.[14]

Our children learn the beauty-is-thin lesson at a disturbingly early age. Studies suggest that by kindergarten, fat children are teased more and included less; thin children are more likely to be chosen as leaders.[15] True, overweight boys are hurt by our culture's fat phobia, yet it is girls, not boys, who more strongly link their weight to their self-esteem. The older the girl, the more likely she is to be worried about her weight. In one study, 50% of the nine-year-old girls were dieting, along with 80% of the ten-year-olds.[16]

This madness maps the list of potential dangers for your daughter: the risk for an eating disorder as she copes with the rounding of her body at puberty; the possibility of becoming a compulsive exerciser or developing metabolic problems. Some studies even suggest that adolescent dieting can lower her metabolism, making it more difficult to maintain a healthy weight later in life.[17]

And worse, she may develop a lifelong habit of linking her self-esteem with weight. Like Geena, she may be driven to define her beautifully evolving self in terms of her size. As she nears adolescence, her growing cognitive skills will alert her to beauty standards set by men.

LESSON 4. MEN SET BEAUTY STANDARDS

Teresa describes an all-too-familiar summer scene. "We brought Zoe [age two] to a swimming party at her grandparents' house. All the men were sitting around, critiquing the women's bodies. As I listened to them, I wondered, 'How am I ever going to help my daughter develop healthy feelings about her body?' "

We don't know if Zoe was listening that sunny afternoon, but we do know girls quickly learn that boys have been to beauty school too. The male curriculum is inspecting and dissecting females as objects of beauty (and desire). Before long, girls have learned to let boys set the standards—and to watch themselves.

All too soon, Zoe will learn that girl-watching is an international pastime—ranging from warm admiration to X-rated street or school harassment. The most damaging part of the lesson is that girls and women are not only watched by males, but are also ruthlessly rated—part by part.

Just ask Geena, devastated by being devalued for her "fat ass," or Hilda, who vowed to get a nose job after a young man at a party pointed to her, saying, "Who's the beak?" As we listen to our daughters, we understand the pain of internalizing the male gaze of beauty judgment.

In Melanie's story, we meet girls who view themselves through the filter of an imaginary audience of harsh, unforgiving men. Now nineteen years old, Melanie recalls herself as a thirteen-year-old, sitting with a group of friends, comparing the shape of her legs. In a mock beauty pageant, girls rated each other on a scale of ten points, with scores for "shape" and "general impression."

"I would give Victoria five out of ten for length and eight for shape, wouldn't you?" Another girl, "Yeah, I reckon so. She wouldn't do too badly with John you know; he likes short shapely ones. . . . And what about Natalie—I'm afraid we're giving you only three for both marks. We have to be fair, you know." Natalie listens to her score. "That's right, I suppose. . . . I could kill my mom for giving me such horrible thighs."[18]

Your daughter's ability to internalize beauty standards set by men exacts the highest price. Not only does it heat up competition among female friends, but you see, once she begins to view her body as an *object,* she watches it instead of lives in it—she cannot feel its hunger or desire. She will be blind to its unique beauty.

When we study these lessons of beauty school, we wonder: How can I balance my attention to my daughter's beauty—and help her win the Looking Glass Wars?

GET OUT OF THE MIRROR

I was in Hannah's room—using her full-length mirror to check my runaway curly hair for the fifteenth time that day. Hannah's eyes locked with mine in the reflecting glass. "Get out of the mirror!" she ordered. I laughed and lowered my gaze—knowing what a struggle it will be for me to stop looking. Because I, too, am a beauty school graduate.

I am the second of four daughters, whose appearance was the source of constant comment and comparison by friends and family. Each one of us was singled out for whispered confessions ("I think *you* are the prettiest—or have the best figure—of *all* the Mackoff girls!").

Our parents emphasized accomplishment, not appearance. Our clothes allowance was limited; our book allowance was unlimited. Yet we were captivated by the culture. I can still see the four of us transfixed by the Miss America Pageant, the perfect cram course of beauty school. In it, women were watched and rated, women competed against each other's beauty, and a woman's wonderful personality was given a consolation prize (the dreaded "Miss Congeniality"). We learned our lessons and dutifully dieted, ironed each other's hair, and knocked our too-round knees.

Determined to make things different for my daughter, I went into action early. From the moment Hannah could turn her head toward the sound of my voice, I took the pledge: I would no longer complain about my bad-hair days or the bump on my nose; I would not mention the "D" word (diet). Although I have succeeded in silencing my current beauty critiques, my daughter can still catch me in the old mirror.

> *Hannah:* Mom, did you ever have straight hair?
> *Me:* No.
> *Hannah:* How about all of those pictures of you at Grandma's?
> *Me:* You're right. When I was younger, I didn't like my hair as much as I do now. I used to try to make it straight.

When we bring our own beauty business into the light, we can join our daughter in defining herself outside of the narrow bounds of slim, blond beauty. Yet how do we get out of the mirror?

BEAUTY BIAS IS NOT PRETTY

When I listen to parents, I hear the different lessons men and women learn. I understand how compromised we all are by being socialized in a culture that overvalues, and constantly watches, feminine beauty and slimness. Do these parents sound familiar?

A mother, raised to be relentlessly self-improving (and self-loathing), regards her long-legged daughter dancing on the beach and comments, *"Thank goodness she didn't get my legs!"* A father, trained by a lifetime of girl-watching says, *"She has the legs of a chorus girl!"* Both scenarios are the result of beauty socialization.

Many women, focused on appearance as identity, may view their daughter as a mirror—a second chance to perfect her version of herself. Many a man (although certainly not all) sees a daughter's beauty as a reflection of his success—a pretty girl on his arm. Such parents see their own image in her beauty; they, too, regard their daughter as a beauty object.

Telling our daughters the truth about beauty means facing our own beauty bias. Because of the differences in men's and women's experiences in learning about beauty, I want to offer a rare instance of sex-segregated parenting tips. I direct the first (and longest) sermon to mothers. As women, schooled to see ourselves as beauty objects, we have a heap of homework—if we want to help daughters win the Looking Glass Wars.

BEAUTIFUL MOTHERS

Louise remembers taking seven-year-old Amanda shopping for jeans. As her daughter pulled on a pair, Louise was startled by her own image in the mirror and blurted, "God, I'm ugly!" Amanda said, "You aren't ugly, Mommy. You look just like me. And you are always saying that." Louise told her daughter she was right and later commented, "Two things changed for me after that experience. One, I don't say I am ugly even when I am feeling that way, and certainly not in front of Amanda and Margarita; two, when I do feel that way, I remind myself that I look like Amanda and I know she is lovely."[19]

A mother who joins daughters in doing battle with our culture's beauty bias has two tasks. The first, as Louise suggests, is the internal work of embracing her own beauty. This work allows her to model beauty behavior that will embolden her daughter to define *her* own beauty. Here are some techniques for tackling both tasks.

• *Write a beauty biography.*[20] Summon memories of your earliest awareness of your appearance. (Were your eyes, hair, height, or weight the focus of a parent's, teacher's, or friend's attention?) Study photos of yourself at five-year intervals. Do the photos reflect various efforts to meet your beauty ideals at the time (permanent waves, fashion victim clothes?). Do you remember a mother, an aunt, a cousin, or a grandma whose beauty behavior made an impression on you? Speculate about the source of your own beauty standards. (Did you covet Candice Bergen's nose?)

• *Read all about beauty and body.* Armed with a revolutionary reading list, you can begin to transform your beauty and body image. You might read *Face Value,* by Robin Lakoff and Racquel Scherr; Rita Freedman's *Beauty Bound;* Roberta Pollack Seid's

Never Too Thin; Naomi Wolf's *Beauty Myth; Fat Is a Feminist Issue,* by Susie Orbach; *Unbearable Weight,* by Susan Bardo; *Transforming Body Image,* by Marcia Hutchinson; *Body Love,* by Rita Freedman; and *Some Body to Love,* by Leslea Newman. For a picture worth a thousand words, rent Henry Jaglom's film *Eating.*

• *Beware of your beauty routine.* If you asked your daughter how much time you spent on beauty and body, what would she say? Examine your beauty routine in terms of what it teaches your daughter: How much time does she see you spending on makeup application, haircare, facials, leg waxing, shopping, putting outfits together? How much money do you spend (proportional to your budget)?

Is your beauty routine fun, expressive, sensual? ("I love this color of lipstick," versus "I'm getting those pencil-thin lines above my upper lip!") Does the process of adornment bring pleasure, or is it a driven pursuit to perfection? ("I love the flow of this jacket," versus "This jacket covers a multitude of sins.")

• *Cut the comments.* Stop woman-watching. Stop the running commentary about your own—and other women's—appearance. Become aware of the inner commentary that critiques all women's beauty. At the very least, don't give it a voice in front of your daughter. Enforce an immediate ban on conversations about body, weight, shape, diet, gray hair, or wrinkles.

• *Find a beautiful self.* Can you expand your idea of beauty to include the gifts that add beauty to the lives of the people in your world: your thoughtfulness, delicious earthy humor, razor sharp ideas, or sense of celebration and generosity?

• *Begin beautiful friendships.* Choose soulmates you can share your whole life story with—the good, the bad, and the ugly—and still know that you are loved.[21] Beware of beauty-bound friendships. Remember that friends don't dress to kill. Instead of asking, "What do I look like?" or "What image do I project?," you can ask, "What difference do I make to the people and the world around me?"

The men in our lives can help with this assignment. In fact, one intriguing study reported that focusing on appearance and concern about face and hair ranked among the top four qualities annoying men about women.[22] Still, before our male pals can join us, I invite them on an eye-opening adventure.

HER FATHER'S WATCH

Writer Charles Simmons admits to a lifetime of watching women as objects. "You realize that all of your life you have screened women out. Too tall, too short, too fat, too thin, ill-dressed. . . . and of course, too mature. A hint in the eye's corner kept the eye moving for the fresh face, the youthful waist between firm hips and bust."[23]

Psychologist Rita Freedman suggests how this trained gaze of men makes both men and women objects. Women are rated piece by piece—like chicken quarters—and men categorize themselves by preferred piece: "they are tit, ass or ankle men." Men watch women, women watch themselves being watched, and both are focused only on beauty and body parts.[24]

Dads, is this making you feel uncomfortable—even insulted? Do you feel I am "stereotyping" your behavior? Do you number yourself among the men who retired from "ranking" women after high school, who never peek at *Playboy,* who wish the beloved women in your life would stop bad-mouthing their bodies?

Welcome to a regrettably small and very wise club; most men I meet admit the burden of beauty-watching. They can't look at a larger-sized woman enjoying ice cream without thinking "try a nonfat yogurt." Still, I insist that all dads—those who have outgrown beauty myths and those who have recognized themselves in the lessons on these pages—to take another look at the way they watch women.

• *Take a history lesson.* Revisit your yearbook, scrapbook, prom pictures, slide collection, or home videos. Think about the young women you dated and danced with. Did you think of them or describe them in parts (big breasts, gorgeous eyes)? Do you remember being limited by your ideas of beauty? Did you ever want to date a young woman but felt she wasn't "pretty enough"?

Do you remember feeling reflected pride as others watched the "pretty" woman by your side? Can you recall being embarrassed by the appearance of your mother, sister, or date? (Can you imagine how you would feel if a young fellow felt embarrassed by *your* daughter's appearance?)

• *Spy on yourself.* Stroll or sit in a public park or café. When a woman of any age walks by, *track your gaze.* Are you drawn to her face, eyes, your preferred body parts? *Assess your adjectives:* Are they appreciative or dismissive—reflective of white, Waspy, thin stereotypes of beauty?

• *Watch behavior, not appearance.* Shift the focus of your woman-watching from her appearance to her actions. How does she respond to her companions? Does her walk bespeak confidence? Does she appear determined, distracted, relaxed? *Imagine her larger life*—where might she work, does she enjoy a circle of loving friends? Is she hurrying off to a critical meeting, to pick up a child at school? Observe how much effort is required to shift your focus.

• *See the male gaze.* Imagine that your daughter is baby-sitting and uncovers a cache of *Penthouse* magazines or vintage *Sports Illustrated* swimsuit issues. What would she learn about how women are viewed? How would you answer her questions: *"Who* reads these magazines?" or *"Why* do people read these magazines? (Hint: Saying "They have good interviews" is not one of the choices.)

Fathers who have explored their own lessons of looking become the most effective allies of daughters and their beauty-driven sisters, friends, and wives. Still, for both parents, the biggest job remains.

JUMP OFF THE SCALE

Of all the questions I have raised in classes and interviews with parents, I found dads and moms to be the least comfortable—and most conflicted—by answering questions dealing with food and weight. Many thoughtful folks linked their behavior with their daughters to their own unfinished beauty business. A sample:

Martha: I lived the life of an overweight kid. I had to clean my plate and couldn't have snacks; I became obsessed with food. Any child of mine will eat on demand—I'll never use food as a reward.

Lydia: I can never forget I was a fat kid in high school; I'd hate to see that happen to Karly. She's short and chunky—like her dad—so I try to limit her sweets and give her water instead of juice. Her dad and I argue about food a lot—he's always giving her ice cream and treats.

Herb: Sarah has been overweight for a number of years. I don't want to make a mountain out of the issue, but I know it's an issue for *me*. I ask myself: What would it mean if my daughter were slim? Will being overweight limit her? Have I not helped? Should I have done a better job?

Each parent suggests their own issues about weight. Martha and Lydia's attitudes are shaped by painful memories. Martha continues a dialogue with her parents about food ("I'll show them the right way to feed a child"), and Lydia wants to protect her child from her past ("She'll never have to hurt like I did when I was a fat teenager!"). Herb's concern about fat shaping his daughter's future is a reasonable one—yet what haunts him is the idea that a fatter child reflects a parenting failure ("Should I have helped more?").

Like you, Martha, Herb, and Lydia are struggling to raise a daughter in a society with sick ideas about food and weight. How else do you explain simultaneous epidemics of obesity and anorexia and bulimia?[25] But struggle we must, because as a daughter grows toward puberty (and as early as six years old), she begins to acquire the fatty deposits that will help her develop her wonderful female form. And if our own issues about weight push us to join her "I'm getting fat" panic, we can't be of much help.

As an alternative, parents who wish to jump off the scale can answer two questions:

What Did I Learn About Food and Weight in My Family?

Educator Leslea Newman, author of *Some Body to Love,* teaches workshops on food and body image for women with eating disorders. "In every class, I ask the women to describe their mother eating a meal. I am amazed at the details they remember."[26] Take a moment and join Leslea's class: What do you remember about your parents' eating habits and values about weight and food?

Did your dad and mom diet, binge, deprive themselves of dessert, exercise obsessively—or urge you to do the same? Was your family a member of the clean-plate, "children are starving in China" club? Were they food dealers ("just one more bite of broccoli," "no dessert without finishing dinner")? Healthier than thou? ("that has salt in it"); alarmists ("high blood pressure runs in our family"); culture snobs ("we have *never* eaten at Burger King")?

What memories come to mind about your family's mealtimes? What rewards or punishments were tied to the dinner table? Was there a winner's circle for slimmer siblings? Did slim kids forgo sweets to "protect" chubbier ones? Did plump kids keep large-sized parents company? Was your parents' approval tied to the size of your waistline? Or did they put you in charge of your eating?

Parents of growing children may find such questions painful—many recall how their parents' food values and fear of fat kept them from feeling loved. Nancy tells me, "I remember at a family celebration, my dad put his hand over my glass to keep me from having another glass of (fattening) wine." Julie remembers, "I wasn't allowed to get my driver's license until I lost twenty pounds."

The pain of childhood experiences with food points parents to the toughest question of all: Is your parenting behavior regarding food and weight an attempt to "show" your parents how they should have parented you? What is the cost of this contest to your daughter? Perhaps your parents could not adore and respect a daughter or son who tipped the scale; *but be assured that you can.*

Begin by throwing out the bathroom scale, and stop counting fat grams and calories like the mantra of mantras.[27] You can teach a daughter to be an independent eater when you stop seeing her (and yourself) in terms of size. To do this, you need the facts about fat.

What Are the Facts About Fat?

All these statements are false: Fat people eat more. Fat people don't exercise. Fat people lack willpower—they could lose weight if they wanted to. A fat six-year-old will be a fat sixteen-year-old.

All these statements are true[28]:

- Studies show that many fat people consume the same amount of food as people of normal weight.
- Research suggests that the difference between fat and slim people is not simply their activity pattern, but that fat folks have a slower metabolism—they burn caloric fuel more slowly.
- Studies confirm that some fat people can lose weight (and keep it off) but only if their metabolism cooperates.
- More and more research points to genetic and biochemical origins of body weight, type, and activity level.
- A *normal* weight spurt—the accumulation of fatty deposits that triggers puberty in girls—can begin at age six or seven.

As nutritionist Ellyn Satter sums up the facts about fat in her marvelous book *How to Get Your Kid to Eat . . . But Not Too Much*: "People who are genetically programmed to be fat are likely to have a relatively high requirement for calories and a relatively low metabolic ability to squander excess calories."[29]

Satter points to the current statistics of childhood obesity and notes that many children are "fatter than nature intended." According to her, "The fastest route to fattening a child is to curb her physical activity, try to control her eating (especially putting her on a diet) or teach her to eat for reasons other than hunger."[30]

In other words, parents who understand that each family member has a genetic blueprint for height, weight, growth pattern, and physical capacity are poised to jump off the scale—and raise a daughter with a healthy relationship to food and her body.

In addition, parents of daughters must have the facts about female fat and normal growth, says Elissa Koff, professor of psychology at Wellesley College. As she explains, "Many parents panic when their daughters have a 'fat spurt' from age 7 to 9; they get scared and then, their daughters get scared. The fact is, the girls *need to grow*. These fat deposits trigger puberty and restrictive eating puts girls at risk for not achieving their full height and for long-term menstrual dysfunctions."[31]

Parents who understand these facts about fat are freer to stop weight watching and raise a joyously active daughter who is an independent eater. But only if they realize the facts also apply to them.

Sports nutritionist Nancy Clark advises adults about making peace with their own size and shape. "Weight, like height, is largely under genetic control. Just as you may wish that you could be five inches taller, you may also wish that you could be five pounds lighter. You probably can accept the fact that you have little control over your height; but can you accept your natural weight and refrain from fruitless dieting practices in pursuit of a model's physique?"[32]

Your daughter has a slim chance of developing a healthy body image if you are constantly critiquing your own size. If she does grow to be a large-sized young woman in this fat-phobic society (where people think she could be thin if she ate less and exercised more), she will need all of your help in loving the body she has.

Parents who confront their unfinished beauty business can become loving guides in teaching a daughter to be beauty wise. Even so, I'm not suggesting this requires to you to live a secret life— whispering diet and beauty tips on the phone with friends at night. But if you can acknowledge your feelings about beauty, you can reflect your daughter's encounters with beauty bias rather than your own.

It helps her when you can say, "I remember wishing I were taller," or "I'm still struggling with liking my ears (or nose or thighs)," and especially, "I was overweight and my parents watched every bite I ate; I may be doing some of that with you, and I'd like to stop."

BEAUTY WISDOM: FINDING TRUTH IN BEAUTY

Miles tells me, "Ever since Rhianna was a toddler, her mother and I have been kissing her goodnight, saying, 'You are strong, intelligent, and beautiful.' " Ah, if only we lived in a culture giving equal time to the many qualities that make our daughters so beautiful to us!

In the next chapter, we will invite a daughter to look beyond the illusion of perfect beauty, and find truth in showing her radiant self.

16

Teach Her to Be Beauty Wise

MARILYN, mother of ten-year-old Leslie, gave me a wonderful example of teaching a daughter to be beauty wise. When Leslie returned from a long visit with her dad, she hugged Marilyn at the airline gate and immediately asked: "Mom, where do you keep your copies of *Playboy*?" It seems that Dad hadn't hidden his habit, and one particular pictorial had captured Leslie's imagination. It showed a woman on a date, removing her clothes. "Leslie kept talking about how beautiful the woman was, how she hoped she would look that beautiful." Marilyn elaborated:

My mind was racing in a dozen directions. What should I react to first: the fact that she *saw* the magazines? The portrayal of women in them? The reason men look at them? I decided to start where she was—*comparing herself to the model*. I explained that she wasn't supposed to look like that because the pictures were an illusion. I told her the woman was certainly beautiful, but that magazines shot pictures through special lenses and were retouched to look perfect. To prove my point, I asked her, "Did you see any moles or freckles or splotches on her skin—normal things we all have?" When she said no, I talked about how rare that kind of beauty is; I asked her if we knew anyone who looked like the woman in the picture.

We talked about it all the way home and couldn't think of a soul who looked like the picture. And I reminded her that we couldn't tell the kind of person a model was from the beautiful picture. I kept stressing that everyone looked different and it was okay not to look like that perfect woman.

With her loving words, Marilyn was able to reveal both the illusion and rarity of ideal beauty. In this way, she encouraged Leslie to accept her own lovely—but less than perfect—appearance. I cannot overemphasize the importance of what Marilyn did, because research confirms our worst fears about a young girl's need to look like the stars she sees.

In one disturbing study, young women who were shown fashion and beauty images reported lowered evaluation of their own appearance after viewing them. In another, a group of teenage girls' exposure to beauty commercials increased their sense of beauty's importance to their personality and popularity.[1]

In this chapter, we consider the ways a daughter can become beauty wise. You must know I won't be offering tips for mother-daughter makeovers. Instead, we begin by exploring what Marilyn did. She understood how Leslie's interest in a picture-perfect beauty had provoked her daughter's uncertainty about her appearance. So she invited Leslie to look behind the mask of media beauty.

UNMASK MEDIA BEAUTY

We must join our daughters to see that ideal beauty is an illusion. As long as girls compare themselves to ideal images, they will frown in the mirror. Ironically, the very models daughters use as standards to berate their own beauty are the first to admit the making of this ideal.

"I'm an optical illusion," said one supermodel. Said another, "I have no breasts, but by holding my body in a certain way I can create cleavage. You can create cheekbones or take a bump on your nose and make it disappear."[2]

I talked about this image-making with Diana, a fashion editor, *Vogue* alumna, and mother of a five-year-old daughter. "You are missing the point," she said. "Forget talking about illusions created by airbrushing and hours of makeup. The worst thing about media beauty is the way women are portrayed—the pressure it creates for young girls to be sexual and to be attractive to men. Some of the images are absolutely gruesome: ten-inch high heels, S&M poses— these are not powerful females! They cannot possibly help our daughters feel good about themselves."

Diana is right. Parents who want to help a daughter become beauty wise must look behind the images that create beauty ideals, and also probe the way women and girls are portrayed. You can start now by trying to see beauty bias through her eyes.

Familiarize yourself with the images that catch her eye. Depending on her age, she might find the latest Disney diva or an MTV queen as a symbol of divine beauty. Flip through the magazine she reads, or watch a music video and ask, "What do you think about the way she looks, moves, dresses, dances?" Notice who is ugly and who is beautiful in her favorite stories, television shows, or movies. Learn what she is learning about ideal beauty. Then, explain these pictures in a thousand words. Try these ideas.

• *Describe the people behind the picture.* Help her understand that women she sees in movies, in magazines, and on MTV are posed images of women—with art directors, stylists, makeup artists, and hair stylists working behind the scenes to prepare them to be photographed and filmed.

• *Define photogenic.* Explain to older daughters the idea that certain models have features that photograph well and create more beautiful pictures. Being photogenic is part of what makes a model's beauty so rare. For a younger daughter, explain "not being photogenic" by asking her to note how much prettier Aunt Sarah looks in person than in her picture.

• *Tell her some tricks of the trade.*[3] Every daughter who has clicked her computer mouse to change a computer drawing can begin to understand some common practices in photographing and filming beauty: airbrushing and retouching to get rid of wrinkles or create creamy skin tone, the trimming of photographic negatives with scissors, the use of gauze or Vaseline over camera lenses to lie about an actor or model's age.

Older daughters may be interested to learn of the widespread use of a "Scitex" machine—a computer graphics machine that alters fashion and glamour images.

• *Get specific about size.* Girls really do need to know that the average model, dancer or actress is thinner than 95% of the population.[4] As noted earlier, many models meet the criteria for anorexia.

Yet the waif of the week may not suffer from an eating disorder. We must also tell our daughters that although many media beauties diet and exercise like madwomen, others have genes that let them eat cake—and never stride the StairMaster. To accept her own size, a daughter needs to know how rare it is to see these slim and toned specimens of women. It's an easy lesson—just go to the beach, or take her to your gym, where she'll see women of all shapes and sizes.

ARGUE WITH ADVERTISING

Two high school girls made a pact to stop buying fashion magazines. One of the girls explained, "When we stopped looking at all of the models in the ads, we felt better about ourselves." Since you may not be able to banish glamour girl magazines from your home, the next best action is to teach a daughter to argue with beauty-biased advertising.

• *Critique commercials.* The older she gets, the more beauty advertising is aimed at shrinking her self-esteem. Ask her, "Have you ever noticed how magazine ads always try to make us feel ugly—or like we need to lose weight or buy something"; or "I wonder why most of the models are white"; or "How come there are never any male makeovers?"

• *Probe portrayals of women in advertising.* Ask older daughters to study men and women in joyless, sexualized activities or poses, and ask a daughter about what she sees. "Do you think these people look happy? Do they love and support each other? Does this woman look like she is strong and happy in her life?" Think out loud: "I wonder why someone would use a picture like this to sell perfume to women?" Offer a second opinion about absurd adornments, "Imagine showing up for school in that outfit."

CREATE BEAUTY IN HER IMAGE

Elana, an African-American mother, talks about her fierce determination to provide a model of beauty that reflects her daughter's own image.

> I will not straighten my hair. I am absolutely opposed to it. Not because intrinsically there is something wrong . . . but because it represents a particular legacy of mine and I think, of most black people. . . . You try to change your hair to look white and as you are doing it, you're affecting your insides, you're saying there is something wrong about you and you communicate that to your kids.
>
> I remember I wanted long, long hair that would come down to my hips and my daughter has that same dream now and she should not. She is continually concerned about her hair, wanting it to be long and fly-away like on the TV ads. I think she has a contradiction. On the one hand, she wants to look like the models, on the other hand, *she wants to believe that there is something right about her.*[5]

For Elana's daughter (and her Asian, Hispanic, and Native American sisters), our culture's beauty bias is even more crushing. Young women of color are forced to contrast the distinctive features of their ethnic legacy with the fair-haired, wide-eyed, white "beauties" who dominate the media. Too often, they feel they don't measure up. Yet the effort to believe "there is something right about her appearance" is a struggle shared by *all* of our daughters—bombarded by media images of impossibly beautiful and thin women.

Here's how we can help create a sense of beauty in her own image.

• *Let her see her reflection.* Buy look-alike toys; surround her with splendid girls who look like her. Buy dark-haired daughters a brunette doll; get Duplo World's multiethnic block people to live in the cities she builds. Buy book and doll sets for daughters to color such as Faith Ringgold's *Tar Beach* or *The Legend of Bluebonnet.* Several catalogs offer multiethnic puppets. Also, *The Playfair Catalog* has multiethnic baby dolls, and UNESCO has a multicultural doll series (available at many art museums).

• *Support her idea of beauty.* If she wants to grow her hair, show her how to tackle the tangles. If she wants to cut it, get her to the scissors. Let her choose treasures (necklace, pins, rings) for adornment. When she reaches the age of makeup: make it fun, experimental, sensual, expressive.

We must also stop "dressing" a daughter as soon as she can talk.

HELP HER DRESS FOR SUCCESS

We are now a year past Hannah's "I only wear skirts" stage. Jeremy and I survived this era by reminding each other: This was her first expression of her own style, skirts didn't seem to keep her from rock climbing and—according to my research—her fashion statement was also part of a preschooler's figuring out what was female. Besides, we discovered some wonderfully patterned reversible skirts; it was fun!

Yet when I look back on that era, I wince to recall how much attention Hannah got for the clothes she wore (and how much it mattered to her). My tip-off was the day last year when she came home from school and sadly announced, "No one said anything about my new jumper today."

This year, Hannah has chosen to live in leggings, and her clothing compliments are few. I find myself wondering how much this simpler attire contributed to her attitude adjustment. For example, last week she told me, "Molly didn't want to play in the woodchips because she was afraid of wrecking her new shoes. I think she cares too much about her clothes."

These conversations with Hannah focused my interest in exploring the part parents play in how much our daughters "care about clothes." I found one study that suggested that the more girls dress up, the more attention they get from adults.[6] But does this automatically *lead* to more investment in her appearance? And so what? Here we are—back at the "what's wrong with a velvet dress at the ballet" question.

The simple answer is that dressing up for special occasions can be a joyous, fanciful experience. It is fun to behold our daughters in feminine finery. Besides, monotone sweats are not the dress code for strong and spirited girls.

You may hate me in the morning, because I've got to ask the tougher question: Don't you think that the more she wears eye-catching, "I can't climb or kick or get these dirty" clothes, the more she will receive attention for *being* beautiful—as compared with *doing* brave, beautiful deeds?

You don't have to listen to me; just tune in to adults and girls at a party. The dressier daughters get clothes compliments, the other girls get asked about school and sports and how they spent their summer vacation.

Parents who want to help a daughter dress for success must steer her away from beauty-bound stereotypes. You can start by bringing your own clothes issues out of the closet. How would you answer these questions?

Do you feel that she (and you) can be beautiful or handsome only when "dressed up"? How much time do *you* spend shopping for clothes? Are you basking in compliments about her beautiful clothes ("Everyone in New York was raving about her hat!") or do you give yourself politically correct points for her unisex attire— you're embarrassed by her passion for pink? How can you shift your focus from how she looks to how she feels?

SUPPORT HER SENSE OF STYLE

Anna Rose didn't wear pants from ages two to six, while Rachel wore the same two outfits so often, her mom sent a note to school explaining that "Rachel has more clothes, she just won't wear them." Matty won't take off her leggings and wear the jumpers her grandma lovingly sewed for her. Each daughter is expressing her style and separateness in her choice of her own dress code.

The preschooler who expresses her fashion authority is less likely to be steered by her peers as a school-ager. Here's how parents can help.[7]

• *Don't make her dress for dinner.* If she refuses to wear the "beautiful" dress you bought her for the party, support her. Don't believe for a moment that she would be happier in a dress, but do inform her that everyone else will be in dresses. If she still declines, let her wear dressy pants to the party. If she is not embarrassed, don't you be. Yet if you are invited to a black-tie dinner at the White House, expect her to rise to the occasion.

• *Don't let pretty mean prissy.* Parents of the daughter who defines herself in dresses have two choices. You can set limits for dressing up (for example, she can't play or go rollerskating in a party dress) or you can let her live in them but not limit her activity. If you choose the second choice, search for a good spot remover and be prepared to let her rip. You might consider secondhand garb; then allow only the finest of finery (say, a flower girl dress for a wedding) to be treated like a museum piece.

• *Remember that style can be shaped by her temperament.*[8] We must honor daughters with a low sensory threshold—the ones who find skirts or tights scratchy, will only wear one pair of shoes, or can't stand belts, sandals, or turtlenecks. Be sure to give your slow-to-adapt daughter an early warning about how she will need to stop wearing shorts before the first frosty fall morning.

You can support her sense of style and still help a daughter "dress her age"—avoiding clothing that creates the pressure to grow up too fast.[9] For example, when Karen's daughter Maggie was seven, she wanted to wear black all the time (a sign of her identification with teenagers). She would point to her four-year-old sister and say, "I hate pink and purple," as if to separate herself from her baby sister. Karen's solution: "I didn't want my seven-year-old walking around in outfits that looked too grown-up. So we started at the bottom, with black leggings, and bright skirts."[10]

DO WE TAKE PRETTY OUT OF THE PICTURE?

Tom tells me, "I finally figured out what to say when strangers make such a fuss over Ellie's appearance. When someone says, 'Oh, your daughter is *soooo* beautiful,' I just nod and then add one of her recent accomplishments. Like I say, 'Yes, and did you know she has just learned to dive off the high diving board?' "

Don't get me wrong—as I said earlier, the answer to her question, "Am I pretty?" is a resounding "Yes! You are beautiful in my eyes." And even: "When I look at you, I see your beautiful ideas and your kindness." As psychologist Rita Freedman explains, "If you *don't* compliment them on their appearance, it heightens their self-consciousness. If you overcompliment them, you inflate the importance of physical dimensions—you underline the idea that they are ornaments."[11]

Here's how parents can find balance, and put her appearance in a healthy perspective.

• *Probe the meaning of being pretty.* Begin a dialogue with the daughter who asks, "Am I pretty?" Freedman suggests we counter her question saying, "Why do you ask?" "What do you think is pretty?" or "Who is pretty in our lives and why?" Then ask, "Is there someone you like and respect who isn't pretty?"

• *Consider your compliments.* Become aware of how many times you use "beautiful" or "pretty"—passive adjectives to describe her accomplishments. For example, does every picture have to be "pretty"? Instead, substitute action words that imply her artistry. "It's awesome, powerful, full of energy. This is the first time you ever combined paint and crayons!" Take care not to praise the *presentation*—neat, pretty printing—more than the *product*. "This is a terrific story."

• *Find new words for beauty.* In their book *Face Value: The Politics of Beauty* Robin Lakoff and Raquel Scherr suggest the promise of using "subjective, nonevaluative" beauty talk. You look "radiant, splendid, beaming, glowing, glorious, sparkling."[12]

• *Refocus your praise.*[13] Refocus your attention in terms of how a daughter's physical self serves her (her legs are graceful, powerful—they win the race). Tell her you can *see* the qualities of inner beauty and self-acceptance ("When I watched you singing, your eyes just sparkled," "You look so happy today," or "You're just glowing.")

• *Model a different kind of praise* with your partner,[14] family, and especially your friends, saying, for example, "It's wonderful to see you looking so relaxed," "I can hear the joy in your voice," "Your haircut will be perfect for swimming this summer," "You seem to have such energy today," and even "It's wonderful to see you enjoying your chocolate sundae with such gusto!"

MIRROR HER BEAUTIFUL SELF

To counter the lessons of beauty school, parents must believe her story. We can confirm her concerns and comparisons of her appearance with ideal images: "I know you wish you had wavy hair" or "I know you would feel more comfortable in a bathing suit if your tummy looked different." Then, we can move beyond her comparisons to find beauty in her deeds—and tell her about them.

We can talk about the treasures she is hiding from the world: her whip-smart wit, her delicious laugh, her idealism, her gifts for friendship or music, her passion for politics or poetry, her vivid imagination or marvelous moves on the dance floor. We can say, "When I look at you, I see the beauty of all your concern for the environment, your smarts, and your sensitivity." We can tell her, "Your body is beautiful because *you* are in it."[15]

CELEBRATE HER BODY

Miles remembers, "When Rhianna was born, I was the one who lifted her out. I immediately looked at her genitals and yelled to my wife Julia, *'It's a woman!'* " As their daughter grew, Miles and Julia continued to celebrate her body's vitality and femininity. As Rhianna approached the age of her first menstrual period, her mother asked her if she wanted to have a ritual when her period began—to invite a group of women to celebrate with her.

Miles describes his role: "Before they arrived, my three sons and I decorated the house. We rolled a red carpet up to our front door and lined it with stones from the river. In the room where she would be sitting, we decorated a large pillow with purple lace and filled the room with bouquets of flowers. We left her a poem and went to the movies."

Not all families share Miles and Julia's joyous sense of ceremony, and not all daughters would be comfortable in this kind of occasion. Yet every parent can join with a daughter in building a sense of truth and beauty about her body. We can teach her to celebrate— rather than critique—her body. When we encourage her to understand and live inside her body, we offer her a vital alternative to girl-watching. Let's start with her vocabulary.

OFFER ANATOMY LESSONS

Astonished by the number of parents who think the term "vulva" refers to a Swedish automobile, psychologist Harriet Lerner wonders, "How could [any woman] feel 'permission' to be a sexual being when she has been taught from childhood that she has a vagina (which is internal and difficult to examine) but not that she has a vulva, which includes the clitoris and the labia? What does it mean for a little girl to discover her clitoris as a prime source of sexual stimulation, but have no label for—or validation of—this reality?"[16]

Parents can join a daughter in understanding her body by naming her genitals. According to pediatrician Betsy Lazoff, the correct answer to the perennial "Do I have a penis?" query is "No, boys have

a penis and testicles and you have a vulva, clitoris and vagina."
Lazoff laments the lack of more casual words for female genitalia.
"It's hard to get comfortable saying 'clitoris' and 'vulva'—they are
so cumbersome, so Latin. But vagina is an *internal* organ so it's just
not the right word to use."

Yet Lazoff is more concerned about girls who have no words for
their genitals, or call them "privates" or "down there." She suggests
that you skip the serious lecture, introducing anatomy in everyday
situations: "Touching your clitoris feels good," or "You need to
wash your vulva when you take a bath."[17]

PREPARE FOR HER FIRST PERIOD

Rob was explaining the menstrual cycle to his five-year-old
daughter Kathy: "Did you know that when you were born, you had
dozens and dozens of eggs—already in your body?" Kathy's eyes
widened and she sat silently. Then: "Shh, Daddy, I think I just
heard one of them cracking."

We all know how to *start* the conversation about her first period.
You will be sitting in a cozy corner with your daughter and casually
say, "You'll probably be getting your first period soon." Ah, but
then what? How much should you explain—and how will you explain it?

In a study where teenaged girls were asked how to tell younger
girls about their first period, they offered this expert advice: Parents
should put away the charts and diagrams and place less emphasis
on what facts of what a period means ("how the egg is released"
and that "your period will occur in the cycle if the egg isn't fertil-
ized"). Rather than telling a daughter that a period means "being a
woman," parents should tell girls "how to deal with it," to give
them support, and focus on how it "feels" with practical info about
how to get and use the necessary products.[18]

ENCOURAGE HER TO LIVE IN HER BODY

I asked Hannah about the best part of the evening we spent with Sarah—an old friend from another school. She told me: "My favorite thing was while the parents were having dessert, Sarah and I took off our underwear, filled them full of sand, and put them back on again." I laughed with her—one part of my brain thinking "bladder infection," the other marveling at the pleasures girls can find from living in their bodies. Consider some ways we can enhance her pleasure.

• *Sing her body electric.* Teach her what her body can do. Direct her toward activities where her body is a vehicle of *accomplishment* rather than *appearance*. Take her climbing, dancing, hiking, rowing, skiing, skating, swimming. Focus her attention on her body's grace and acuity. ("I love to watch you speed through the water," or "How did it feel to make that three-point basket?")

• *Support her sensuality.* Acknowledge her sense of desire, pleasure, and tender touch. Appreciate how she luxuriates in the feeling of soft fabrics or a pet's fur, savors the taste of her food, smells pizza a mile away, and loves to cuddle, tickle, or massage. Confirm her gleeful discovery of her clitoris. Become comfortable with her exploration of her body—along with a caveat about exploring in private.

• *Teach her to protect her privacy.* Convey a sense of her body's integrity—teaching her that her body, and her feelings about her body, *belong only to her.*

• *Confirm and then challenge her body blues.* Don't simply argue with her critiques ("Oh, honey, your legs aren't fat"). First, mirror and acknowledge her longing ("You'd feel more comfortable on the beach if you liked your thighs better"). As one mom put it: "You are not fat; you are getting hips and you are getting breasts. That's normal and it's sexy and it happens to every girl."[19]

• *Next, share your gender glasses:* "It would be easier if we didn't live in a world where people cared so much about being thin!" And finally, let a daughter see her body through your eyes. "When I look at your legs, I think of you running down the beach and jumping happily into the surf—you look beautiful to me."

Yet the biggest step in challenging her body blues—and encouraging her to live with her body—is teaching her to trust the wisdom of her body when she eats.

RAISE AN INDEPENDENT EATER

George is raising his daughter to be an independent eater. He told me, "In our family, we put a premium on healthy eating for both sexes. *The emphasis is on health, not weight.* We teach our daughter to respect her body by good eating—we talk about satisfying hunger with good food. But we let *her* make the choices and see the consequences."

George points out the keys to a daughter's independent eating: keeping food and nutrition issues separate from those about weight, teaching her to recognize hunger, giving her information about healthy food, and most important, respecting her decisions about food.

Yet teaching a daughter to be an independent eater in a culture obsessed with thin women requires great parental discipline (especially if you are obsessed with your own battles of the bulge). Still, offering her independence as an eater is absolutely essential in teaching her to trust the wisdom of her body.

Instead of watching her weight from the *outside* ("Am I too fat?" "How many calories are in this?"), we can help teach her to listen to her body's *internal clues*. ("Am I hungry?" "Am I full?")

A number of clinicians, such as nutrionist Ellyn Satter, suggest that listening to her body's cues to make her own food choices will help make her less vulnerable to the current epidemic of eating disorders—and disordered eating—among young girls. In her smart book *Child of Mine,* Satter describes the division of labor that leads to a child's healthy relations with food.[20]

- Parents are responsible for *what is presented to eat* and *the manner in which it is presented.*
- Children are responsible for *how much* and even *whether* they eat.

Satter suggests that the same principle that applies to babies—you give them a milk feeding and they let you know if they are hungry or full—is a model for a parent-child feeding relationship through young adulthood.

In this feeding relationship, parents must redefine the meaning of a "good eater." The answer to the question "Is she a good eater?" can be: "Yes, she eats when she is hungry and stops when she is full. And over a course of a few meals, she eats enough healthy food."

An impressive array of research affirms that children are capable of regulating their own intake of food.[21] So our job is to provide healthy food and to teach them to be in touch with their natural cues of hunger, appetite, and enjoyment and fullness. Try these techniques:

• *Stop food fights.* You already know the answer to these questions: "Aren't you going to eat your broccoli?" and "Don't you want a little more chicken before dessert?" Instead of making meal deals, think of nutritious eating as taking place over a period of days, rather than one sitting.

Before you utter the parent perennial "No dinner, no dessert," remember Tuesday, when she had two helpings of salad and was too full for dessert. Don't make dessert divine; this gives the message that it is the "best" food. As an alternative, offer a small portion of a healthy dessert *with* dinner. You'll be amazed to discover she won't always gobble her whole dessert first.[22]

• *Don't use food as a parenting tool.* Don't use food to reward, punish, distract, or comfort her. Each time you offer a cupcake for cleaning her room, leave brownies when you have to work late, pass the popcorn when you are talking on the phone, or break out the sugar snacks when she's sad, you encourage patterns of eating for reasons other than hunger or pleasure. Join her in sharing delightful food as part of family celebrations, but don't link your approval to her appetite. If you do, she will begin to connect eating with being loved.

• *Don't use food to console her.* Of course, you will share the occasional cup of cocoa and sympathy as you listen to her tale of woe. Just don't offer her a pint of mint chocolate chip ice cream with a tablespoon.

• *Refuse to police food.* Calculating fat grams and calories are adult math problems. Daughters do need information about nutrition. Show her the food pyramid that states "Use oil and sugar sparingly"—and skip the lecture about hardened arteries. Describe junk food as simply "less healthy" or offering "less energy." Even overweight daughters can be honored as independent eaters, especially since studies show that the more parents police what kids eat, the more the kids overeat.[22]

A BEAUTIFUL BALANCE

As you have seen, parents who tell their daughter the truth about beauty have three tasks. First, to acknowledge her confusion and fears about her appearance. Next, we must help her see that she lives in a culture with a beauty bias—it provokes her feelings. Then, we must tell her that we see her beautiful self. As we listen to Claire, we hear this beautiful balance.

Claire describes her daughter Christina's "awkward stage," and a vacation day when two beach boys had teased her about being skinny: "I thought no one would bother me here," she cried. Her mother confirmed how much the comments hurt—but told her that she couldn't change the way Christina looked—or the world that cared so much about beauty.

Claire explained, "I also told her that she was going through a growth spurt that was awkward, that she didn't look like the cute kid she used to be. I knew she would continue to change and come through this time—but I had no idea of how she would look. While I knew it might not make her feel any better, I told her some of the reasons why she was special and unique. I told her what I saw in her."[23]

Then, Claire bowed to our culture's concern with looks by asking Christina what bothered her about her appearance, and letting her try out different hair styles and clothes. At the same time, Christina decided to become a swimmer and make a commitment to developing her strength.

Christina's feelings about her mother's help sum up how we can succeed in telling our daughters the truth about beauty: "I really appreciate my mom's helping me with how I look and for helping me think about it. *I felt she was really on my side."*

KEY IDEAS

Strategy 6
Tell the Truth About Beauty

How to teach your daughter to see beyond ideals of perfect beauty—and celebrate her beautiful self

- Beware of beauty bias, and don't let your daughter judge her worth by her appearance.
- Get out of the mirror. Explore your own unfinished business about your body and beauty.
- Unmask media beauty. Show her that ideal beauty is an illusion—created by camera crews, airbrushing, and computer graphics.
- Create beauty in her image: buy look-alike toys, support her sense of style, and let her choose her clothes.
- Consider your compliments. Avoid using words such as "pretty" and "beautiful" to describe her accomplishments.
- Stop food fights; respect her food choices. Teach her to recognize hunger and fullness.
- Celebrate her body. Name her body parts, prepare for her period, cheer her sensuality.

Strategy 7

LEARN WHAT SHE LEARNS

*How to Discover Your Daughter's
Strengths as a Learner and Build on
Her Natural Interest in Math,
Science, and Computers*

17

⌘

Teach Her to Learn Through Play

SCENES from the October potluck lunch for Hannah's new pre-school: parents brought salads and companionably compared notes. Has he given up his nap? Did she show you the sign language she learned? Weren't those "brain stem" puppets great? Our kids laughed and talked easily together, painting frosting on the Hallow-een cupcakes and dashing out of the community center building to play. When Jeremy and I had finished lunch, we followed the kids outside and discovered two distinct playgroups. The boys were playing touch football on the front lawn; the girls were on the swings and merry-go-round in back.

Jeremy was steamed, "Can you believe this? The same thing hap-pened at Alan's birthday! I think they should leave the footballs at home, or at least make an effort to include the girls in the game." And even I—who have been writing for months about how early sex segregation begins—shared his shock to see it in full force a year before kindergarten. So I stood with Mackenzie's mom, Kay, and we plotted to take our daughters to a coed T-ball team in the spring.

Later, when I replayed the scene, what stunned me was how we, as parents, had reinforced the dramatic differences in what girls and boys were learning in their play. On the front lawn, parents cheered the boys, who were competing joyously against friends—yelling full throat, ordering each other around—pushing, shoving, and getting messy to reach their goals. They had their parents' permission to learn the lessons of competing to win.

Parents on the back playground watched passively as Hannah and three girls were unsuccessfully trying to order each other out of the two available swings. The girls alternated between shouting and sulking. Then, a couple of parents, including (gulp) me, intervened with various suggestions on turn-taking. While the boys were learning to compete on the team, our girls were learning lessons of fairness and nonrowdy cooperation (also known as "being nice").

In this final strategy section, we will join our daughters to level the learning and playing fields. When we learn about what a daughter learns, we discover how the sex typing of the preschool picnic can follow her into the classroom. Here, she struggles to get equal teacher time—and wonders why subjects such as math and science can seem like a boys' club.

Yet I promise not to whine about the risks of a sex-skewed education for our daughters. Equalist parents cannot simply focus on taking her where the boys are; we must also nurture a daughter's sense of wonder and possibilities, and teach her about her unique qualities as a learner. When we do, we light the path for her to know herself best.

In this chapter, we explore the lessons of play. We begin by asking what a daughter misses when she doesn't play ball.

NOT MAKING THE TEAM

An eleven-year-old daughter tells us how it feels to be left out of the sports scene.[1]

> I like playing outside, but some of the boys are ball hogs. I was almost going to quit and I was crying yesterday because I spent the whole recess just sitting out on the gym floor, saying, "Hey, I'm open!" and no one would pass it to me. They just think they are the best and they just take the ball down the court and

they score everything; it's like, great, I'm glad you scored, but there's no point in my being here so . . .

As I considered her experience, I thought back to Hannah's preschool picnic—the striking contrast between the boys' competitive team play and the girls' cooperative, turn-taking play. Once again I wondered: Besides not getting the ball, what are girls missing?

As you know, the subject of what girls lose (or gain) by not making the team has received millions of words in print.[2] Still, without suggesting that girls be like boys, parents should review the lessons learned by boys in team sports—and what their daughter may be missing.[3]

- Practice in accepting criticism.
- Experience in risk-taking, making mistakes.
- Strategic thinking.
- Perseverance, playing for results.
- Teamwork: working for the good of all.
- How to play against friends and with nonfriends.

Carol, the mother of two daughters, describes how these lessons play out. "Both of my daughters are on competitive softball teams. What strikes me most is how every accomplishment or mistake is acknowledged in playing the game. Every play is credited to *somebody*—whether it's a hit, a catch, a strike, or an error. There's a real sense of 'I did it!' And play moves go fast; they don't have time to dwell on their mistakes."

In Carol's comment, we see that team play can contribute to a daughter's independence. In this play, she is an active agent, constantly exposed to making mistakes and repeating tasks until she gets them right. More important, she sees her influence on the outcome. *Through sports, girls can learn to attribute success to skill, and not luck.*[4]

What holds daughters back from sports? And why does sports participation drop so sharply as girls approach the age of the glass mezzanine? To understand why, we must round up the usual suspects.

WHY GIRLS WON'T PLAY

Here's a short sample of how sports socialization limits daughters: Girls are treated as fragile ("You'll get hurt!") or cautioned to stay clean (sweating isn't pretty or polite). They are not encouraged to learn basic moves (such as throwing, aiming, and jumping) that are the basis for sports skills—such as dribbling and catching.[5] And their gym teachers may expect boys to play best—they offer more praise and correction to the guys.[6]

Girls begin to wonder where the sportswomen are playing. They see 92% of the sports coverage on television is of male events, they meet more male coaches, and they notice that women are missing in action in sports books and magazines.[7] Also, adults can give them mixed messages. Which should they believe—that sports are great, or men don't like women with too much muscle?[8]

For all these reasons, your daughter may become a girl who decides that sports aren't feminine. How can you give her a sporting chance.

PARENT STRATEGIES: A WHOLE NEW BALL GAME

We just got a new, taller basketball hoop for Hannah. I miss the smaller one—I was a better shot—but this one really lets her see when and why she scores and misses. During a recent after-school game, she proudly informed me, "There are three kinds of passes: chest passes, cross-court passes, and behind-the-back passes." I was delighted to apply this new information (since I had shot more baskets with Hannah than in the whole rest of my nonathletic life). As I watched her delight in the game, I wondered how we could build upon her sense of fun in learning about sports—and make it a foundation for life-long learning.

As parents, we can't afford to ignore the lessons of sports. Because the evidence is building that sports are linked to self-esteem and self-reliance. High school girls who play sports are significantly less likely to get pregnant, become involved in drugs, and more likely to graduate from high school.[9]

Try these ideas to get and keep her in the game.[10]

• *Get an early start.* Research suggests that the early bird makes the team. As soon as she can reach, select toys that encourage the sporting life. There are rubber or plastic toddler versions of every possible piece of sports equipment. Get her balls of all sizes, a plastic bat, a T-ball, and a soft rubber ball for her room.

• *Select the right sport.* Explore the possibilities by taking her out to the ball games: to women's soccer, volleyball, and basketball, as well as co-ed softball and soccer (local high school and university teams are easier on the wallet). Find out what interests her, what she thinks her strengths are. Recognize that some daughters prefer being on a "team" where each individual performs (e.g., swimming).

• *Consider the coed question.* Although many athletes urge participation in coed teams, you must consider your daughter's temperament, strengths, and the advantages of each experience. Single-sex teams provide learning and leadership in a less-pressured environment, and girls spend less time on the bench in an all-girl team. On the other hand, coed teams can lessen barriers between the sexes as they compete and cooperate with each other.

• *Question the coach.* Ask about the goals of the team: Are teams made up of girls (and boys) of equal skill, weight, and ability? Are the best kids always picked first? Is the focus on fun as well as winning?

• *Celebrate her skill.* Lead the cheers by offering specific feedback about her achievements. This encourages her to be the author of her accomplishments. Begin by offering her a *compliment* ("That was a nice level swing."), followed by an *error correction* ("Next time, make sure you step toward the pitcher"), and conclude with *encouragement* ("Your batting is really improving").[11]

• *Research role models.* Create a family sporting tree: gather photos and background about the sports her aunts, cousins, mother, grandmothers, or great-grandmothers enjoyed or excelled in. Ask your librarian about books that tell the tales of female athletes (such as soccer player Julie Foudt). Plant sports images as early as possible with preschool picture books (like Nancy Carlson's *Luanne Pig Makes the Team*. Collect photos and posters of sportswomen. Write your newspaper to ask for more coverage of girls' and women's sports.

Now that you have joined her team, it's time to check her toy chest.

TOYS AS THE GREAT DIVIDE

Lee explains: "My new neighbor had just brought home a baby boy and I wanted to bring a small present. I stood for ten minutes in the store, looking at rattles—pink, blue, clowns, dolls, trains. I liked the clown best, but it was pink. So I played it safe and got a blue and red train rattle."

Lee reminds us of just how early we begin to offer our children the lesson of "sex-appropriate" toys. We use playthings as one of our earliest ways of teaching kids what it means to be a girl or a boy.[12] As we select toys, we plant the first seeds for the separation of the sexes: we begin to teach girls and boys to view themselves as being unlike each other.

Yet the trouble with talking about toys is that the conversation digresses in three directions: rehashing of nature vs. nurture arguments, dissing dolls, or overvaluing boys' toys. Allow me to interest you in a more promising question. What does your daughter learn (and not learn) from the toys that you—and she—select?

WHAT TOYS TEACH

Picture yourself in a marvelous toy emporium. Think F.A.O. Schwarz minus the military music and $800 stuffed animals; or Toys "R" Us sans fluorescent light and shelves labeled by sex. Imagine toys in a rainbow of boxes—without pictures of girls or boys as owners. In this toyland, toys are arranged by the skills learned by playing with them. Setting aside computer games, here is a sample of the shelves:

Spatial Skills—three-dimensional space, distance: Blocks, Tinkertoys, Legos, Erector sets, Lincoln Logs, bowling sets, basketballs, T-ball, puzzles, Duplos, transportation toys: trains, trucks, cars.

Relationship/Nurturing Skills—roleplaying, empathy, caretaking: Dolls, puppets, stuffed animals, and animal figurines.

Science Skills—collecting, identifying, observing, classifying: Magnets, chemistry sets, ant farm, magnifying glass, binoculars, telescope, shell or rock collections.

Verbal Skills/Linguistic Skills—spelling, vocabulary, reading: Alphabet puzzles and games, puppet theater, Scrabble.

Mechanical Concepts Skills—tinkering, fixing assembling: Model trains, tool kits, model car and airplane kits.

Math Skills—estimating, counting, distance, weight, volume, patterns: Dominoes, Chutes and Ladders, Candyland, cooking sets.

Creativity—story telling, picturing, portraying: puppets, modeling, paints, crayons, crafts kits.

*Strategic Problem solving—*tic-tac-toe, Uno, Connect Four, chess, checkers.

Next, imagine this: As you drive home with your purchases, you pass a playground teeming with boys and girls. Picture each child with a T-shirt that spells out what s/he learns as s/he plays. Shirts worn by children playing jacks, jumping rope, or swinging would read, "I'm learning small and large motor movements, hand-to-eye coordination, cooperation, and turn-taking."

Kids playing basketball, softball, and football would wear shirts proclaiming, "I'm learning how to compete," or "I'm learning math in the ratio of batting averages and in seeing relationships between time, distance, and speed. And even, "I'm learning physics as my eye is calculating a ball's direction, speed, and velocity."[13]

When you get home, go to your daughter's room.

THE CURRICULUM OF CHILD'S PLAY

Survey her scene. Is your daughter's room filled with the traditional fem-four: dolls, horses, cooking, and crafts? What skills and interests are being nurtured in this play? What skill areas are missing? Do the toys you buy suggest your own stereotypes? (For example, do they assume greater verbal skills and little interest or skill in sports, math, and science?)

At this point, you may object, "But these are just *toys*—aren't they supposed to be fun?" Or even, "Is this going to be another essay about football-as-future-corporate-curriculum?" The short answer: the more toys, the merrier. For a longer answer, equalist parents must learn that *all* toys are educational toys—they teach rules and roles.

Just consider how buying sex-type toys plants the idea that girls and boys can't be friends. Fascinating studies have described how playing with sex-typed toys leads boys and girls to develop different playing styles. (Then we see girls who festoon trucks with jewelry or boys who take apart mechanical dolls.) Then, since kids choose playmates who play the way they do, boys and girls begin to prefer same-sex friends—and may stop inviting each other to their birthday parties.[14]

Sometimes gender segregation can lead to amusing accusations—throwing the ball "like a girl." But we have also seen how it can create cross-sex contempt. And worse, it can channel girls and boys into separate corners in the classroom and in career choice.

PRACTICE IN PLAY

Toy training can translate into missed opportunities in math and science for schoolgirls. Because traditional boys' toys (model airplanes, tool and chemistry sets) lead to math and science readiness, boys enter the classroom with years of practice in play. Then, the self-fulfilling cycle begins: Boys have more comfort and competence from play practice. Then, teachers assume boys are natural leaders and daughters live up to their teachers' not-so-great expectations.

In her book *Equal Their Chances,* Catherine Hunenberg suggests how daughters get discouraged—and come to accept that they are not expected to enjoy science and math. She writes, "Girls become frustrated with math and science—where their inadequate play experiences put them at a disadvantage. Over time, they step aside and let the boys become the leaders, and eventually their betters. *They become the watchers, the helpers, the secretaries* who record the findings while boys struggle with concepts and equipment."[15]

Clearly, this curriculum will not result in a daughter's Nobel Prize in Physics. We see how the designation of math and science as male domains can grow from the self-fulfilling seeds of toys and play. When computers join the classroom, once again, boys are prepared by play. They have been taking apart toasters and admiring their Erector sets. We see how the gender gap in learning grows.

Now then, what can parents do to ensure the fair play that can keep a daughter's options open?

PARENTS WHO PLAY FAIR

Equity educators Myra and David Sadker tell the story of the father who attended one of their parenting workshops and went home to check his daughters' toy box. He found a cast of a thousand Barbies and no sign of the science and chemistry sets he had bought. When he confronted his daughters, they admitted that they had made a swap. Said one daughter: "We didn't know why you bought us those things and we didn't like some of them and we didn't know how to work the science things. So we gave them away and got Barbies instead."[16]

Teach your playful, wide-eyed daughter how to play with a variety of toys that can enhance her pleasure, self-confidence, and options for future learning. As you shop for toys—or listen to her "must have" list—ask yourself: What is she learning (or not learning) from participating in this play? Here are some suggestions[17]:

• *Don't dismiss dolls.* Every child can learn from the drama of dolls: the chance to relish relationship play, practice loving care, enrich empathy, verbalize, and role-play problems—and solutions—to sticky situations with family and friends. The key is in helping her focus on the *nurturing* side of doll play rather than the *accessorizing* side.

Discourage doll play that focuses exclusively on grooming and appearance. Avoid an emphasis on new outfits or expensive accessories; it reflects our culture's preoccupation with consumerism and perfect feminine beauty. Encourage her dolls to get busy—buy "Dr. Barbie" rather than the "Hollywood hair" version. And would someone please get her Snow White doll a pair of leggings so she can climb a tree?

• *Cross the gender divide by mixing something old and something new.*[18] If it seems she is only interested in the "fem-four," expand her learning base by using her interests as a launching point to new, fun learning. This means you could use her cooking set to focus on fractions, volume, and chemistry (why baking soda causes cupcakes to rise). Sharpen her observational skills with a book about horses (she can learn to identify different markings on her toy horse collection), or she can use a hammer and nails to build a horse barn.

Have her measure and compare different dolls' heights or measure a wall in her dollhouse to cut and paste wallpaper. She can wire the lights for the streets in a toy village. Choose puzzles that picture her passions (dinosaurs or birds or kids). Or make a puzzle by blowing up and mounting a picture of her with a favorite friend or toy.

• *Have a block party.* Encourage her to experience three-dimensional space by providing a variety of building blocks (Legos, waffle or wooden blocks, empty boxes). If she is short on ideas, suggest buildings that reflect her interests or recent experiences. When an animal-loving daughter returns from the zoo, invite her to join you in "building the zoo." Suggest that she build corrals, or cities, or houses that her horse dolls, dinosaurs, or stuffed animals can live in or visit.

• *Comment on commercials.* Don't expect television commercials to participate in expanding her toy horizons; TV surrounds her

Teach Her to Learn Through Play 221

with Stone Age stereotypes. If she must watch them, offer your "second opinions." "Why aren't there any girls with hammers?" "That doll could never climb a tree like you do." Also, let her in on the secret agenda of commercials: they are filmed to make kids pester their parents for more toys and to spend several billion dollars of their allowance on them.[19]

• *Check your catalogs.* Toy catalogs are notorious for their gender-typecast portraits of toys. Since kids love to thumb through catalogs, cancel the ones that still offer boys as doctors and consumers of food cooked by girls. Among the best: Play Fair Toys, 1-800-824-7255.

• *Talk up toys that create cross-sex bonds.* Tell her that Nate's mom got him a T-ball, so maybe they can play. Or tell her you noticed that James brought his tank engines to school—maybe she could bring hers.

• *Let them bring gifts.* Encourage the people she loves and respects to bring her nontraditional presents. A model train or airplane kit, a magnifying glass, a set of magnets, a microscope or telescope (as demonstrated by Grandpa) is likely to become a focus of interest and fun. A chess set from a beloved aunt (who makes a date for a game together) sets up a great expectation for learning and pleasure. A chemistry set or tool kit from an esteemed brother or sister is a vote of confidence in her new curriculum.

Yet even parents who understand the power of play may resist toys that lead to math and science readiness.

WHAT'S SO SPECIAL ABOUT BEING A ROCKET SCIENTIST?

Sometimes a parent will tell me, "My daughter is much more artistic and creative—she doesn't need math and science to succeed." Other parents offer, "I find traditional boys' play is highly overrated—bats and balls and science kits leave me cold. I love watching the more nurturing and imaginative play of my daughter and her friends with their dolls and puppets and horses." Both parents are offering yet another version of the "girls are kinder and gentler" theory. Just look at the consequences of this theory in practice.

Since the early 1970s, researchers have focused on how math becomes what Lucy Sells calls a "critical filter"—filtering and narrowing the path of learning, and restricting choices in higher education, occupational choice, and earning power. In Sells's classic study, 92% of the women had taken so little math, they were, in effect, limited to five majors: humanities, music, social work, elementary education, and guidance and counseling.[20]

This math filter will cost her money. Data from a U.S. Department of Education longitudinal study of the high school class of 1972 suggested that women who took at least eight credits of college math earn an average of 16% more than men with comparable education.[21]

The math filter quickly becomes a science filter and narrows for females early in their education. This means that if your daughter didn't take four years of math in high school, she can't take calculus in college (which is, in itself, a prerequisite for most science, math, and economics classes). And these are the courses that prepare her for careers in medicine, engineering, fast-developing technologies, and other top-paying jobs.

Yet by the time she gets to high school, her self-confidence and competence may have fallen prey to the familiar pattern—the longer a girl stays in school, the greater the gender gap in math and science. You can see what's at stake—studies show that girls and boys who enjoy math and science have a greater sense of their own importance, like themselves better, feel better about family and school, and have more professional goals.[22]

Parents must expand their definition of the role of math and science in a daughter's future. Is she an artist with a delicious imagination? Then offer her the playful lessons and learning so that her options widen to include becoming a painter, chemist, writer, physicist, or inventor. Think Leonarda da Vinci.

18

~~*~~

Study Science, Math, and Technology

A<small>T</small> the Holyoke, Massachusetts, Girls Club, nine-year-old Anna-belle approached a table set out with batteries, bulb wires, and switches. She turned to the coordinator and asked, "Can I have a quarter, Elyse, so I can call my brother? He knows how to do this." Instead of giving her the coin, Elyse offered coaching and questions. Then, Annabelle was able to complete the circuit and make a lightbulb: "I can do this myself!" she said.[1]

Like Annabelle, many girls see science, math, and computers—and the self-reliance they imply—wearing a male face. They are subjects for fathers, brothers, and the boy next door. It is easy to understand how a loss of confidence and competence can occur when girls view these subjects as boys' clubs.

In this chapter, you'll find a curriculum to study science and math along with your daughter. As we explore why a girl can become invisible in these subjects, we can learn how to encourage her to "do it herself." Let's start by meeting the science guy.

MR. SCIENCE

In a recent "Draw a Scientist" test, 100% of the boys and 84% of the girls drew a man.[2] Is it any wonder girls don't see themselves as scientists? Chances are her science teacher is a man, just like Mr. Wizard, Beakman, and Bill Nye. Then, consider the Marie Curie Syndrome: Textbooks that ignore the contributions of women in science (with a token mention of Madame Curie) or picture boys doing lab experiments and girls watching clouds and watering plants.[3]

These male images describe the classroom perfectly: A study of science classes found that when teachers selected a student to assist in a demonstration, 79% of them picked boys.[4] The boys do not only the demonstrating, but also the fixing. Which brings us to Mr. Fix-it.

When a tape recorder, VCR player, or film projector malfunctions, most teachers look for the nearest male.[5] It is not hard to imagine the self-fulfilling direction of the Mr. Fix-it phenomenon. Boys, who have spent some time tinkering, are eager and confident about messing with machines, they are willing to figure a new one out—and even break it trying. So why aren't girls AV operators?

Educator Catherine Hunenberg tells us why. Girls—with less experience playing with machines and operating them in the classroom—give up. "Having made up their minds that the mere operation of a machine is too difficult for them, it is not surprising that they also consider it useless to attempt to understand how these machines actually work."[6]

But there's more to the equation. Science, along with math and computers, shares a reputation among girls of being cold-hearted, logical, unsexy—nerdy. Seventeen-year-old Rebecca, who is the only girl in her computer seminar, explains: "If you're female and you excel as a student—especially in a subject like science, you are thought of as kind of weird. Guys feel intimidated by you and that can really hurt your social life."[7]

Rebecca's explanation goes a long way toward explaining why, at age nine, more girls than boys express interest in science-related activities—but by age seventeen, boys are the predominant gender in terms of interest.[7] Rebecca's attitude—shared by many girls—is particularly disturbing in light of a recent study of children in seventeen countries that demonstrated that in science, more than any other subject, children's achievements were affected by their attitude.[8]

As we have seen, a change in a daughter's attitude toward math and science in adolescence comes before her drop in achievement. Thus we understand the urgent need to help girls see themselves in the picture. So how can parents help create science in her image? You might start by getting a substitute teacher.

PARENT STRATEGIES: MS. FRIZZLE—A FEMALE FACE IN SCIENCE

By the time Joanna Kerns's *Magic School Bus* books became a hot series on PBS, they had already sold more than 7 million copies worldwide. One reason was the woman behind the wheel. She is Ms. Frizzle—a science teacher extraordinaire—with the magical ability to make science fun and to involve girls and boys in the adventure. Hannah and I were glued to our chairs during the Sunday morning series.

For the first time in my life, I enjoyed my encounters with physical and biological science. It was a joy to watch Hannah: role-playing the part of Ms. Frizzle, delightedly discussing digestion, pointing to the planets in the mobile she had previously ignored in her room. The best part was hearing Hannah echo Ms. Frizzle's oft-repeated mantra: "Take chances! Make mistakes! Get messy!"

Ms. Frizzle's science slogans echo the spirit of New York–based "Operation Smart," established by The Girls Clubs of America in 1985 to encourage girls' interest in math, science, and technology. Here is how Ellen Wahl, its founding director, described their work in putting female faces in science.

First, says Wahl, "We thought about the qualities of a scientist: persistence, invention, creativity, risk-taking, self-direction, singular pursuit of an idea, willingness to fail and learn from mistakes. Then, we theorized that the mandate to listen to directions, be neat, clean and ladylike prevents girls' engagement with science and the physical world. It was this thinking that led to our slogans: *Create, Discover, Take Risks, Get Messy.*"[9]

Parents can be inspired by the spirit of Ms. Frizzle and Ellen Wahl of Operation Smart. When we invite our daughter to happily use the tools and questions of the scientific method, we help her see herself as a scientist.

For this mission, parents need a simpler definition of science—one that doesn't elevate our blood pressure. Try this: *Science is understanding the world around us.* Now our job is to point our daughters in the direction of delightful discovery.

Here's a list of suggestions.[10]

• *Give her interest in science a name.* Let her know when her interests or passions are part of science. When she examines a spider's web, tell her, "This is the science of entomology." Add to her delight in spotting a bird's nest, "People like you who are interested in studying birds are ornithologists." Focus her fascination with cloud shapes—"People who study what clouds do are called meteorologists."

• *Teach her how to use the tools.* Get her a magnifying glass ($1–$5) or a microscope ($20–$200). Bring a magnifying glass to a picnic; study the grass and the ants. Collect water at the ocean, pond, or pool and take it home to study it on a slide under her microscope. Don't forget other inexpensive scientific tools such as funnels, magnets, binoculars, prisms, and thermometers.

• *Stimulate scientific questions.* Educator Barbara Sprung has suggested that parents can turn familiar activities into experiments by asking, "What would happen if?" or "What do you think is going on here?" and "How do you explain?"[11]

Don't focus on her answers. Focus on her observations and predictions. (Do you think your ball will sink or float in the pool? When? Why?)

• *Encourage mistakes and messiness.* Let her touch worms, take apart a broken toaster or clock, spill water, get greasy and muddy. Focus on the process, testing ideas, the excitement of being wrong and trying again.

• *Show her women in science.* Talk about and visit friends or relatives whose jobs involve science. Encourage her to identify with the success of women in science through biographies of scientists such as Barbara McClintock and Rosalyn Yalow. One of the best resources is *The Scientist Within You: Experiments and Biographies of Distinguished Women in Science,* by Rebecca Lowe Warren and Mary H. Thompson (available from the Women's History Project).

• *Strike a balance with her books.* Begin early to select science fiction with a brave heroine to introduce principles of physics and astronomy. (For example, for preschoolers try *The Universe Is My Home,* by Bill and Sally Fletcher, or the prepuberty perennial *A Wrinkle in Time,* by Madeleine L'Engle. Encourage a mix of nonfiction books that follow her interest. When she peppers you with questions about the moon, check out an astronomy book from the library. Help her browse in the nonfiction science sections—in most libraries, they start with Dewey decimals in the 500s.

• *Get together with the girls.* Consider all-girl science and math experiences, where girls can play leadership roles and experiment with newfound scientific expertise—all without managing their impression around boys. Contact Operation Smart (science, math, and relevant technology) at your local chapter of the American Association of University Women, or Girls Incorporated, 300 East 33rd Street, New York, NY 10016-5394, to learn of opportunities in your neighborhood.

• *Take family field trips.* Combine the fun of being together with the joy of discovery. Why not try whale, eagle, or swan watching; botanical gardens; archeological digs; ice caves; visits to space centers such as Cape Canaveral.

But why wait for vacation?

Sunday Night Science

A parent in one of my workshops told me about a wonderful way her family shares the fun of science: They do a "Sunday Night Science Experiment." Of course, I couldn't wait to try this idea but my first experiment with Hannah was a disaster!

We took a glass pitcher of water and started adding different things (spices, baking soda) to see the reaction. I urged her to look at how the water was changing. Unfortunately, I also suggested that she smell our additions, and in the case of the spices, this resulted in spasms of sneezing and itchy eyes.

Soon after this awkward beginning, I discovered some terrific books for our science curriculum. I think you will enjoy: *Floating and Sinking,* by Terry Jennings; *Simple Science Experiments,* by Andrea McLoughlin; *Einstein's Science Parties,* by Shar Levine and Alison Grafton; *The Berenstain Bears Science Fair,* by Stan and Jan Berenstain; *The "Hello" Reader Science Series* (Scholastic Books); *The World of the Microscope,* by Chris Oxlade and Corinne Stockley; *Science Arts,* by Mary Ann Kohl and Jean Potter; and Vicky Cobb's books: *Science Experiments You Can Eat, Gobs of Goo,* and *Lots of Rot.*

But let's not forget the science of numbers, another scene where girls are missing in action.

MOM'S NOT GOOD IN MATH

In her compelling book *The Difference,* journalist Judy Mann confessed to a scenario that may hit uncomfortably close to home. Her sixth-grade daughter, Katherine, had asked for help with her math homework. Mom (Mann) answered, "See if Dick can help you. I'm in the middle of cooking dinner, and, *besides, I can't do math."* Almost immediately, Mann understood the dreadful economy of her words.

> In one fateful exchange, I had told her that her stepfather was more competent to help her at math than I was, that I was cooking dinner—translated as men do math and women cook—and to top it off, that it was okay not to be able to do math since I had just announced that I couldn't do it, with no apparent shame or remorse. . . .
>
> Without realizing it, I was modeling the worst possible set of attitudes and behavior toward math for my daughter, and I was typical of mothers and female teachers—the very people who have the best chance to break the chain of science and math anxiety that keeps women out of the best paying jobs.[12]

Much later, Mann recounted her comment to biologist Marsha Lakes Matyas, who responded: "It's okay for a girl to get by by not knowing as much about math and science. . . . you'd never hear someone at a cocktail party say, 'I'm illiterate,' but it's okay to say, 'I can't do math.' "[13]

As you will see, the lack of women as models in math is only one of the reasons a daughter—already poorly prepared by play for math—may view math as a male subject. Still let's not blame Mom; she may be the legacy of five generations of math anxiety. Our real mission is to understand how parent and teacher expectations contribute to a girl's believing and behaving as if she "can't do math."

Our concern is focused on a well-documented pattern—the longer girls stay in school, the less interest, competence, and confidence they show in both math and science. And as we noted earlier, there is a circular link between enjoyment of math, self-esteem, and greater career choices.[14]

Let's go straight to the source of these not-so-great expectations of girls and math.

THE MYTH OF THE MATHEMATICAL MIND

Sheila Tobias, the fairy godmother of conquering "math anxiety," has joked that no history teacher tells a student who writes poor exams that they don't have "a historical mind.[15] Yet parents of girls—often armed with outdated statistics from the sex differences debate—*expect* their daughters to be nonmathematical.

And research reports that children's beliefs about their abilities in math *are more strongly influenced by their parents' expectations than by their own past performance*. Even the girls who had higher standardized test scores and teacher ratings had parents who believed math was harder for girls. As you might expect, such girls had lower confidence in math ability—lesser expectations about a future success in math.[16]

We see how a parent's attitude can defeat a daughter's success in math. It's a self-fulfilling process. If you don't expect your daughter to have a mathematical mind, when she does well, you attribute it to extra effort (and praise her for it). The message she hears is that her hard work—*and not her competence*—is the source of her success. How can she stand on such a slippery rock?

Psychologist Jacqueline Eccles elaborates: "If parents believe the stereotype [of lower female math ability] and say to a girl, 'It's because you are working hard.' And they say to a boy, 'You are working hard and *you are talented,*' over time he will come away with more confidence in his ability."[17]

And when a girl opens her books, she finds few models of women in math. She may never learn about mathematics such as Mary Sommerville, Emily Noether, and Evelyn Granville.[18] Even worse is that girls appear less often in text illustrations and they are often shown as needing the boys' help in math.[19]

The idea that math is for males is a belief that ripens with age. In one disturbing study, math skills were labeled as both masculine and feminine by elementary school kids. Yet once they entered adolescence, male and female students labeled math ability as a masculine trait.[20] This poses a special problem for daughters who display mathematical ability.

As daughters approach adolescence, they may suffer from what Lynn Rosen calls "The Feminine Mathtique."[21] At this age, the female mathematician becomes a must-avoid role model: she's too cold and impersonal; she doesn't care about people; she wears a plastic pocket for her pens. She's like her sister, the oh-so-weird scientist. For girls, socialized to be "people centered"—and especially for adolescent girls, focused on how they appear—this is not the image they want to see in the mirror.

Here is where parents enter the picture, by redefining the meaning of "doing math."

PARENT STRATEGIES: MATH WITH A SMALL *m*

I am one of those parents who had to cheat to get a D in Algebra. Even after I got my doctorate, I still dreamed that I wouldn't graduate from high school unless I took geometry. Jeremy is an architect who can't subtract. Between us, we can't balance a checkbook. We often ask each other: Who is going to help Hannah with her math? How do we keep from modeling math anxiety? She is in the blissful

"I love to count" stage of life; but what about life after counting the squares on the Chutes and Ladders board?

My first clue came while we were making Chanukah cookies. Jeremy was rolling out the dough and Hannah and I were using the cookie cutters. I found myself mentally estimating how many cookies we could fit on each roll-out, and I quickly invited Hannah to see how many cookies she could cut on the rolled dough. Suddenly, I had a shock of recognition: *I was helping Hannah with math*. We were estimating, counting, and doing visual mapping.

As I explored the work of math educators, I found a similar theme emerged. Their message: Parents can help their kids enjoy and understand math when they convey a sense that math is a part of everyday life. If we can think about math with a small *m*, we can increase our comfort and identification with it. We help a daughter see that math is not for boys only; we can show her that she is *already* "doing math."

Because even the youngest daughter is already a delighted mathematician. Watch her skip along the sidewalk, stepping on every other square, sorting her Halloween candy, arranging her sandwiches in a pattern, saving her allowance, or counting the months, days, and hours until her birthday. Like most children, and all mathematicians, she has a strong desire to find order and patterns in her world.[22]

As parents, we can help her to build on her natural comfort and joy in math—and leave our own math histories behind. Depending on her age, you might try these ideas to help her see math in her own image.[23]

- *Ask mathematical questions.* In his book, *Innumeracy: Mathematical Illiteracy and Its Consequences,* John Allan Paulos suggests that parents ask fanciful questions to simulate mathematical thinking, estimating, and improvising fractions: How many leaves are on that tree? How many hairs are on Grandpa's head? How many nickels would it take to reach the top of that building? How many quarts of water are in the bathtub? How would you divide this cake with three friends? How many times a day do we open the refrigerator?

- *Number her days.* As you move through your life and work, count out loud. Talk about the fractions as you follow a recipe, calculate the cost of a meal or a trip, try to estimate whether you can fit into a parking space, or how many people can fit at the Thanksgiving table.

• *Pass the time.* Keep track of time in a number of ways: Ask your daughter when she thinks a minute has passed, time how long it takes to walk from her room to the front door, have her estimate how long it takes her to tie her shoes or set the table.

• *Make measuring fun.* Measure odd things around the house: the length of the cat's tail, your daughter's nose to her belly button. Use items in the house for standard measurement. For example, if the living room couch is six feet and you read that a saguaro cactus measured thirty-six feet tall, you can say, "That's six times as long as the couch."

• *Teach her to read maps.* Start with a *Bird's-Eye View: A First Book of Maps,* by Harriet Wittels and Joan Greisman. She'll learn to figure out distance, read a compass, and develop visual spatial skills.

• *Give her female models in math.* Check out biographies of women in math, or buy an inexpensive set of portraits of women mathematicians such as Mary Sommerville (the Women's History Project).

• *Read math stories.* Explore basic math concepts in story form with Scholastic Books' *Hello Math Readers* (ages 3–9).

• *Play math games.* From youngest to oldest: Hi-Ho! Cherry-O, Candyland, Chutes and Ladders, dominoes, Boggle, or Uno.

• *Open a bank account for her.* A bank or credit account (with a low limit) offers hands-on addition, subtraction, and practice with percentages. Balancing the statement with the check register can be a real eye-opener.

• *Find a female tutor.* When your daughter's need to learn reaches beyond your ability to help, introduce her to a female tutor. Placing an inexpensive ad in a university paper or canvassing your neighborhood can help you find someone to guide her through the nitty-gritty numbers.

• *Learn math as a family.* You might explore the possibility of starting a "Family Math Course." Materials are available from the EQUALS project at the University of California in Berkeley. A typical family math class involves *both* parents and children to build on their understanding of mathematics. Contact EQUALS, Lawrence Hall of Science, University of California, Berkeley, CA 94720, 510-642-1823.

Now that you have nurtured her interest in science and math, you will both be emboldened to approach the male machine.

THE MALE MACHINE: WHY COMPUTERS AREN'T NEUTER

Writer David Laskin was excited to find a computer in his daughter Emily's new kindergarten class. After a month had passed and she still hadn't used it, Emily explained, "Computers are for boys. They really know what to do with them." Struggling for an explanation, Laskin imagined, "Maybe a gang of leather-clad, pint-sized male hackers were standing shoulder to shoulder around the terminal." When he suggested this to his daughter, she replied, "Nah, I just don't feel like using it."[24]

The reasons why your daughter might not "feel like" using the computer mirrors the gender gap in math and science. A girl may lack play practice with machines—she hasn't been tinkering with her toys. Also, computer science can create a public relations problem with an adolescent girl (she doesn't wish to see herself as a hacker or computer nerd).[25] And sure enough, studies show that the gender gap in computer interest, confidence, and ability widens with age.

Sociologist Ronald Anderson, co-author of the report *Computers in American Schools,* reports that boys and girls are equally interested in computers until about the fifth grade, a time when boys' interest rises and girls' interest drops. Anderson's explanation: "This is a time when tremendous sex-role learning is going on. Computers, machines and technology are viewed as more for boys than girls."[26]

Why the Chips May Be Down for Your Daughter

Jo Sanders, author of *The Neuter Computer,* has catalogued a list of reasons why computer skills and interest decreases for daughters, including the computer's association with both math and machines—where girls may lack experience and comfort; self-fulfilling parent actions (for example, expecting boys to be more interested, and sending them to computer camp); sex-slanted software—and the lack of female role models in magazines and texts.[27]

Sanders notes that even girls who *are* interested may lack the assertiveness to claim their right to computer time in the classroom. Yet parents must recognize the consequences for daughters who don't compute.

First of all, she will be handicapped in her homework. Then, as our economy becomes more computerized, her choices will be limited in the job market. Jo Sanders warns, "People who avoided the computer during childhood are likely to have a hard time overcoming their negative attitudes in learning computer skills as adults. The way things are going now, a disproportionate number of these people will be women."[28]

How can parents build this essential computer confidence?

PARENT STRATEGIES:
GETTING GIRLS ON-LINE

Publisher Nancy Evans has written about becoming a computer coach.

It was a big deal when I moved up to an electric typewriter and I left my trusty Smith-Corona behind. And it was kicking and screaming that I finally moved on to a computer. So how did it happen that I am here, with no tutor to lean over my shoulder, learning the new-fangled art of CD-ROM?

A big part of the answer has to do with my child. The vision of me stuck at the side of the information superhighway while my child goes zooming by has got me scrambling to learn. . . . The good that can come from this new technology, I'd like to share with my daughter. And have her share with me. What's bad, I'd like to steer us clear of.[29]

Like Evans, parents who understand the consequences of the computer gender gap try a variety of routes to narrow it.[30]

• *Log more hours with her.* If resources allow, buy a computer for home use. Give her time to make mistakes away from peers in the comfort of home. Play games as a family, work on projects together (a family holiday card, a spreadsheet for the family budget). Or visit libraries, computer stores, or computer trade shows to use computers and try out new software. Visit friends who have computers or ask to use their office on a holiday.

• *Trade in her models.* Connect her with women in computing, from Ada Lovelace, one of the first computer programmers, to Grace Hopper, who led the team that created COBOL. Introduce her to vital women in computer science.

Alter her image of the computer nerd by showing her how computers are part of most careers. Casually point to computers as you visit "people" places, such as hospitals, doctors' offices, police departments, and museums.

• *Make it social.* Since some preadolescent girls may emphasize the social rather than the mechanical in their lives, teach them to use E-mail or suggest that their school use connective team projects such as publishing a newsletter.

• *Make a pact with parents.* Since only the bravest girl will dare to be different from her friends, band with other parents to try to make computers "cool." For example, have parents organize a group of girls to go to a computer fair or inexpensive computer afternoon program or camp. Agree to give software as holiday presents, or arrange to buy it to "share" among friends.

• *Put it in the mail.* Subscribe to computer magazines in her name. One of the best is *Family Computing.*

• *Include her interests.* Your math whiz will enjoy spreadsheet programs—she can keep track of her grades, or create a budget for her allowance. The designing daughter can use graphics programs to create posters, invitations, wall hangings, and banners. Many movies or popular books now have software tie-ins. If she loved the movie, her enthusiasm may happily hook her into the software program.

• *Share your discoveries.* Share your software finds with your daughter's teacher. Donate or loan a copy of *The Neuter Computer* to the school library. Order a number of low-cost pamphlets (for example, Jo Sanders's "Do Your Female Students Say 'No Thanks' to the Computer?") and distribute them to her teachers.

• *Avoid fluffware.*[31] Purchase or borrow software that avoids a gender-typed cast: girls as cooks and damsels in distress. Search for software where girls and women are active. Some suggestions: *Millie's Math House* (Edmark, preschool), *Trudy's Time and Space House* (Edmark, ages 6–9); *Tree House* (Brøderbund, ages 5–8), *The Little Turtle* (Computer Curriculum Corporation [Davidson], ages 3–8), *The Magic School Bus* (Microsoft, ages 5–12).

• *Buy science and math software.* Get her programs that encourage science and math skills. For example, *Math Blaster* (Davidson, ages 6–12 and 8–13), *Kid's Cad 3-D Building Kit* (Davidson, ages 7–adult), *Sammy's Science House* (Edmark, ages 4–6).

• *Increase your own comfort with computers.* It is absolutely critical that a daughter see both parents using computers. Let her play on your office computer on a Saturday. Or if you are one of many parents who are computer-phobic, try to ask for a free demonstration at a computer center, get a student tutor from the university, or form a parent learning group.

Even better, let *her* teach you. In her role as teacher, she will be able to model the competence that will increase her confidence in using computers.

Parents can join daughters in tackling subjects that seem marked for males only. Yet we can't just show her where the boys are. In the final chapter, let's discover your daughter's strengths as a learner— and how she can use her unique gifts to meet challenges in the classroom.

19

Teach Her Teacher

JACQUELINE Sadker's mother and father—Myra and David—wrote a best-selling book about how schools shortchange girls.[1] Her parents' research revealed the dangers of the classroom: teachers who ignore girls, call on boisterous boys, and regard them as better students. They believed girls were cheated in the classroom—and the result was lasting damage to a daughter's self-regard. Yet when Myra Sadker died, twenty-one-year-old Jacqueline warmly remembered the solutions her mother had taught her, rather than the problems.

Jacqueline wrote, "She taught me how to get more attention in class. Based on her research, she told me I should sit in the front row or one of the middle seats, an area called the Terrific T, to catch the teacher's eye. My mother encouraged me to raise my hand often, and *to never let it waver*."[2]

In this chapter, we, too, will focus on solutions to the widely publicized problems of schoolgirls. Yet we can't simply catalog complaints about how teachers dote on boys. We will also study our daughters—to discover and celebrate their unique intelligence and learning styles. Armed with an understanding of a daughter's strengths as a learner, we will have much to teach her teacher.

CALLING ALL BOYS!

Dan Blum is a parent and teacher who refuses to accept what he calls "the unspoken agreement" between teachers and female students. "We say: If you don't bother me, I won't bother you. So girls are silent; they don't cause any trouble; and it's easier not to push them, to challenge them, to question them." But Blum doesn't buy into this bargain. "I tell my female students: *I'm not going to let you be silent in my classroom.*"[3]

Sadly, most studies suggest that Dan Blum may be in the minority. One comprehensive study, summarizing twenty years of classroom observation—from nursery school to graduate school—found the following: white males consistently received more teacher time, encouragement, probing, precise feedback, and praise.[4]

In one study of elementary and middle school classrooms, boys were seen to call out eight times more than girls. Teachers responded—whether or not their comment was on target. In some studies, teachers called on boys two to twelve times more frequently than girls. Yet girls who called out were frequently reminded to raise their hands.[5]

As we study these statistics, we see yet another example of stereotyped assumptions in action. Boys' disruptions are tolerated, even expected: "It's testosterone!" Girls, the "kinder, gentler" classmates, are expected to be docile rather than disruptive; they must raise their hands.

The limiting consequences for daughters are clear. When teachers are calling on boys, they ignore the needs of many girls, especially those who may need more "wait time," and who are less likely to risk giving the wrong answer.[6] As a result, girls get less practice in the lessons of speaking out or learning by trial and error. They learn to let the boys answer.

The story behind the statistics for African-American girls is even more disturbing.[7] Even when black girls' achievements were equal to white boys', teachers attributed the girls' success to hard work, and the boys were upbraided for not working at their full potential. This group of girls received the least amount of feedback about academics. We see how the assertive, alert black girls of primary grades can become the least visible members of the classroom in high school.[8]

Still, counting the number of teachers' responses is only one way to see how girls are missing in the action. We must also look at the nature of the responses they receive. Myra and David Sadker have mapped four kinds of teacher reaction: *Praise* (commenting on doing it right: "Good job!"); *remediation* (encouragement to change an answer, or expand on an idea: "Think for a while and give it another try."); *criticism* (stating what's wrong: "That *J* is backward"); *acceptance* (acknowledging the right answer: "Okay, um-hmm. All right.")

In their studies, *boys received more of all four reactions* with the gender gap widest in boys' receiving more criticism, remediation, and praise. When girls received a response, it tended to be an acknowledgment without elaboration. Other studies found African-American females received the least amount of feedback about academics in the classroom.[9]

The lessons of this unequal curriculum are chilling. Boys learn how to assert and value their opinions, how to deal with criticism, how to interrupt or steer a conversation, and how to persevere.

Girls learn to reserve their opinions, to expect to be ignored, to accept being interrupted, to be unfamiliar with criticism, to give up easily—to wait for a boy to bring it up. Boys learn to be the squeaky wheel; girls learn to hand them the grease.

How can parents change this pattern?

PARENT STRATEGIES: BRINGING IT ALL BACK HOME

Dan Blum's daughters, Jenna, eleven, and Jessica, nine, are anything but invisible in the classroom. "Jessica will go into a gym and say, 'Look Dad, they've got eight guys playing basketball, only one woman and she's a cheerleader.' She's thinking quite a bit; I'm proud she is."[10]

Here's how to break your own silence about bias in the gym or in your daughter's classroom.[11]

• *Form a parent-teacher association.* Don't knock down her teacher's door, waving a videotape from a TV newsmagazine that targets teachers who call on boys. As an alternative, you might copy a magazine article on the subject, loan her a copy of the AAUW report—or a copy of the Sadkers' book *Failing at Fairness,* saying, "I found this book (or article) fascinating. I'd like to get your thoughts on the subject."

• *Direct attention to your daughter.* If you suspect bias, talk to her teacher; but make the subject your daughter, not his/her teaching. Myra Sadker has suggested, saying "Whenever there are a lot of noisy boys, Laura gets withdrawn. How can we help her get more involved?"

• *Share information.* Let her know what you have learned about your daughter. You might say, "One of the things we notice at home—especially when our son keeps interrupting—is that if we wait a few extra seconds, Laura will respond. She really seems to need that 'wait time.' Have you noticed that too?"

• *Set up a seminar.* Contact your neighborhood bias-busting organization (most likely it will be the American Association of University Women; 1-800-362-AAUW, ext. 1) and encourage your daughter's principal or administrator to organize a seminar on equal education.

• *Let her practice at home.* Create a safe conversational climate in your family—one where she can blurt out ideas, risk being wrong, offer an opinion that's different from yours, think out loud. You can help her practice visibility at home by monitoring the air time given to Dad, son, and Grandpa. Wait for her answer, but don't fall into the fragile flower routine. Give her crisp and caring feedback; encourage her to play out her ideas and amend her answers.

When parents study scenarios where a daughter's learning potential is lowered, it is easy to feel overwhelmed. You might even find yourself musing about a school in an old house in Paris that was covered with vines—where twelve little girls stood in two straight lines. Well, what about the strategy of a single-sex school?

THE SINGLE-SEX STRATEGY: IS MORE SEGREGATION BETTER?

Wouldn't it just be easier to send your daughter to an all-girl school? Parents who read the research find various answers to this question. For starters, the reports are contradictory. Some studies suggest that girls at same-sex schools have greater confidence, more assertiveness, a stronger interest in math and science, and superior academic performance.

Yet other researchers have noted schools where teachers coddle all-female classes—and where female students then respond with help-seeking, risk-avoiding behavior. Still others have documented "male bashing" at all-girl schools.[12]

Such studies raise more questions than they answer: Do segregated schools shelter girls from sexism—allowing them to grow stronger during vulnerable growing years? Or does a lack of experience with sexism in school leave girls without gender glasses to deal with bias?

Do same-sex schools nurture individuality? Or do they reinforce the notion that all girls are alike (kind, cooperative, in need of nurturing)? Does an all-female environment breed girl power or cross-sex contempt—by cultivating and contributing to the so-called differences between girls and boys?

The question of whether or not single-sex schools are good for girls does not yield a simple answer. And since many all single-sex schools are private (read: expensive) schools, it makes sense for equalist parents to explore short-term, all-girl groups. "The key," says Elsa Bowman, president of the National Coalition of Girls Schools, "is giving girls a chance to experience a world in which females are in charge."[13]

Here are some experiences to explore.

• Encourage your daughter's teacher or principal to form short-term, single-sex learning groups—particularly in traditionally male domains of math, science, or computers. Here she won't have to manage her impression with boys; she can be free to take chances, make mistakes, and get messy.

• Enroll in after-school, all-day seminars or summer programs for girls only. Among the best are Operation Smart, the Girl Scouts, and the American Association of University Women's "New Horizon" Science Fair.

These experiences focus on how to get girls into the picture—and make them powerful players on the playground and in the classroom. Yet you may not have a clear picture of your daughter's power and profile as a learner. Next, let's study your daughter, and she how smart she is.

STUDY YOUR DAUGHTER: DISCOVER HER LEARNING STYLE

Christine and Jay have been struggling to find a way to show Ana (age twelve) the many ways she is strong and smart. Christine told me, "Ana was getting so many negative messages at school and she would tell us, '*You* say I'm smart, but you are *my parents*!' So we had to help her find a way to see what she could do—let her get feedback away from home. Sports were a godsend; she could see what a great soccer player she was. We encouraged her artistic ability and when she excelled in drawing, sculpting and making jewelry; her talents and pride were affirmed."

Ana's parents understood a critical key to a child's education: that being smart is not restricted to the traditional schoolhouse abilities of words and numbers. Psychologist Howard Gardner, in his jewel of a book *Frames of Mind*, has suggested that all children have "multiple intelligences," though not equal amounts of each.

Each child demonstrates a pattern of strengths in one or more of eight different kinds of intelligence. These include linguistic, logical-mathematic, spatial, musical, bodily-kinesthetic, naturalist, interpersonal, and intrapersonal.[14]

Since Gardner's original work, educators have used the concept of multiple intelligences to understand how different smarts create distinctive learning styles in children. When we can understand and honor a daughter's learning style, we join her on an adventure of self-discovery.

THE MAGNIFICENT EIGHT: EIGHT WAYS SHE MAY BE SMART

To understand the eight ways kids are smart, think about your daughter and her sisters or friends. Rachel tells great ghost stories (linguistic); Martha is always counting and questioning (logical-mathematical); Ellie looks up from her painting or Legos to remember where you left your keys (spatial). Brenda is always humming—she enjoyed opera when she was four (musical). Rose is captain of the soccer team and a hot-dog skier (bodily-kinesthetic). Emma knows the name of every water bird in the lake (naturalist). Deborah organized the car wash; she's the one friends call for advice (interpersonal). Virginia is a lone ranger, always writing her thoughts in her diary (intrapersonal).

To discover your daughter's unique learning style, remember that she has all these intelligences in different proportions. While it is tempting to locate your daughter in one of the eight, you will begin to see that several descriptions fit her. The great ghost story teller may also be able to calculate sales tax in her head. The goal is not to narrow your definition of her intelligence—but to expand it. When we study the magnificent eight, we discover clues about how she learns best.[15]

1. Linguistic

Is your daughter in love with words? She delights in puns, rhymes, sounds. She's a storyteller, a reader, a good speller, a crossword puzzler. She has a strong memory for sounds; she's a quick study, and if you drop a word reading, she'll know. *One way this daughter learns is by verbalizing, being able to see and hear words.*

2. Logical-Mathematical

Does your daughter think in concepts, enjoy working with numbers, and explore relationships and patterns? She asks questions you can't answer (such as when clouds first appeared). She sorts her Halloween candy by category, beats you at chess, and has to be coaxed away from the computer. *She will learn by translating ideas into numbers or by classifying and categorizing.*

3. Spatial

Does your daughter think in pictures? She's actively engaged in art activities—drawing, designing, building. She loves maps and mazes, never gets lost, remembers landmarks on vacation, recognizes a place she's been to only once before. She's a daydreamer, a moviegoer, a machine lover—maybe an inventor. *She can learn best by working with images, visualizing, drawing, and imagining.*

4. Musical

Is your daughter a singer, hummer, whistler? She sings on key, remembers the melody, can tell an oboe from a French horn, plays an instrument—or wants to. She's got the beat, she hears the bee buzz (when no one else does). *Her optimal learning environment would have background music and let her express her ideas through music or dance.*

5. Bodily-Kinesthetic

Do you have a daughter who can't sit down, who trusts her "gut feelings," who has amazing grace? She was the first kind in her class to tie her shoelaces or ride a two-wheeler. She's an actor who does a devastating imitation of Great-Aunt Myra. She's first in line for the rollercoaster, captain of the swimming team, and excels in handcrafts. *She will learn best by hands-on learning, building a model, dancing, or acting things out.*

6. Naturalist[16]

Can she name every dinosaur, recognize species of birds, flowers, and trees? She's a keen observer of nature, and needs to play outside. *To help her learn, bring the outside in and use plant and animal props to guide her learning of math and language.*

7. Interpersonal

Is your daughter people wise? She's the first to notice your mood change—and express empathy. She loves to role-play, plan parties, go out in groups. She mediates feuds among her many friends; she's an organizer, a leader who is good at getting her way. *Her best learning environment may be in a group—where she can share, compare, and cooperate.*

8. Intrapersonal

Is her self-knowledge and personal style striking? She can tell you exactly why she's mad or sad and she knows her strengths and limitations. She's an individual, an original—definitely not a team player. She needs a room of her own—she wants to be alone; she has a secret hobby or a diary. *This daughter may learn best by working alone, in a program she defines—at her own pace and in her own territory.*

Do remember that each daughter has each of the intelligences in different amounts. Parents who understand the theory of multiple intelligences are careful not to use limiting labels. ("Oh, she's a number-cruncher.") Instead, we can discover the unique combination of strengths and weaknesses in each area of intelligence that create her learning style.

When we put our theory into practice, we can enrich her education and deepen her knowledge—and belief—in herself.

PARENT STRATEGIES: SHARING A VISION OF HOW SMART SHE IS

My ten-year-old niece, Chloe, and I are sitting at an empty table, talking. She is fashioning a skullcap made of the empty gold-foil wrappers from chocolate Chanukah gelt candy. Suddenly, she exclaims, "My head is always full of art!" Intrigued, I ask her to explain. She says, "Sometimes I'll be sitting in class and I'll have these visions—like I can picture a scissors and how I want to cut something."

I am struck with Chloe's wonderful description (and understanding) of her unique gift of spatial intelligence. She has always been an inventive, articulate, and empathic person. As I listen to her, I share her vision of herself. I am reminded of the challenge for parents who can see a daughter's unique talents and abilities. How can we help her use her gifts to meet the challenges of the classroom?

For starters:

• *Tell her how smart she is.* Introduce the idea of eight kinds of smart at the earliest possible age. Preschoolers can be told, "You have a great ear for music!" and preteens will delight in recognizing themselves (and their friends) in a simple article on the subject. At Hannah's school, the preschoolers are studying the Eight Smarts— Don't worry, five-year-olds don't say "linguistic intelligence"; they say, *"I'm word smart."*

• *Tell her teacher; plant a positive prophecy.* Share your knowledge of your daughter's unique profile as a learner. Offer an article on the subject and let her know what you've discovered. You might say, "Sarah has a great sense of space and loves to visualize; we have found she learns best when she can draw something she is learning."

• *Get help with her homework.* Once you discover her dominant learning style, you can use her gifts to help her gain confidence in other, less developed areas. As an example, Thomas Armstrong suggests a variety of ways you might teach multiplication. *Linguistic learners* could use toothpicks grouped by twos, threes, and fours—to discover principles of multiplying. *Musically minded learners* could chant or sing the times tables.[17]

• *Acknowledge separate styles.* As you understand a daughter's unique intelligence, you will also gain insight into your own ways of being smart. Armed with the knowledge of your own learning style—and how it might clash with hers—you will stop expecting her to learn in the ways you do. For example, an *intrapersonally smart* dad, who had to study in solitude, can quit insisting that his musically smart daughter turn off the tunes when she studies.

• *Get smart with gender glasses.* Don't assume that a daughter will be verbal and empathic—unable to understand fractions or read a map. Remember that every child has each kind of intelligence, and each kind of intelligence can increase. Since girls are often discouraged from developing their smarts in logic, space, and math, we must remember to nourish their learning in those areas.

MOZART'S BIRTHDAY

It seemed like a long time between Chanukah and Valentine's Day; so I thought we should celebrate Mozart's birthday. After all, I told Jeremy, Hannah had been listening to Mozart all her life. Before Baby Beluga swam into her tape deck, Wolfgang's soothing piano sonatas were Hannah's goodnight music. And later, she loved to listen to a "Classical Kids" version of the opera *The Magic Flute,* called *Mozart's Magic Fantasy.*

We had great fun preparing for the party. We played the Mozart tape on the way to school. We read a book called *Young Mozart* ("Did you know he had a sister named Nannerl?"), and plastered the dining room windows with pictures of instruments. Hannah drew a Happy Birthday banner and we decorated musical cupcakes with licorice notes.

On the morning of the party I splurged—and bought a full-length CD of *The Magic Flute.* I put the music on when Hannah and I were setting the table. Several minutes into the opera, Hannah raised one eyebrow and shouted, "That's the Queen of the Night's song!" As the music played on, I could see her excitement in recognizing so many of the melodies.

When I watched her delight, I could believe that Hannah would never lose her pleasure or pride in learning. As Hannah listened to the music, I could imagine her growing into a woman who would always hear the song in her heart.

KEY IDEAS

Strategy 7
Learn What She Learns

How to discover her strengths as a learner and build on her natural interest in math, science, and computers

- Get an early start with sports. Buy her sports equipment, take her out to the ball game, show her sportswomen.
- All toys offer lessons, so consider what she is learning in her play. Bridge the gender gap by giving her nontraditional toys.
- Don't model math anxiety. Number her days, make measuring fun, show her how to read maps, play math games.
- Give science a female face. Show her women in science and encourage her to take chances, get messy, and make mistakes.
- Build computer confidence: Avoid fluffware, include math and science programs, and share software among friends.
- Teach her how to get a teacher's attention—to sit in the "Terrific T" and to raise her hand and keep it aloft.
- Discover her strengths as a learner. Teach her teacher what you have learned about your daughter.

Epilogue:
The Girl in
the Elevator

As I look through the glass doors, I can see Hannah and Jeremy, crossing the street toward the lobby of my office building. Hannah is chatting merrily, with her new Lassie puppet covering her right hand. The two of us are meeting for a picnic in my office—to celebrate my finishing the book. We hug hello, bid Jeremy good-bye, and hop into the elevator. As the door closes, she asks, "When can I see your book?"

It has been months since she visited my office—it has been a mountain of manuscript pages. So she surveys the scene with interest; remembering how her drawings festoon the walls, and how my beige chair makes a great merry-go-round. Then, we open the box with my completed manuscript. We talk about what the bound book will look like; and I read several "stories" about her. (She tells me she loves the Barbie story, because "You tell how you really feel.")

As she holds the book in her hands, I realize it has been almost three years since I began to think about writing a book to help us raise our brave new daughter. When I show her these pages—filled with stories and strategies—my fondest wishes find a voice.

For you, dear reader, my wish is that you have found practical, joyous paths to explore with your daughter. And for you, my dear daughter, I hope I will find the wisdom to honor your life with what I have learned.

NOTES

Prologue. The Girl in the Elevator

1. *Shortchanging Girls, Shortchanging America*—Executive Summary. Washington, D.C.: American Association of University Women, 1991.

2. *How Schools Shortchange Girls*. Washington, D.C.: American Association of University Women. Educational Foundation, 1992.

3. *Hostile Hallways: The AAUW Survey on Sexual Harassment in American Schools*. Washington, D.C.: American Association of University Women, 1992. *Secrets in Public: Harassment in Our Schools*. Wellesley, Mass.: Wellesley Center for Research on Women, Wellesley College, 1992.

4. Daley, Suzanne. "Little Girls Lose Their Self-Esteem on the Way to Adolescence, Study Finds." *New York Times,* Jan. 9, 1991.

5. *A Call to Action: Shortchanging Girls, Shortchanging America*. Washington, D.C.: American Association of University Women, 1991, pp. 24–26. The "finding" Diamant referred to comes from a widely reported and discussed 1991 survey of 3,000 schoolchildren, commissioned by the American Association of University Women. *A Call to Action* summarizes the study's alarming data on self-esteem:

In a crucial measure of self-esteem, 60% of elementary school girls and 69% of elementary school boys say they "are happy the way I am." But, by *high school, girls' self-esteem falls 31 points to only 29%,* while boys' self-esteem falls only 23 points to 46%.

Girls are less likely than boys to say they are "pretty good at a lot of things." Less than a third of girls express this confidence, compared with almost half the boys. A 10-point gender gap in confidence in abilities increases to 19 points in high school.

The study also found a gender gap in the area of self-concept and competence: Boys are twice as likely to list their talents as what they most liked about themselves; girls listed their appearance.

Parents have found these numbers (only 29% of girls are happy with themselves at adolescence) dutifully reported in every article about girls since 1991—often without some of the study's most fascinating findings. For example, at adolescence, African-American girls reported higher self-esteem than their Caucasian or Hispanic classmates (whose self-esteem plummets to the lowest level of all three groups).

6. Diamant, Anita. "The Good Fight." *Parenting,* April 1994, pp. 72–73.

7. O'Reilly, Jane. *The Lost Girls. Mirabelle,* April 1994, pp. 117–18.

8. Gilligan, Carol, Lyons, N., and Hammer, T. *Making Connections: The Relational Worlds of Adolescents at Emma Willard School.* Cambridge: Harvard University Press, 1990.

   Gilligan, Carol; Rogers, Annie; and Tolman, Deborah. *Women, Girls and Psychotherapy: Reframing Resistance.* New York: Haworth Press, 1991.

   Gilligan, Carol, and Brown, Lyn Mikel. *Meeting at the Crossroads.* New York: Ballantine, 1992.

9. Sommers, Christina Hoff. *Who Stole Feminism?* New York: Simon & Schuster, 1994, p. 146.

   Sommers, Christina Hoff. "The Myth of Girls' Low Self-Esteem." *Wall Street Journal,* Oct. 3, 1994.

Of particular note is the fur that flew following the publication of Christina Hoff Sommers's book *Who Stole Feminism?* In her book, Sommers insists that the American Association for University Women's self-esteem study is badly flawed—grist for AAUW's political agenda. In a well-documented (but mean-spirited) attack, she pursues the original study (as conducted by Greenberg/Lake Associates), and does a different math:

We are told about how many boys and girls responded *"always true"* to "Happy the way I am." We are not told that *this was only one of five* possible responses, including "sort of true," "sometimes true/sometimes false," "sort of false," or always false and that most responses were in the *middle range. . . .*
   In addition to the 29% of girls who checked "always true," 34% checked "sort of true" and another 25% "sometimes true/sometimes false"—a *total of 88%, compared to 92% of the boys.* The AAUW claims a 17 point gender gap in adolescent self-esteem [p. 146].

Introduction. Equalist Parents: 7 Strategies for Raising Stronger, Spirited Daughters

1. Dunn, Rita, and Dunn, Kenneth. *How to Raise an Independent and Professional Successful Daughter.* Englewood Cliffs, NJ: Prentice-Hall, 1977.

2. New York: Doubleday, 1990. Examples include books like Sally Hegensen's *The Female Advantage* and Connie Glaser and Barbara Smalley, *Swim with the Dolphins.*

3. Debold, Elizabeth; Wilson, Marie; and Malave, Idelisse. *Mother Daughter Revolution.* New York: Addison-Wesley, 1993, p. 154.

4. Ibid., pp. 16–20.

5. Sadker, Myra, and Sadker, David. *Failing at Fairness: How America's Schools Cheat Girls.* New York: Scribners, 1994.

6. If we examine the history of sex differences dressed as best-sellers, we find book after book that suggest profound difference between adult men and women. On this list we find cult classics like *Women's Reality* by Anne Wilson Schaef, *Women's Ways of Knowing,* by Mary Blenky et al., as well as more recent entries such as *Women Who Run with Wolves* by Clarissa Pinkola Estés, *You Just Don't Understand, Talking 9–5* by Deborah Tannen, and especially the marital therapist's cash cow: *Men Are from Mars, Women from Venus.*

7. Women's historic caretaking roles (and a daughter's unbroken connection with her mother) have created ways of being that are *not only different from men, but superior to them.* This belief is the core of what is now called "gender feminism" or "differences feminism":

   Writer Lindsy Van Gelder sums up the sentiment, "As traditional caretakers, women in this culture easily affiliate and identify with others, value people's feelings and tend to base moral codes on the good of the entire good. . . . These traditional values are our best shot at changing our culture and saving the world." (As quoted in Carol Tavris, *The Mismeasure of Women.* New York: Simon & Schuster, 1992, p. 58.)

8. My friend Jane is referring to the macrobiotic notion of male/female foods, but it is ironic to note that many people who argue that "women are protein" refer to Carol Gilligan's book, *In a Different Voice* (Cambridge: Harvard University Press, 1982). But Gilligan's work began as a challenge to using only male subjects in psychological studies—she offered a model of including the experiences of *individual* women. She did not suggest that all women speak in one superior-sounding voice.

Strategy 1. Discover Your Own Stereotypes

Chapter 1. Approach the Gender Puzzle

1. Sadker, Myra, and Sadker, David. *Failing at Fairness: How America's Schools Cheat Girls.* New York: Scribners, 1994, p. 253.

2. Condry, Sandra, and Condry, John. "Sex Differences: A Study of the Eye of the Beholder." *Child Development,* 1976, 47, as cited in Olga Silverstein and Beth Rashbaum, *The Courage to Raise Good Men.* New York: Viking, 1994, p. 29.

3. Harrison, Barbara Grizutti. *Unlearning the Lie: Sexism in School.* New York: Liveright, 1973, pp. 6–7.

4. Herman, Judith, and Lewis, Helen Block. "Anger in the Mother Daughter Relationship," in *The Psychology of Today's Women,* eds. C. Bernay and D. Cantor. Cambridge: Harvard University Press, 1989, pp. 142–58.

5. Honig, Alice Sterling. "Research in Review: Sex Role Socialization in Early Childhood." *Young Children,* September 1983, Vol. 38, No. 6, pp. 57–70.

6. "Beginning Equal Project." *Beginning Equal: A Manual About Nonsexist Childrearing.* New York: Women's Action Alliance, 1983.

7. The information on sex role cognition comes from the following sources: Jeanne Brooks-Gunne and Wendy Schemp-Matthews, *He and She: How Children Develop Their Sex Role Identity.* Englewood Cliffs, NJ: Prentice-Hall, 1979, pp. 115–16; Carol Tavris and Carole Wade, *The Longest War: Sex Differences in Perspective,* San Diego: Harcourt Brace Jovanovich, 1984, pp. 216–17.

8. Maccoby, Eleanor. "Social Development: Psychological Growth and the Parent Child Relationship." New York: Harcourt Brace Jovanovich, 1980, as cited in Tavris, "The Mismeasure of Women."

9. Brooks-Gunne and Schemp-Matthews, p. 116.

10. Garrett, C. D., et al. "The Development of Gender Stereotyping of Adult Occupations in the Elementary School Child." *Child Development,* Vol. 48, 1977, pp. 507–17.

11. Rogers, Annie. "Voice Play and the Practice of Ordinary Courage in Girls' and Women's Lives." *Harvard Educational Review,* August 1993.

12. Debold, Elizabeth; Wilson, Marie; and Malave, Idelisse, *Mother Daughter Revolution.* New York: Addison-Wesley, 1993, p. 52.

13. The idea of impression management as a strategy for dealing with

stereotypes is drawn from Susan Bascow's *Gender Stereotypes: Traditions and Alternatives*. Pacific Grove: Brooks/Cole, 1986, p. 13.

Chapter 2. Study Sex Differences

1. A point made by Katha Pollitt, "Why Boys Don't Play with Dolls." *The New York Times Magazine*. Oct. 18, 1995, p. 46.

2. Maccoby, Eleanor, and Jacklin, Carol. *The Psychology of Sex Differences*. Stanford: Stanford University Press, 1974.

3. Discussions of brain lateralization and the sexes appear in: Ann Moir, *Brain Sex,* New York: Dell, 1989; Laskin and O'Neill, *The Little Girl Book,* pp. 13–16; Anne Fausto-Sterling, *The Myths of Gender,* New York: Basic Books, 1985; and Gina Kolata, "Men and Women Use Brains Different, Study Discovers," *New York Times,* Feb. 16, 1995.

4. Feingold, Alan. "Cognitive Gender Differences Are Disappearing." *American Psychologist,* 43, pp. 95–103. Alan Feingold's studies offer data indicating that gender differences in SAT scores have declined greatly in the last forty years with boys catching up in verbal scores and *girls catching up in abstract and numerical abilities and cutting the difference in mechanical and spatial relations reasoning in half.* Hyde, Janet. "How Large Are Cognitive Gender Differences?" *American Psychologist,* Vol. 36, 1981, pp. 892–901.

5. Goldstein, A. G., and Chance, J. E. "Effects of Practice on Sex Related Differences in Performance on Embedded Figures." *Psychonomic Science,* 1965, 3, pp. 361–62, as cited in Rhoda Unger, *Male and Female, Psychological Perspectives,* New York: Harper & Row, 1979, p. 83.

6. Hood, Kathryn; Draper, Patricia; Crockett, L., and Petersen, A. "The Ontogeny and Phylogeny of Sex Differences in Development of Biophysical Syntheses." *Current Conceptions of Sex Role and Sex Typing: Theory and Research,* Bruce Caplan, ed. New York: Praeger, 1987, as cited in Laskin and O'Neill, *The Little Girl Book.* These studies suggest *that specific differences could alter the direction of brain development.* Their point: "Sex typed socialization sufficiently constrains the activities and experiences of boys and girls to produce sex typed cognitive performances."

7. Sadker, Myra, and Sadker, David. *Failing at Fairness: How America's Schools Cheat Girls.* New York: Scribners, 1994, p. 95.

8. See, for example, Thorne, Barrie, *Gender Play: Boys and Girls in School.* New Brunswick, NJ: Rutgers University Press, 1993.

9. Laskin, David, and O'Neill, Kathleen. *The Little Girl Book,* p. 15.

10. Psychologist June Reinish's studies discussed in Faust-Sterling, Anne:

Myths of Gender: Biological Theories About Women and Men. New York: Basic Books, 1992.

11. Money, John, and Ehrhardt, Anke. *Man and Woman, Boy and Girl,* as cited in Tavris and Wade, *The Longest War,* p. 143.

12. Fisher, Alan. "Maternal and Sexual Behavior Induced by Intracranial Chemical Stimulation." *Science,* 1956, Vol. 124, pp. 228–99, as cited in Tavris and Wade, *The Longest War,* p. 161.

13. Natalie Angier reported on the work of Dr. Christine Wang at UCLA in: "Does Testosterone Equal Aggression? Maybe Not." *The New York Times,* June 20, 1995, p. A1. In Wang's studies, when men with low testosterone levels were given testosterone replacement, *their aggression and agitation decreased* and a sense of optimism and sociability increased.

14. Condry, John, and Ross, David. "Sex and Aggression: The Influence of Gender Labels on the Perception of Aggression in Children." *Child Development,* Vol. 56, No. 1, 1985, pp. 225–33.

15. Maccoby, Eleanor, and Jacklin, Carol. *The Psychology of Sex Differences.*

16. Conrad, Eva. "Girls Read Emotion." *Working Mother,* October 1994, p. 30.

17. Shapiro, Laura. "Guns and Dolls." *Newsweek,* May 28, 1990, p. 61.

18. Feshbach, Norma, and Feshbach, Seymour. "The Young Aggressors." *Psychology Today,* April 1993, pp. 90–95. In their study of first-graders' responses to the new kid on the block, *they found boys supportive and girls aggressive.* They wrote, "One of the girls even set out to terrorize the newcomer. She spilled a box of pickup sticks and, taking one up, began to stalk the new boy around the room."

19. Judith Smetana, at the University of Rochester, found that girls received more verbal explanations of why misbehavior (like biting or toy-grabbing) was unacceptable and boys were simply stopped and punished. (Girls gained emotional insight into behavior.)

20. As reported in Shapiro, p. 62.

21. Bem, Sandra, and Bem, Daryl. "Training the Woman to Know Her Place." In *Sexism and Youth,* ed. Gersoni-Edelman, Diane. New York: Bowker, 1974, pp. 15–16.

22. Psychologist Rhoda Unger sums up this idea in her book *Female and Male.* New York: Harper & Row, 1979, p. 19. "Sex differences are used to justify asymmetries in attitudes toward, and treatment of, males and females. In fact, differential treatment is never justified

since individual potential is still a far better predictor of behavior than membership in a particular racial, ethnic or sexual group."

23. As quoted in Laskin, David, and O'Neill, Kathleen, *The Little Girl Book.* New York: Ballantine, 1992, p. 15.

24. For example, psychologist June Reinisch, who studied the effects of male hormones on females, wrote, "The differences in male and female brains are really quite small, but are amplified by the different socialization boys and girls receive." As quoted in Laskin and O'Neill, *The Little Girl Book,* p. 15.

Chapter 3. Let Girls Be Girls

1. Tronick, Edward, and Adamson, Lauren. *Babies as People: New Findings on Our Social Beginnings.* New York: Collier, 1980.

2. Ibid., p. 85.

3. Silverstein, Olga, and Rashbaum, Beth. *The Courage to Raise Good Men.* New York: Viking, 1994, pp. 28–29.

4. A number of "Baby X" stories are summarized in Alice Sterling Honig, "Research in Review: Sex Role Socialization in Early Childhood." *Young Children,* September 1983, Vol. 38, No. 6, pp. 57–70. Other sources include: Jeffrey Robin, Frank Provenzo, and Zella Lura, "The Eye of the Beholder." *American Journal of Orthopsychiatry,* Vol. 44, No. 4, July 1974.

5. Carmichael, Carrie. *Non-sexist Childraising.* Boston: Beacon Press, 1977.

6. Silverstein and Rashbaum, *The Courage to Raise Good Men,* p. 4.

7. Pomerleau, Andree; Bolduc, Daniel; Gerard, Malcuit, and Cossette, Louise. "Pink and Blue: Environmental Gender Stereotypes in the First Two Years of Life." *Sex Roles,* Vol. 22, Nos. 5–6, 1990, p. 365.

8. Quindlen, Anna. "Birthday Girl." *The New York Times,* Nov. 21, 1993.

9. In mapping out these five parent paths, I was very influenced by discussions of "Public and Private Domains" and the notion of the "Paths of Least Resistance" as found in Elizabeth Debold, Marie Wilson, and Malave Idelisse, *Mother Daughter Revolution,* New York: Addison-Wesley, 1993. In addition, the insights about sex differences and women's superiority were inspired, in part, by discussions in Carol Tavris, *The Mismeasure of Women,* New York: Simon & Schuster, 1992.

10. Gruver, Nancy. *New Moon Parenting,* November–December 1993, Vol. 1, No. 2, p. 2.

11. A term used by psychologist Dana Jack in a conference workshop "In Her Own Voice" given at Forest Hills School in Bellevue, Washington, on May 17, 1993.

12. Carmichael, *Non-sexist Childraising*, p. 3.

Strategy 2. Believe Her Story

Chapter 4. Make Her the Authority

1. Smith, Beverly Jean. "Raising a Resister." *Women, Girls and Psychotherapy*. eds. Carol Gilligan, Anne Rogers, and Deborah Tolman, Binghamton, NY: Haworth Press, 1991, p. 138.

2. The notion of listening to girls as authorities about their own experiences appears in: Lyn Brown and Carol Gilligan, *Meeting at the Crossroads*, New York: Ballantine, 1992, pp. 1–4.

3. Ibid., p. 61.

4. Brown, Lyn Mikel. "Telling a Girl's Life," in *Women, Girls and Psychotherapy*, p. 78.

5. Lerner, Harriet. *The Dance Of Deception*. New York: HarperCollins, 1993, pp. 83–84.

6. Rogers, Annie. "Voice, Play, and the Practice of Ordinary Courage in Girls' and Women's Lives." *Harvard Educational Review*, August 1993.

7. Kohut, Heinz. *The Restoration of the Self*. New York: International Universities Press, 1977, pp. 12–13, 171.

8. Ginott, Haim. *Between Parent and Child*. New York: Avon, 1965, p. 40.

9. See Goleman, Daniel, *Emotional Intelligence*, New York: Bantam, 1995, for a description of "atonement" and empathy, pp. 116–17.

10. Miller, Alice. *The Drama of the Gifted Child*. New York: Basic Books, 1981, p. 16.

11. Cohen, Betsey. *The Snow White Syndrome: All About Envy*. New York: Macmillan, 1986.

12. Fraiberg, Selma. "Ghosts in the Nursery." *Journal of the American Academy of Child Psychiatry*, 1975, Vol. 14, pp. 387–424.

13. Lustman, Jeffrey, as quoted in Schoen, Elin, *Growing with Your Child*. Doubleday: Garden City, NY, 1994, pp. 18–19. He expanded his comments in a personal communication, June 1994.

14. The technique of "naming feelings" appears in Faber, Adele, and Mazlish, Elaine, *How to Talk So Kids Will Listen.* New York: Avon, 1980, p. 15.

15. Ginott, Haim. *Between Parent and Child,* p. 30.

16. Ibid., pp. 37–38.

17. Faber and Mazlish, *How to Talk So Kids Will Listen,* p. 16.

18. Ibid.

19. Greenspan, Stanley. *Playground Politics.* New York: Addison-Wesley, 1993, pp. 26–27, 92–93.

20. Samalin, Nancy, and Whitney, Catherine. "Mom, You're Not Listening." *Parents,* February 1995, p. 49.

Chapter 5. Discover Her Temperament

1. The idea of temperament was defined by Chess, Stella, and Thomas, Alexander, in their book: *Know Your Child: An Authoritative Guide for Today's Parents.* New York: Basic Books, 1987.

2. Personality preferences, including "introverted" and "extroverted," are introduced in Carl Jung's *Psychological Types; The Collected Works of Carl Jung,* Vol. 6. Princeton: Princeton University Press, 1971.

3. The idea of preference match is discussed in Chess and Thomas, *Know Your Child,* pp. 54–70.

4. The following sources suggested ways in which temperament and behavioral style can be used as discovery tools:

   Keirsey, David, and Bates, Marilyn. *Please Understand Me.* Del Mar, Ca.: Prometheus Books, 1984.

   Kurchinka, Mary Sheedy. *Raising Your Spirited Child.* New York: HarperCollins, 1991.

   Tureki, Stanley, and Tonner, Leslie. *The Difficult Child: A Guide for Parents.* New York: Bantam, 1989.

5. Goleman, Daniel. *Emotional Intelligence.* New York: Bantam, 1995, pp. 215–28.

6. Kagan, Jerome, et al. "Initial Reactions to Unfamiliarity." *Current Directions in Psychological Science,* December 1992, as cited in Goleman, Daniel, pp. 220–21.

7. Preferred styles of responding in nine categories are finely detailed in Chess and Thomas, *Know Your Child,* pp. 28–31.

8. Kurchinka, Mary. *Raising Your Spirited Child,* p. 27. [Pronouns added.]

9. In describing this balance of coaching and confirming, I was very influenced by Mary Kurchinka's view of labeling and mastery in *Raising Your Spirited Child,* as well as my conversations with Seattle psychiatrist Diane C. Stein and psychologist Laura Kastner.

Chapter 6. Explore Her Energy

1. As explained in Von Franz, Marie Louise, and Hillman, James, *Jung's Typology.* Dallas: Spring Publications, 1971.

2. Spoleta, Angela. *Jung's Typology in Perspective.* Sigo Press: Boston, 1990. People who take the Myers-Briggs Type Indicator can make the mistake of typecasting themselves ("I'm an Introvert," "I'm a Feeler"). But in fact, these pairs draw on habitual or *preferred* behavior, not exclusive orientations. As Angela Spoleta explains in *Jung's Typology in Perspective,* "Being extroverted does not prevent an individual from introverted behavior, nor vice versa; *but a person seems more comfortable and feels truest to him or herself in one attitude rather than another.* It is a matter of agreeing and harmonizing with something taken as natural to, and distinctive of personality [p. 23]."

3. Ibid.

4. Kroeger, Otto, and Thuesen, Janet, *Type Talk,* New York: Delta, 1989, talks about some of these contrasts.

5. Keirsey, David, and Bates, Marilyn. *Please Understand Me: Character and Temperament Types.* Del Mar, Ca.: Prometheus Books, 1984, p. 100.

6. Ibid., p. 101 [pronouns added].

7. The idea of unconscious assumption of likeness is found in Keirsey and Bates, *Please Understand Me,* p. 97.

8. A view of overprotection was provided by Dr. Laura Kastner, Associate Professor of Psychology, University of Washington, in a personal communication.

9. Chess, Stella, and Thomas, Alexander. *Know Your Child.* New York: Basic Books, 1987, pp. 54–70.

10. Kurchinka, Mary. *Raising Your Spirited Child.* New York: HarperCollins, 1991, p. 53.

11. A number of these ideas were influenced by Kurchinka's work in *Raising Your Spirited Child.*

12. An idea explored with Dr. Laura Kastner in a private communication.

Strategy 3. Declare Her Independence

Chapter 7. Consider Her Conditioning

1. A quote from a speech given by Ellen Wahl, Director of Operation SMART, "Girls and Technology: Stories of Tools and Power." Presented at the American Educational Research Association, April 8, 1988.

2. A point made by Judith Bardwick in "Ambivalance: The Socialization of Women" in *Readings in the Psychology of Women*. New York: Harper & Row, 1972.

3. Dowling, Colette. *The Cinderella Complex*. New York: Summit Books, 1981.

4. Hoffman, Lois. "Early Childhood Experiences and Women's Achievement Motives." *Journal of Social Issues,* Vol. 28, No. 2, 1972.

5. Moss, H. A. "Sex, Age and State as Determinants of Mother-Infant Interaction." *Merrill-Palmer Quarterly,* Vol. 13, 1967, pp. 19–36, as cited in Hoffman, "Early Childhood Experiences," p. 140.

6. Rubenstein, J. "Maternal Attentiveness and Subsequent Exploratory Behavior in the Infant." *Child Development,* Vol. 38, 1967, pp. 1089–1100, as cited in Hoffman, "Early Childhood Experiences," p. 140.

7. Hoffman, "Early Childhood Experiences," p. 141.

8. Dowling, Colette. *The Cinderella Complex,* p. 108.

9. Burns, Allison; Mitchell, G., and Obradovich, Stephanie. "Of Sex Roles and Strollers: Male Attention to Toddlers at the Zoo." *Sex Roles,* Vol. 20, 1989, pp. 309–15.

10. Collard, E. D. "Achievement Motive in the Four Year Old Child and Its Relationship to the Expectancies of the Mother." Unpublished doctoral dissertation, University of Michigan, 1964, as cited in Hoffman, "Early Childhood Experiences," p. 142.

11. Sadker, Myra, and Sadker, David. *Failing at Fairness*. New York: Scribners, 1994, pp. 80–81.

12. Serbin, Lisa, and O'Leary, Daniel. "How Nursery Schools Teach Girls to Shut Up." *Psychology Today,* July 1975, pp. 56–57, 102–3.

13. Janzen, Marta Cruz. "A Case Study of Gender Interactions in a Bilingual Early Childhood Education Classroom." National Institute of Education, Washington, D.C., as cited in Sadker and Sadker, *How Schools Shortchange Girls,* p. 80.

14. Fennema and Peterson, as quoted in Mann, Judy, *The Difference*. New York: Warner, 1994, pp. 105–6.

15. This idea was inspired by Letty Pogrebin's notion of "Parity Parenting" in *Growing Up Free*. New York: McGraw-Hill, 1980.

Chapter 8. Encourage Her Competence

1. Marston, Stephanie. *The Magic of Encouragement*. New York: Pocket Books, 1990.

2. Hoffman, Lois, as quoted in Dowling, Colette, *The Cinderella Complex*, pp. 112–13.

3. An idea suggested by Nancy Samalin in *Loving Your Child Is Not Enough: Positive Discipline That Works*. New York: Penguin Books, 1987.

4. Marston, Stephanie. *The Magic of Encouragement*, p. 113.

5. A point made by developmental psychologist Robert Kegan.

6. Many of the suggestions were influenced by the work of Stephanie Marston as discussed in *The Magic of Encouragement*.

7. This is a theme discussed in Orenstein, Peggy, *School Girls*, New York: Doubleday, 1994.

8. Ryckman, David, and Peckham, Percy. "Gender Differences in Attributions for Success and Failure Situations Across Subject Areas." *Journal of Educational Research,* Vol. 81, November–December 1987, pp. 120–25, as cited in Sadker and Sadker, *How Schools Shortchange Girls*, pp. 96–97.

9. Bascow, Susan. *Gender Stereotypes: Traditions and Alternatives*. Pacific Grove: Brooks/Cole, 1986.

10. A notion of "learned helplessness" is described in the work of Martin Seligman, particularly in his classic book *Helplessness*. San Francisco: Freeman, 1975. His descriptions of "learned optimism" in *The Optimistic Child*, New York: Houghton Mifflin, 1995, should be required reading for parents who want to nurture a daughter's mastery and independence.

11. An idea developed in behavior therapist Debora Phillips's book *How to Give Your Child a Great Self Image*. New York: Penguin, 1991.

12. Viorst, Judith. *Necessary Losses*. New York: Fawcett, 1987, p. 247.

Chapter 9. Find Safety in Self-Reliance

1. Marone, Nicky. *How to Father a Successful Daughter*. New York: Fawcett Crest, 1988.

2. Statman, Paula. *On the Safe Side*. New York: HarperCollins, 1995.

3. Martin, Barclay. *Anxiety and Neurotic Disorders.* New York: Wiley, 1971, as quoted in Dowling, *The Cinderella Complex,* p. 110.

4. Marone, *How to Father a Successful Daughter,* p. 169.

5. Ibid., p. 152.

6. Statman, *On the Safe Side,* pp. 66–86.

7. Ibid., p. 85.

8. The information and resources about becoming streetwise were drawn from the following sources:

   Israeloff, Roberta. "How to Teach Street Smarts." *Parents,* September 1994, pp. 84–86.

   Wright, Lenore. "What to Do When a Stranger Says Hello." *Family Life,* September–October 1994, p. 38.

   Statman, Paula. *On the Safe Side.*

   "Child Protection." The National Center for Missing and Exploited Children, 2101 Wilson Boulevard, Arlington, Virginia 22201.

9. Statman, *On the Safe Side,* pp. 113–38.

10. Mayer, Linda. *Safety Zone.* Charlotte, NC: Kids' Rights, 1984.

11. *Hostile Hallways: The AAUW Survey on Sexual Harassment in American Schools.* Washington, D.C.: American Association of University Women, 1992.

    "Secrets in Public: Harassment in Our Schools." Wellesley, Mass.: Wellesley Center for Research on Women, Wellesley College, 1992.

12. Kelly, Joe. "Sexual Harassment in School." *New Moon Parenting,* Vol. 1, September–October 1993, pp. 1–9.

13. Manning, Anita. "Sexual Harassment at School." *USA Today,* March 22, 1994, p. 2.

14. These ideas are in reference to strategies suggested in Shannon, Sally, "Why Girls Don't Want to Go to School," *Working Mother,* November 1993; and Kelly, Joe, "Sexual Harassment in School," pp. 7–8.

15. Simpson, Louis, as quoted in Viorst, Judith, *Necessary Losses,* pp. 227–29.

Strategy 4. Bring Home Heroines

Chapter 10. Review Role Models

1. Kastner, Dr. Laura, Ph.D., from a keynote address, "Girls' Adolescent Slump: What's a Parent to Do?" Giving Girls Their Voice Forum, Forest Ridge School, Bellevue, Washington, March 26, 1994.

2. Shapiro, Laura. "Guns and Dolls." *Newsweek,* May 28, 1995, p. 56.

3. Douvan, Elizabeth. "The Role of Models on Women's Professional Development." *Psychology of Women Quarterly,* Vol. 1, No. 1, 1976, pp. 5–20.

4. Brooks-Gunn, Jeanne, and Schempp-Matthews, Wendy. *He and She: How Children Develop Their Sex Role Identity.* New Jersey: Prentice-Hall, 1979.

5. Kerr, Barbara. *Smart Girls, Gifted Women.* Dayton: Ohio Psychology Press, 1992.

6. Like Mother, Like Daughter data can be found in the following sources:

   Speizer, Jeanne. "Role Models, Mentors and Sponsors: The Elusive Concepts." *Signs,* Vol. 6, No. 41, pp. 692–712.

   Shreve, Anita. *Remaking Motherhood.* New York: Viking, 1987, pp. 84–87.

   D'Amico, Ronald, et al. "The Effect of Mother's Employment on Adolescent and Early Adult Outcomes of Men and Women" in *Children of Working Parents.* National Academy Press: Washington, D.C., 1983, as cited in Shreve, *Remaking Motherhood.*

   Alington, Diane. "Social Change and Equality: The Role of Women and Economics" in *Women in Midlife,* ed. J. Brooks-Gunn, New York: Plenum, 1984.

7. Flex, Vicki; Fidler, Dorothy; and Rogers, Donald. "Sex Role Stereotypes: Developmental Aspects and Early Intervention." *Child Development,* Vol. 47, 1976, pp. 998–1007.

8. "Ellie" is a fictional name as quoted by Sadker, Myra and Sadker, David, *Failing at Fairness: How Schools Cheat Girls.* New York: Scribners, 1994, p. 69.

9. Thomas, Marlo; Steinem, Gloria; and Pogrebin, Letty. *Free to Be You and Me.* New York: McGraw-Hill, 1974. Available in book and audiocassette form. The Atalanta story is also included on the videocassette, issued by Children's Video Library.

10. Kerr, Barbara. *Smart Girls, Gifted Women,* p. 70.

11. Levinson, Daniel. *The Seasons of a Man's Life*. New York: Knopf, 1978.

12. Webb, Marilyn. "Our Daughters, Ourselves: How Feminists Can Raise Feminists." *Ms.*, November–December, 1992, p. 31.

Chapter 11. Find Great Girls and Wonderful Women

1. Ruething, Ann, as quoted in Schoen, Elin, *Growing with Your Child: Reflections on Parent Development*. Garden City, NY: Doubleday, 1995, p. 111.

2. Ibid., p. 112.

Chapter 12. Model Choices

1. For a full discussion on studies of working and stay-home moms, see Shreve, Anita, *Remaking Motherhood*. New York: Viking, 1987.

2. Holcomb, Betty. "No, We're Not Going Home Again." *Working Mother*, November 1994, p. 28.

3. Shreve, Anita. *Remaking Motherhood*, pp. 192–200.

4. Swasy, Alecia. "Stay-at-Home Moms Are Fashionable in Many Communities." *Wall Street Journal*, July 23, 1993, p. 1.

5. Smith, Beverly Jean. "Raising a Resister," in Carol Gilligan, Annie Rogers, and Deborah Tolman, eds. *Women, Girls and Psychotherapy*, Binghamton, NY: Haworth Press, 1991, p. 143.

6. A point made by Debold, Elizabeth, et al. in *Mother Daughter Revolution*. New York: Addison-Wesley, 1993, and Laura Kastner, "Girls' Adolescent Slump."

Strategy 5. Wear Gender Glasses

Chapter 13. Show and Tell Her About Sexism

1. Kegan, Robert. *The Evolving Self*. Cambridge: Harvard University Press, 1982.

2. Debold, Elizabeth; Wilson, Marie; and Malave, Idelisse, *Mother Daughter Revolution*. New York: Addison-Wesley, 1993, pp. 152–155.

3. Gilligan, Carol. "Women's Psychological Development: Implications for Psychotherapy," in Gilligan, Carol; Rogers, Anne; and Tolman, Deborah, eds., *Women, Girls and Psychotherapy*, p. 16.

4. As published in *New Moon: The Magazine for Girls and Their Dreams,* March–April and May–June 1993.

5. Parents' comments were published in *New Moon Parent,* May–June and July–August 1994, p. 3.

6. As quoted in Kegan, *The Evolving Self.*

7. Debold et al., *Mother Daughter Revolution,* p. 117.

8. Diamant, Anita. "The Good Fight." *Parenting,* April 1994, pp. 72–73.

9. Best, Raphael. *We've All Got Scars: What Boys and Girls Learn in Elementary School.* Bloomington: Indiana University Press, 1983, p. 90.

10. Gilligan, "Women's Psychological Development," pp. 23–24.

11. Mann, Judy. *The Difference.* New York: Warner Books, 1994, p. 279.

Chapter 14. Counter the Culture

1. This means a daughter can develop her own version of what bell hooks calls "the black woman's oppositional gaze." For an explanation, see Robinson, Tracy, and Ward, Janie, "A Belief in Self Far Greater Than Anyone's Belief: Cultivating Resistance Among African American Females," in Gilligan and Rogers, eds. *Women, Girls and Psychotherapy,* p. 97.

2. Diamant, Anita. "The Good Fight." *Parenting,* April 1994, pp. 72–73.

3. Psychologist Dana Crowley Jack in a personal communication, June 1994.

4. Shuker-Haines, Fanny. "On the Homefront." *Parenting,* April 1994, pp. 75–76.

5. Sommers, Christina Hoff. *Who Stole Feminism?* Simon & Schuster: New York, 1994, pp. 41–42.

6. O'Reilly, Jane. "The Lost Girls." *Mirabella,* April 1994, pp. 117–18.

7. Debold et al. *Mother Daughter Revolution,* p. 154.

8. Dr. Dana Crowley Jack in a personal communication, June 1994.

9. A suggestion made by Letty Cottin Pogrebin in *Growing Up Free,* New York: McGraw-Hill, 1980.

10. An idea developed in Lakoff, Robin, *Language and Woman's Place.* New York: Farrar Straus and Giroux, 1976.

11. Carmichael, Carrie. *Non-sexist Childraising*. New York: Beacon Press, 1977. pp. 119–21.

12. Seattle psychologist Maria Root in a personal communication, June 1994.

13. Dr. Dana Crowley Jack, in a personal communication, June 1994.

14. Carmichael, *Non-sexist Childraising*, p. 84.

Strategy 6. Tell the Truth About Beauty

Chapter 15. Beware of Beauty Bias

1. Rubin, J., Provenzano, F., and Luria, Z. "The Eye of the Beholder: Parents' Views on Sex of Newborns." *American Journal of Orthopsychiatry*, Vol. 44, 1974, pp. 512–19.

2. Freedman, Rita. *Beauty Bound*. New York: Free Press, 1986, p. 130.

3. Bernard, Jessie. *The Female World*. New York: Free Press, 1981, p. 479.

4. Una Stannard gives a girls' eye view of beauty in her essay "The Mask of Beauty" in *Woman in Sexist Society,* eds. Gornich, Vivian, and Moran, Barbara. New York: Basic Books, 1971.

5. Freedman, Rita Jackaway. "Reflections on Beauty as It Relates to Health in Adolescent Females." *Women and Health*, Vol. 9, 1984, pp. 29–45.

6. A point made in Wolf, Naomi, *The Beauty Myth*. New York: William Morrow, 1991.

7. Freedman, Rita. *Beauty Bound*, p. 130.

8. Berscheid, Ellen, and Dion, Karen. "What Is Beautiful Is Good." *Journal of Personality and Social Psychology,* 1972, Vol. 24, No. 3, pp. 285–90.

    Dion, Karen. "Young Children's Stereotyping of Facial Attractiveness." *Developmental Psychology*, 1973, Vol. 9, No. 2, pp. 183–88.

    Adams, Gerard, and Crane, Paul. "An Assessment of Parents' and Teachers' Expectations of Preschool Children's Social Preference for Attractive or Unattractive Children and Adults." *Child Development*, 1980, No. 51, pp. 224–31.

9. Freedman, Rita. *Beauty Bound*, p. 125.

10. Pogrebin, Letty Cottin. "The Power of Beauty." *Ms.*, December 1983, pp. 73–78.

270 *Notes*

Dion, Karen. "Physical Attractiveness and Evaluation of Children's Transgressions." *Journal of Personality and Social Psychology,* Vol. 24, No. 2, 1972, pp. 207–13.

Clifford, M., and Walster, Elaine. "The Effect of Physical Attractiveness on Teacher Expectations." *Sociology and Education,* No. 46, 1973, pp. 248–58.

11. Freedman, *Beauty Bound,* p. 28.

12. Ibid., p. 65.

13. Pipher, Mary. *Reviving Ophelia.* New York: Putnam's Sons, 1994, p. 55.

14. Wiseman, Claire, and Gray, James, et al. "Cultural Expectations of Thinness in Women: An Update." *International Journal of Eating Disorders,* Vol. 11, No. 1, 1992, pp. 85–89.

15. Fontaine, Karen Lee. "The Conspiracy of Culture. Women's Issues in Body Size." *Nursing Clinics of North America,* Vol. 26, No. 3, September 1991, p. 673.

16. Seligmann, Jean. "The Littlest Dieters." *Newsweek,* July 27, 1987, p. 48.

17. Freedman, "Reflections on Beauty," p. 35.

18. A story told in Debold, Elizabeth; Wilson, Marie; and Idelisse, Malave. *Mother Daughter Revolution,* New York: Addison-Wesley, 1993, p. 201.

19. Ibid.

20. Inspired by a suggestion in Hutchinson, Marcia Germaine, *Transforming Body Image: Learning to Love the Body You Have.* The Crossing Press: Freedom, Cal., 1985.

21. Finding beautiful self and friendships as suggested in Kearney, Cook, and Streigel-Moore, Ruth. "Through the Looking Glass." *Shape,* July 1992, pp. 98–101.

22. Wolf, *Beauty Myth,* p. 169.

23. Simmons, Charles. "The Age of Maturity." *New York Times Magazine,* Dec. 11, 1983, p. 114, as cited in Freedman, *Beauty Bound,* p. 204.

24. Freedman, *Beauty Bound,* p. 38.

25. Pipher, *Reviving Ophelia,* p. 185.

26. Leslea Newman, personal communication, January 1995.

27. Wolf, *The Beauty Myth,* p. 124.

28. Robinson, Beatrice. "The Stigma of Obesity: Fat Fallacies Debunked." *Melpomene Report,* February 1985, pp. 10–13.

Satter, Ellyn. *How to Get Your Kid to Eat . . . But Not Too Much.* Palo Alto: Bull Publishing, 1987, p. 312.

Melpomene Institute for Women's Health Research. *The Body Wise Woman.* New York: Prentice-Hall, 1991, p. 5.

29. Satter, *How to Get Your Kid to Eat,* p. 300.

30. Satter, Ellyn, personal communication, January 1995.

31. Elissa Koff, Professor of Psychology, Wellesley College, personal communication, February 1995.

32. Clark, Nancy. "Women and Weight." *The Physician and Sports Medicine,* Vol. 20, No. 3, March 1992, p. 41.

Chapter 16. Teach Her to Be Beauty Wise

1. Tan, A. S. "TV Beauty Ads and Role Expectations of Adolescent Female Viewers." *Journalism Quarterly,* 1979, pp. 56, 283–88.

Martin, Mary, and Kennedy, Patricia. "Advertising and Social Comparison." *Psychology and Marketing,* Vol. 10, No. 6, November–December 1993, pp. 513–30.

Cash, Thomas; Walker, Diane; and Butters, Jonathan. "Mirror, Mirror on the Wall . . . ?: Contrast Effects and Self-Evaluation of Physical Attractiveness." *Personality and Social Psychology Bulletin,* Vol. 9, No. 3, September 1983, pp. 351–58.

2. Lakoff, Robin Tolmach, and Scherr, Raquel. *Face Value: The Politics of Beauty.* Boston: Routledge & Kegan Paul, 1984, p. 111.

3. Wolf, *Beauty Myth,* pp. 6, 82–83.

4. Ibid., pp. 11, 185.

5. Lakoff and Scherr, *Face Value,* pp. 274–75.

6. Joffe, C. "Sex Role Socialization and the Nursery School: As the Twig Is Bent." *Journal of Marriage and Family,* Vol. 33, pp. 467–75.

7. I was very influenced by the discussions of clothing as a parenting issue in Flusser, Marilise, *Party Shoes to School and Baseball Caps to Bed.* New York: Simon & Schuster, 1994. Many of her suggestions appear in this section.

8. Ibid., pp. 90–93.

9. These ideas come from the work of Elkind, David, *The Hurried Child,* as discussed in Flusser, *Party Shoes to School,* p. 11.

10. A parent story as told in Flusser, *Party Shoes to School,* p. 19.

11. Freedman, Rita, in a personal communication, January 1995.

12. Lakoff and Scherr, *Face Value.*

13. Freedman, Rita, in a personal communication, January 1995.

14. Ibid.

15. Wolf, *Beauty Myth,* p. 205.

16. Lerner, Harriet Goldhor. *The Dance of Deception.* New York: HarperCollins, 1993, p. 54.

17. Lazoff, Dr. Betsy, Director of the Center for Human Growth and Development of the University of Michigan, personal communication, February 1995.

    Fraley, Cecile; Nelson, Edward; Wolf, Abraham, and Lazoff, Betsy. "Early Genital Naming." *Developmental and Behavioral Pediatrics,* Vol. 12, No. 5, October 1991.

18. Recommendation based on a study reported in Koff, Elissa, and Rierdan, Jill. "Preparing Girls for Menstruation: Recommendations from Adolescent Girls." Working paper, Wellesley College, February 1995.

19. Satter, *How to Get Your Kid to Eat,* p. 66.

20. Satter, Ellyn, *Child of Mine: Feeding with Love and Good Sense.* Palo Alto: Bull Publishing, 1986, p. 409.

21. For example, Kleinman, Ronald, and Jellinek, Michael, *Let Them Eat Cake.* New York: Villard, 1994.

22. Satter, *Child of Mine: Feeding with Love and Good Sense.*

    Costanzo, P. R., and Woody, E. Z. "Domain Specific Parenting Styles and Their Impact on the Child's Development of Particular Deviance: The Example of Obese Proneness." *Journal of Social and Clinical Psychology,* Vol. 3, 1985, pp. 425–45.

23. Debold, Elizabeth, et al. *Mother Daughter Revolution,* p. 211.

Strategy 7. Learn What She Learns

Chapter 17. Teach Her to Learn Through Play

1. Jaffee, Lynn, and Manzer, Rebecca. "Girls' Perspectives, Physical Activity and Self Esteem." *Melpomene Journal,* Vol. 11, No. 3, 1992, p. 19.

2. The lessons of sports are highlighted in a number of books including Hennig, Margaret, and Jardim, Anne, *The Managerial Woman,* Pocket Books: New York, 1976.

Harragen, Betty. *Games Your Mother Never Taught You.* Rawson Associates: New York, 1977.

Heim, Pat, and Golant, Susan K. *Hardball for Women: Winning at the Game of Business.* Los Angeles: Lowell House, 1993.

3. "Sporting Chance: Ten Principles of Girl's Sports Participation." The Girls Clubs of America, Inc., 1986.

4. Jaffee and Manzer, "Girls' Perspectives," p. 14.

5. An idea developed in "Sporting Chances," The Girls Clubs of America, p. 3.

6. See, for example, Sadker and Sadker, *Failing at Fairness,* p. 65.

7. Jaffee and Manzer, p. 19.

Besson, Lisa. "On the Playing Field." *Parenting,* April 1994, pp. 92–93.

8. Harris, Dorothy. "Fallacies About Women in Sports." *Strategies: A Journal for Sport and Physical Educators,* Vol. A, No. 6, 1993, pp. 13–17.

9. Besson, "On the Playing Field," p. 92.

10. Suggestions for involving daughters in sports are drawn from the following sources:

"Breaking Barriers: National Girls and Women in Sports Day Brochure."

Women's Sports Foundation, 342 Madison Avenue, Suite 728, New York, NY 10173.

"Girls, Self-Esteem and Sports." Melpomene Institute, 1010 University Avenue, St. Paul, MN 55104.

Yu, Victoria. "Portrayals of Females in Sports Picture Books." *Melpomene Journal,* Vol. 12, No. 3, Autumn 1993, pp. 14–19.

11. A model of feedback inspired by Lirgg, Cathy, and Feltz, Deborah, "Female Self-Confidence in Sport." *Journal of Physical Education, Recreation and Dance,* March 1989, pp. 49–54.

12. Kacerguis, Mary Ann, and Adams, Gerald. "Implications of Sex Typed Child Rearing Practices, Toys, and Mass Media Materials in Restricting Occupational Choices of Women." *The Family Coordinator,* July 1979, pp. 369–75.

13. An account of how boys learn more math-related concepts in play appears in Tobias, Sheila, *Overcoming Math Anxiety,* Boston: Houghton Mifflin, 1978.

14. Coates, Patricia, and Overman, Steven. "Childhood Play Experiences of Women in Traditional and Nontraditional Professions." *Sex Roles,* Vol. 26, Nos. 7–8, 1992, pp. 261–71.

    Liss, Marsha. "Patterns of Toy Play: An Analysis of Sex Differences." *Sex Roles,* Vol. 7, No. 11, 1981, pp. 1143–50.

15. Shapiro, June; Kramer, Sylvia; and Hunerberg, Catherine. *Equal Their Chances: Children's Activities for Non-Sexist Learning.* Englewood Cliffs, NJ: Prentice-Hall, 1981, p. 61.

16. Sadker, Myra, and Sadker, David. *Failing at Fairness.* New York: Scribners, 1994, p. 256.

17. These suggestions are variations on ideas presented in Shapiro et al.'s *Equal Their Chances.*

18. Ibid.

19. Collins, Clare. "Fighting the Holiday Ad Blitz." *New York Times,* Dec. 1, 1994, p. B1.

20. Sells, Lucy. "Mathematics: A Critical Filter." *The Science Teacher,* Vol. 45, No. 2, February 1978. As cited in Tobias, *Overcoming Math Anxiety,* p. 26.

21. Mann, Judy. *The Difference.* New York: Warner, 1994, p. 94.

    Fox, Lynn, and Turner, Laura. "Gifted and Creative Female: The Middle School Years." *American Middle School Education,* Vol. 4, 17–18, 1981. As cited in Marone, Nicky. *How to Father a Successful Daughter.* New York: Fawcett Crest, 1988.

22. Sadker, Myra, and Sadker, David, *Failing at Fairness,* p. 97.

Chapter 18. Study Math, Science, and Technology

1. Wahl, Ellen. "Girls and Technology: Stories of Tools and Power." A paper presented at the American Educational Research Association Symposium "Women and Technology: New Perspectives on Design and Use," April 8, 1988.

2. Sadker and Sadker, *Failing at Fairness,* p. 123.

3. Shapiro et al., *Equal Their Chances,* pp. 72–73.

4. See, for example, Pelz, William, "Can Girls + Science-Stereotypes = Success?" *The Science Teacher,* December 1990, pp. 44–48.

5. Shapiro et al., *Equal Their Chances,* pp. 69–70.

6. Ibid., p. 70.

7. Prufer, Diana. "In the Classroom." *Parenting,* April 1994, pp. 79–80.

8. Peltz, "Can Girls + Science-Stereotypes = Success?," pp. 44–48.

   Bloom, B. S. *Human Characteristics and School Learning.* New York: McGraw-Hill, 1976, as cited in Shapiro et al., *Equal Their Chances,* p. 65.

9. Wahl, "Girls and Technology," p. 1.

10. Suggestions are drawn from a variety of sources, including:

    Kohl, Mary Ann, and Potter, Jean. *Science Arts.* Bellingham Washington: Bright Ring Publishing, 1993.

    Shapiro, June, et al. *Equal Their Chances.*

11. Sprung, Barbara; Froschl, Merle; and Campbell, Patricia. *What Will Happen If: Young Children and the Scientific Method.* New York: Educational Equity Concepts, 1985.

12. Mann, *The Difference,* p. 93.

13. Ibid.

14. Orenstein, Peggy. *School Girls.* Garden City, NY: Doubleday, 1994, p. 18.

15. Tobias, *Overcoming Math Anxiety.*

16. A study of British psychologists D. C. Entwhistle and D. Baker, as cited in Mann, *The Difference,* p. 99.

17. Ibid., p. 100.

18. For more information about women in math, consult Lynn Olsen's *Women in Mathematics,* available through the Women's History Project.

19. Shapiro et al., *Equal Their Chances.*

20. Marone, Nicky. *How to Father a Successful Daughter.* New York: Ballantine, 1988, p. 37.

21. Tobias, *Overcoming Math Anxiety,* p. 89.

22. A point made by Thomas Armstrong in *Awakening Your Child's Natural Genius.*

23. Suggestions for joining daughters in understanding math are drawn from several sources, including:

Armstrong, *Awakening Your Child's Natural Genius.*

Sternmark, Jean; Thomson, Virginia, and Cossey, Ruth. *Family Math.* Berkeley: Regents of University of California, 1986.

Allison, Linda, and Weston, Martha. *Eenie Meenie Miney Math!* Boston: Little, Brown, 1993.

24. Laskin, David, and O'Neill, Kathleen. *The Little Girl Book.* New York: Ballantine, 1992.

25. A point developed by Turkle, Sherry, "Computational Reticence: Why Women Fear the Intimate Machine," in Cheris Kramerae, ed. *Technology and Women's Voices.* New York: Pergamon Press, 1986.

26. University of Minnesota sociologist Ronald Anderson, in a telephone interview, Dec. 4, 1994.

27. Sanders, Jo. *The Neuter Computer.* New York: Neal Schuman Publishers, 1986.

28. Sanders, Jo. "Does Your Daughter Say 'No Thanks' to the Computer?" New York: Women's Action Alliance, 1989.

29. Evans, Nancy. "Catching Up to Our Children." *Family Life,* March–April 1994, p. 9.

30. Strategies for girls and computers are drawn from a number of sources including Sanders, Jo, "Do Your Female Students Say 'No, Thanks' to the Computer?" New York: Women's Action Alliance, 1987.

Sanders, *The Neuter Computer. op. cit.*

Kantrowitz, "Men, Women & Computers," pp. 51–52.

31. Brady, Holly, and Slesnick, Twila. "Girls Don't Like Fluffware Either." *Classroom Computer Learning,* April–May 1985, pp. 22–28, as cited in Sanders, *The Neuter Computer.*

Chapter 19. Teach Her Teacher

1. Sadker and Sadker, *Failing at Fairness.*

2. Sadker, Jacqueline. "Mom, Malibu Barbie and Me." *New York Times Magazine,* December 31, 1995, p. 24.

3. Manning, Anita. "Teacher's Daughters Drive the Point Home." *USA Today,* February 5, 1994, p. D3.

4. "How Schools Shortchange Girls: A Study of Major Findings on Girls and Education." American Association of University Women, Educational Foundation, 1991, pp. 68–74.

Sadker, Myra, and Sadker, David. "Sexism in the Classroom: From Grade School to Graduate School." *Phi Delta Kappa,* Vol. 67, No. 7, 1986, pp. 512–521.

5. Sadker and Sadker, *Failing at Fairness,* pp. 42–45.

6. Ibid., pp. 57–58.

7. Grant, Linda. "Black Females' 'Place' in Desegregated Classrooms." *Sociology of Education,* Vol. 57, No. 2, 1984, pp. 97–110.

8. Orenstein, *Schoolgirls,* p. 181.

"How Schools Shortchange Girls," pp. 70–71.

9. Sadker and Sadker, *Failing at Fairness,* p. 54.

10. Manning, p. 50.

11. A number of these suggestions were inspired by the work of Myra and David Sadker and the findings of AAUW's "How Schools Shortchange Girls."

Prufer, "In the Classroom," p. 80.

12. The issue of single-sex schools is debated in a variety of sources, including:

Laskin and O'Neill, *The Little Girl Book,* pp. 153–56.

Mann, *The Difference,* pp. 117–28.

Sadker and Sadker, *Failing at Fairness,* pp. 226–50.

Jimenez, Emmanuel, and Marlaine, Lockheed. "Enhancing Girl's Education Through Single-Sex Education: Evidence and Policy Conundrum." *Educational Evaluation and Policy Analysis,* Vol. 2, No. 11, 1989, pp. 117–42.

13. Prufer, Diana. "The Case for Single Sex Schools." *Parenting,* April 1994, p. 80.

14. Gardner, Howard. *Frames of Mind: A Theory of Multiple Intelligence.* New York: Basic Books, 1993.

15. Information and examples of the seven kinds of intelligence are drawn from the following sources:

Armstrong, Thomas. *7 Kinds of Smarts.* New York: Plume, 1993.

———. *In Their Own Way: Discovering and Encouraging Your Child's Personal Learning Style.* New York: Jeremy Tarcher, 1987.

Faggela, Kathy, and Horowitz, Jane. "Different Child, Different Style." *Instructor Magazine,* September 1990.

LaFarge, Phyllis. "7 Keys to Learning." *Parents,* February 1994, pp. 118–24.

16. "Your Child's Intelligences," *Scholastic Parent and Child.* Vol. 3, No. 3, Spring 1996, p. 37. Gardner's original idea was seven intelligences. He recently includes the "Naturalist."

17. Armstrong, *In Their Own Way,* pp. 64–65.